Russia and Europe: Conflict or Cooperation?

Also by Mark Webber

CIS INTEGRATION TRENDS: RUSSIA AND THE FORMER SOVIET SOUTH
THE ENLARGEMENT OF EUROPE (*with S. Croft, J. Redmond and G. Wyn Rees*)
THE INTERNATIONAL POLITICS OF RUSSIA AND THE SUCCESSOR STATES

Russia and Europe:
Conflict or Cooperation?

Mark Webber
Lecturer in Politics
Loughborough University

First published in Great Britain 2000 by
MACMILLAN PRESS LTD
Houndmills, Basingstoke, Hampshire RG21 6XS and London
Companies and representatives throughout the world

A catalogue record for this book is available from the British Library.

ISBN 0–333–73388–6

First published in the United States of America 2000 by
ST. MARTIN'S PRESS, LLC,
Scholarly and Reference Division,
175 Fifth Avenue, New York, N.Y. 10010

ISBN 0–312–23489–9

Library of Congress Cataloging-in-Publication Data
Webber, Mark.
Russia and Europe : conflict or cooperation? / Mark Webber.
    p.   cm.
Includes bibliographical references and index.
ISBN 0–312–23489–9 (cloth)
1. Russia (Federation)—Foreign relations—Europe. 2. Europe—Foreign
relations—Russia (Federation) 3. Europe—Foreign relations—1989– I. Title.

D1065.R9 W43   2000
327.4704—dc21

00–027253

This book is printed on paper suitable for recycling and made from fully managed and sustained
forest sources.

10   9   8   7   6   5   4   3   2   1
09 08 07 06 05 04 03 02 01 00

Printed and bound in Great Britain by
Antony Rowe Ltd, Chippenham, Wiltshire

Contents

List of Tables and Figures

Tables

Figures

Preface

If one is to believe the headlines, then Russia's relations with Europe appear to have lurched from crisis to crisis since the brief 'honeymoon' period of the early 1990s. In December 1991, Russia's first democratically elected President, Boris Yeltsin, made an apparently serious declaration that Russia would one day join the North Atlantic Treaty Organization (NATO). Three years later, however, he was warning that any enlargement of NATO's membership to include the states of east-central Europe would provoke the risk of what he dubbed a 'cold peace'. By the time of NATO's bombing campaign against Serbia/Yugoslavia in the spring of 1999, he had gone a step further, hinting darkly that Europe stood on the brink of a general war, a war in which Russia would, if pushed, take up arms against the NATO states.

The headlines, however, do not always tell the full story. Away from the rhetoric, Russia has, in fact, engaged in a wide range of cooperative activities with the states of Europe. It has negotiated all manner of arrangements with NATO and the European Union; has become a full member of the Council of Europe; has engaged in an unprecedented process of disarmament facilitated, in part, by the Conventional Forces in Europe Treaty; has been an active participant in the Organization for Cooperation and Security in Europe; and has largely remained within the international consensus on action in the former Yugoslavia.

Russia's engagement with Europe has, then, displayed elements of both cooperation and conflict and, therefore, the question posed in the subtitle of this volume elicits no simple answer. That said, it is the purpose of the following chapters to elucidate some of the major areas of the relationship, focusing in the main on how Russian policy toward Europe (and sometimes, by extension, the West more broadly) has developed since the end of the Cold War and the disintegration of the Soviet Union. The book's working premise is that cooperation has endured throughout all the vicissitudes of Russian domestic political and economic upheaval and at a time of flux in the international relations of the European continent. This cooperation, it is true, has often been fragile and has been accompanied by some not inconsiderable disagreements and tensions. Its prospects, moreover, are far from assured. Yet survive it has, the consequence of a complex mix of factors, not least the fact that Russia and Europe have increasingly 'routinized' their relationship in a range of formal multilateral arrangements.

The chapters in this volume were first presented at a workshop at Loughborough University in July 1998. They have been revised subsequently and take into account events up to August 1999.

MARK WEBBER
Loughborough University

List of Abbreviations

ACV	Armoured Combat Vehicle
ATTU	Atlantic-to-the-Urals (region)
CFE	Conventional Forces in Europe (Treaty)
CIS	Commonwealth of Independent States
CMEA	Council for Mutual Economic Assistance
COE	Council of Europe
CPSU	Communist Party of the Soviet Union
CSBMs	Confidence and Security Building Measures
CSCE	Conference on Security and Cooperation in Europe
EBRD	European Bank for Reconstruction and Development
EC	European Community
ECE	East Central Europe
ECHR	European Convention on Human Rights
EU	European Union
FRY	Federal Republic of Yugoslavia
FSU	former Soviet Union
GATT	General Agreement on Tariffs and Trade
I-For	Implementation Force
IMF	International Monetary Fund
INF	Intermediate Nuclear Forces
KLA	Kosovo Liberation Army
MD	Military District
NACC	North Atlantic Cooperation Council
NATO	North Atlantic Treaty Organization
OSCE	Organization for Security and Cooperation in Europe
PACE	Parliamentary Assembly of the Council of Europe
PCA	(Russia–EU) Partnership and Cooperation Agreement
PfP	Partnership for Peace
PJC	(Russia–NATO) Permanent Joint Council
S-For	Stabilization Force
START	Strategic Arms Reduction Treaty
TACIS	Technical Assistance to the CIS
TCA	(Soviet–EC) Trade and Cooperation Agreement
TLE	Treaty Limited Equipment
TNW	Tactical Nuclear Weapon
UN	United Nations

UNPROFOR   United Nations Protection Force
WEU   Western European Union
WTO   World Trade Organization

Notes on the Contributors

Michael Andersen is a visiting lecturer at L'viv State University in Ukraine, teaching for the Civic Education Project. He was previously at the University of Glasgow. A former NATO Research Fellow, he has published on NATO–Russian relations, as well as Russian and Ukrainian foreign policy.

Derek Averre is a Research Fellow at the Centre for Russian and East European Studies (CREES), University of Birmingham, and convenor of the CREES-based East European Security Research Group. His main work is in the fields of Russian security and defence policy and industry, science and technology in the Soviet successor states. He is currently working on a book related to these topics and has published articles in *European Security* and *Contemporary Security Policy*.

Mike Bowker is Lecturer in Politics at the University of East Anglia, Norwich. His research interests are Russian foreign policy and the Cold War, and his publications include: *Superpower Detente: a Reappraisal*, with Phil Williams (1988) and *Russian Foreign Policy and the End of the Cold War* (1997).

Jackie Gower is Honorary Senior Lecturer at the University of Kent at Canterbury and joint Review Editor of the *Journal of Common Market Studies*. Her reseach interests are EU enlargement and Russian–EU relations. Recent publications include an edited book with John Redmond, *Enlarging the European Union: the Way Forward* (1999), and 'EU Policy toward Central and Eastern Europe' in K. Henderson (ed.), *Back to Europe: Central and Eastern Europe and the European Union* (1999).

Caroline Kennedy-Pipe is Reader in Politics at the University of Durham. She is the author of *Stalin's Cold War* (1995) and *Russia and the World* (1998). She is also editor of the journal *Civil Wars*.

Dov Lynch is Lecturer at the Department of War Studies, King's College London. He has been a Research Fellow at the Royal Institute of International Affairs, and at St Antony's College, Cambridge. He is the author of *Russian Peacekeeping Strategies towards the CIS* (1999) and the coeditor of *The Euro-Asian World: a Period of Transition* (1999).

Mark Webber is Lecturer in Politics at Loughborough University. He is the author of *The International Politics of Russia and the Successor States* (1996) and co-author of *The Enlargement of Europe* (1999).

1
Introduction: Russia and Europe – Conflict or Cooperation?

Mark Webber

For some four and a half decades after 1945 the Cold War dominated the landscape of European affairs. However, in the space of a few short years after 1985, Europe's economic, political and military division was overturned. The suddenness and scale of this process owe almost everything to developments initiated in the then Soviet Union. The opening to the West under Mikhail Gorbachev and Moscow's consent to the removal of communism in east-central Europe (ECE) were defining events of the Cold War's end. The unintended collapse of the Soviet Union itself in 1991 meanwhile served to demonstrate still further that, at that point in time, Moscow constituted a pivot around which much of Europe's history was unfolding.

Russia, the largest of the states to emerge from the ruins of the Soviet Union, hardly qualifies as a successor of similar stature and influence. The political, economic and military reconfiguration of Europe that has taken place over the last decade has not, however, occurred in its absence. Contemporary Russia – like the Soviet Union, and indeed, Tsarist Russia before it – has claimed an important role in Europe and has actively sought an involvement in the affairs of the continent.

In what follows the structural bases of Russia's relationship with Europe will be delineated (Russian policy as such will only be touched upon, it being the subject of the following chapters).[1] This is done by presenting two contrasting views of that relationship. The first sees it as characterized by disparity, distance and even estrangement. Here cooperation is not ruled out but it tends to be shallow, short-lived and ultimately overshadowed by more competitive and conflictual dynamics. The second view is quite different. It suggests a relationship that is much more inclusive, one in which the 'Europeanness' of Russia is recognized. Russia certainly retains unique features (as, of course, do all 'European' states) and, in many

1

respects, lies on the continent's geographic, political and economic periphery. Nonetheless, its position is not seen as an inevitable well-spring of conflict with other European states and where differences do exist these can be regarded as open to accommodation. By this view, the relationship between Russia and Europe contains the possibility for a good deal of cooperation.

These two views are, in some senses, ideal types and it may well be the case that Russia's relationship with Europe is far too complex and far too ambiguous to be pigeon-holed into either one or the other. The relationship may, in fact, display features of both. That said, it is the assumption of this volume that the second view provides at least as helpful a means of identifying and understanding its underlying features.

Russia and Europe (I)

This first view suggests that historically, Russia's standing with regard to Europe has not been a comfortable one. Russia's status as a European state has not always been recognized, either in Europe itself or, indeed, by Russia's own leaders and opinion formers. Moreover, Russian/Soviet involvement with Europe has often been regarded as temporary, contingent or at the service of some mischievous foreign policy design. That its more telling or prolonged forays into European affairs have been executed at times of war or have been sustained by coercive means (as in ECE during the period of the Cold War) has served only to strengthen this impression.

Here then, Russia is viewed as separate from Europe, a disjuncture that is a consequence of enduring European and Russian circumstances. This is a state of affairs not predisposed toward cooperation.

Europe

Defining Europe is not easy. It is simultaneously a geographic, historical, political and cultural entity, the borders of which are ill-defined.[2] Yet among these different Europes, in political terms at least, one view more than another has tended to dominate. The shape of Europe has, to use Norman Davies' phrase, been strongly influenced by the 'Allied Scheme'. This is a view of Europe (and of the international system more broadly) that is derived from Allied victories in 1918, 1945 and 1989. It holds to a belief in the superiority of 'western' values and practices (democracy, the rule of law and the operation of a free market economy) and assumes that these constitute the basis of international order, good government and economic progress.[3] Tellingly, this view of things has even won a degree of acceptance at the pan-European level. The 'Paris Charter' signed by all 35 member states of the then Conference on Security and Cooperation in Europe (CSCE) in 1990, for instance, outlined an unabashed commitment to democracy, the rule of law and economic liberalism. With the demise of communism well advanced in ECE and the then Soviet Union, no state was able to mount a defence of political or economic alternatives and the Charter marked the first time in the history of the CSCE in which the values associated with western democratic capitalism were posited as the preferred political and economic standard for all the states of Europe.[4] Yet the elevation of such values has carried with it subsequently an implicit form of discrimination, suggesting as it does a benchmark against which 'Europeanness' is to be measured. Europe, by this view, has become divided into western and eastern spheres with the latter regarded as that much more backward given its motley collection of former communist countries, all labouring to varying degrees of success with the tasks of political and economic transition toward the Western norm.

The triumph of western values, moreover, has carried over into the manner in which Europe has been organized. Rather than dismantling the institutional structure created during the period of the Cold War, the west European states (supported in some measure by the United States (US), an honorary European[5]) have viewed its continued existence as essential to meeting the new demands of post-Cold War Europe. Bodies of a west European origin such as the European Union (EU), the North Atlantic Treaty Organization (NATO) and the Council of Europe (COE) are seen as encapsulating those values that triumphed in 1989 and as embodying tried and tested, and, therefore, indispensable practices of regional organization. The fact that the momentum for the strengthening and/or enlargement of these organizations has come as much from states outside them as from their long-time members adds to the impression that the western part of the continent has acted as both a magnet and model for Europe as a whole.[6]

Russia

This rather exclusivist picture of Europe has important implications for the status of contemporary Russia. Although in some senses the political élite centred around Boris Yeltsin benefited from the defeat of communist ideology in 1989 and, of course, was a direct beneficiary of one of its later consequences (the collapse of the Soviet Union and the juridical birth of Russia as a state in the international system), Russia nonetheless found itself in 1991 politically and organizationally speaking on the wrong side of Europe's divide. Its political and economic systems were, despite the inheritance of reforms begun in the Gorbachev period, still far removed from the standards of governance and stability seen as axiomatic in Europe's western sphere. Its ability to act as a shaper of Europe's broader affairs, meanwhile, was hamstrung from the very outset by its exclusion from European-based international organizations (the CSCE, in which Russia inherited the Soviet seat, being a rare exception).

As well as the specific circumstances of the post-Cold War dispensation, other, arguably more enduring Russian, characteristics also account for what might be seen as Russia's peripheralization. In the first place, there is the obvious fact of geography: territorially speaking the bulk of the Russian Federation is east of one of Europe's commonly accepted geographic boundaries, the Ural mountains. Russia, consequently, is a country more Asian in location than European. This was also true of the Soviet Union. However, whereas the Soviet state enjoyed a direct proximity to Europe via the Union Republics of Ukraine, Belarus, Moldova and the Baltics (and, by proxy, through the communist states of ECE) virtually all of this has been lost to Russia (since 1991, only Belarus can be regarded as unashamedly sympathetic to Moscow). Russia is, in other words, now at some remove from the centre of the continent. As one Moscow-based commentator has ruefully noted '[i]t has been thrown out of Europe into the sixteenth century'.[7]

This geographic position, in turn, has had a significant influence on the foci of Russian foreign policy. Not only does it reconfirm the importance of an Asian dimension (with regard to China, the Indian sub-continent and east Asia) but requires an attention to a whole new category of relations with the Soviet successor states. Such concerns need not rule out a European direction. They do, however, imply that Russian interests ought to be balanced between Europe and other regions around its periphery. This position has been rationalized in Russia through ideas associated with 'Eurasianism' and 'multipolarism'. The former identifies Russia's unique position as a bridge between Europe and Asia. The latter points to the need for a foreign policy that is not unidirectional (i.e. one fixated on the US) but one that is focused rather on multiple centres of power – Europe, but also China, India and so on. (How these notions have affected the Russian foreign policy debate is covered in Chapter 2.) Yet whatever the intellectual rationale, it is also clear that Russian policy has been driven by certain inescapable practical realities: the prevalence of local conflicts around Russia's southern borders, lingering economic and military interdependencies with the Soviet successor states and the supposition that Russia can play the role of regional hegemon. These all demand of Moscow a close attention to matters away from Europe. Add to this the fact that Russia's closest relations with the successor states other than Belarus, have been with Armenia (in the Transcaucasus) and some states in Central Asia, and Russia's extra-European position becomes even more obvious.

As well as geographic separation, Russia's distance from Europe has also been seen to reside in a sense of political and cultural distinctiveness. This relates simultaneously to how Russia is regarded in Europe and to how Europe is regarded in Russia. In both cases, Russia is held to possess a unique set of qualities that mark it off as Europe's 'Other',[8] its distance from the far-reaching European movements of the Renaissance, the Enlightenment, the Reformation and the liberal-democratic transformations of the nineteenth and twentieth centuries having left it in its own peculiar slipstream of development. Russian Orthodoxy, pan-Slavism, the evolution of Russian nationalism since the eighteenth century and even Bolshevism/Soviet communism (understood here as a uniquely Russian variant of Marxism) have all contributed to a Russian self-definition that is, in part, juxtaposed to, rather than in accord with, European influences.[9] The fact also that the Soviet Union spent some 70 years in the pursuit of an alternative model of political, economic and societal development, the credentials of which were laid down in ideological defiance of western Europe (and, indeed, the West more generally) only reinforced the idea that the Russia it then encapsulated had parted company with Europe.[10]

It remains moot whether post-Soviet Russia can overcome this heritage. Many of the strains long apparent in Russian thought and practice have in fact reasserted themselves during the 1990s. The Soviet collapse has had the effect of generating a debate on Russian national identity which is yet to be resolved. What is clear, however, is the movement which has occurred during the 1990s toward 'statist' and nationalist ways of thinking. Chapter 2 will cover this in more detail, but in the current context it is important to note one element of this shift, namely a reassertion of cultural distance between Russia and what is viewed as a global culture epitomized by the US and western Europe.[11]

Trends in post-Soviet reform have also tended to emphasize the peculiarities of Russian development. Although sometimes seen as part and parcel of a continent-wide group of similar post-communist political and economic systems, Russia can, in fact, be regarded as almost a case apart. The fact that the Soviet model held sway for some seven decades (much longer than in ECE) and that the end of communism in the Soviet Union was occasioned not simply by regime transformation but by state collapse, means that the challenges of post-communism have been particularly profound and unsettling. The consequent turbulence of Russia's political and economic transition, and the seeming uncertainties of its eventual outcome have thus served to confirm Russian 'otherness' not just from settled west European states, but even from the majority of post-communist states. Russia is associated with the 'chaotic periphery' of Europe,[12] its political instability and economic collapse feeding social tensions, organized crime, brigandage and, as in the case of Chechnya, civil war. In this light, it has more in common with centres of instability such as Albania and Bosnia than it does with the likes of Poland, Hungary and the Czech Republic, states which have navigated the straits of transition relatively successfully and whose incorporation into the European political and economic mainstream appears that much more assured.

Conflict

A view of Russia somehow divided from Europe tends to assume that there is an inherent tendency toward friction and competition in its relationship with the continent. Leaving aside for the moment the specific policy issues which might be used to illustrate such a contention (these are touched upon in the ensuing chapters), such frictions can be seen to emanate from at least three sources.

In the first place one should recognize that, notwithstanding the demise of the Cold War, enemy images have not been totally eradicated on either side of the former divide.[13] In general terms, studies of foreign policy formulation have shown that the frame of reference of policy-makers (and, by extension, of anybody with a view on a foreign policy matter) is strongly shaped by prior experience. Consequently, there may well be cognitive resistance to a change of outlook even when the objective circumstances in the policy environment alter in a fundamental way.[14] In the specific circumstances of the Russian–European relationship this has meant a periodic revival of Cold War terminology and imagery (nowhere more obvious than over the issue of NATO enlargement).

Second, it has been suggested that the broader context of the relationship encourages a predisposition toward mistrust and competition. This is the view associated with a neo-realist analysis of European security. It argues that the Cold War divide – characterized by a rough parity of military power between NATO and the Warsaw Pact – did, in fact, produce stability in Europe and contributed to a period of 'long peace' on the continent after 1945. The end of the Cold War has removed this balance, thereby returning Europe to what are viewed as the historically more typical conditions of 'fluid regional balances of power, occasional power vacuums, untidy alliance blocs and competitive national interests'.[15] In such a context, rivalry is seen as the natural condition between states; national security is a constant preoccupation and states accord a priority to promoting their relative power positions.[16] Here, Russia, even though economically and militarily prostrate, retains its great power credentials by virtue of its nuclear capacity, its legal status as the *de jure* 'continuing state' of the Soviet Union and its claims to involvement and influence in areas well beyond its borders. Consequently, it is viewed with considerable caution by those states in ECE and the Baltic region with direct experience of past Soviet/Russian aggression (a number of these having sought NATO membership in response).[17] It also remains a concern of west European states (Germany in particular) who feel the need to guard against the long-term eventuality of a revival of Russian power.[18] Yet by the same token, Russia itself has been placed in an embattled position. If one is to regard developments in Europe through the prism of power politics, then the post-Cold War order is clearly not to its advantage. Russia's position has declined relative to the major powers of France, Germany and the UK, and NATO and EU enlargement have had (or will have) the effect of diminishing it still further. In these circumstances, it is seen as almost inevitable that Russia's relations with most of Europe will be tainted by suspicion and a competitive edge, and that Russia will oppose institutional arrangements on the continent which accord it only a marginal role.[19]

Third, friction can also be regarded as a consequence of Russia's domestic weakness. The breakdown of order in Russia, while precluding a direct Russian threat to Europe, has generated all manner of anxieties concerning the spillover of lesser dangers (unchecked migration, organized crime, illegal arms trafficking and the security of Russia's civilian and military nuclear capability) onto the continent. The gravity, scale and intractability of these problems could, in the long term, have two mutually reinforcing effects: to disqualify Russia from playing a lead role in European affairs and to justify on the part of western Europe an abandonment of the country as a hopeless case.[20] The upshot of both would be to increase Russia's alienation from Europe and to transform issues of mutual concern into issues of tension and mutual recrimination.

Russia and Europe (II)

This second view suggests that Russia and Europe cannot be regarded as distinguishable parts: Russia is a European country. When considering

Russia's relations with Europe the two parties are not in juxtaposition. Just as one can speak of 'Britain and Europe' or 'Germany and Europe', so too can one talk of 'Russia and Europe'.[21] Furthermore, whereas the political, economic and military divisions of the Cold War had precluded extensive cooperation, these can, in retrospect, be regarded as temporary. A post-Soviet Russia *in* Europe is also a Russia open to the opportunities for cooperation *with* Europe.

Europe

The distinction between Russia and Europe noted in the previous section can only be neatly drawn if one accepts the equation of Europeanness with just one of its parts, that of western Europe. Such arrogation, however, hardly does justice to what is a complex and disputed concept; in terms of geography, shared history and the development of a common cultural and civilizational process, Europe is about far more than its western half.[22] Even if one concentrates simply on the manner in which Europe has found political expression, a privileging of the western states still remains problematic. To suggest that liberal-democracy is the defining characteristic of Europe is to ignore recent history; for much of the twentieth century a significant number of European states – such as Germany, Italy and Spain, now stable democracies – viewed fascism and communism as equally valid systems of political, economic and social organization.[23] It is also to assert a questionable moral superiority; some of Europe's contemporary democracies were, after all, responsible for visiting continent-wide warfare upon Europe on two calamitous occasions in the twentieth century and for exporting world-wide a now morally discredited form of rule in the shape of colonialism.[24]

If one dispenses with the equation 'Europe equals western Europe' then Russia can more easily be embraced. Russia, of course, still remains distinctive but this is not incompatible with a European identity. On one reading Europe is, in fact, typified by the diversity of its nation-states, a state of affairs which is central to understanding both the history and the contemporary development of the continent.[25] In this sense, assigning Russia the status of Europe's 'Other' is somewhat arbitrary and says more about the need to ascribe difference than it does about what it is to be European. The fact that Turkey, Spain and even Germany have been posited in like manner seemingly bears this out.[26]

This more inclusive conception of Europe also has implications for the manner of Europe's organization. Rather than only viewing bodies of western origin, such as the EU, NATO and the COE, as appropriate to the ordering of the continent, a more explicitly pan-European body such as the Organization for Security and Cooperation in Europe (the CSCE became the OSCE in January 1995) might be regarded as equally relevant. True, as noted above, the OSCE now embraces values associated with the West, but just as significant is its embodiment of general principles of inter-state conduct such as the renunciation of force, respect of territorial integrity and the peaceful settlement of disputes set forth most notably in the Helsinki Final Act of the CSCE in 1975.[27] If these are taken as the cornerstones of a European community of states then Russia's inclusion is far more straightforward and indeed politically relevant, for the OSCE is one major European organization in which Russia has full membership.

Russia

In light of the above, the separation of Russia from Europe can, it seems, be easily exaggerated. Russia is in fact not at all distant from the continent. Notwithstanding the peculiarities of Russia's development noted above, it has been clearly linked to the development of European civilization. Its cultural contribution – not least in art, music and literature – to a European canon is beyond dispute.[28] Similarly, in historical terms, Russia has, since at least the end of the eighteenth century, been a major actor in European affairs. This was apparent through, first, its impact on the continent's major wars from the Napoleonic onward; second, through its involvement in various arrangements of attempted European order (the Concert of Europe of the nineteenth century and, during the Soviet period, the Yalta settlement of 1945 and the *détente* process of the 1970s); and third its participation in European-based alliances (the nineteenth-century Holy Alliance, the Triple *Entente*, the Nazi–Soviet pact and the post-war Warsaw Pact).

Moreover, and of some importance to this volume, Russia's connection to Europe has been, and still is, apparent in geopolitical terms. Even allowing for the geographic effects of the Soviet Union's dissolution, Russia and western Europe still enjoy direct contact (the 1300 km Russian–Finnish border is one of Europe's most extensive land frontiers). In addition, the independence of the former Union Republics as well as severing Russia from certain of its European territories (principally Ukraine) has also meant the amputation of the Central Asian region as an economic and political appendage of Russia. This has had the effect of pulling Russia closer to Europe.[29] As for Russia's own 'Asian' regions east of the Urals, these do account for the bulk of Russian territory but make up a diminishing proportion of the Russian population (at present just 22 per cent). The greater part of this population, moreover, has settled through a process of migration and forced movement and thus can hardly be considered indigenous to the region; its self-identity while perhaps not strongly European can neither be regarded as Asiatic.[30] Indeed, a similar generalization may also be made for the self-identity of Russia's population as a whole. Asian cultures are that much more distant from the Russian majority than are those of Europe. And while Islam may be a resonant influence for a significant minority, whatever small influence it has enjoyed in Russian culture and opinion more generally has been damaged by the war in Chechnya.[31]

Russia's connection to Europe carries with it certain very important implications. First, Russia inherited from the Soviet Union military capabilities and treaty commitments (principally the 1990 Conventional Forces in Europe (CFE) Treaty) with a heavy focus on European contingencies. These have subsequently been refashioned by virtue of the withdrawal from ECE, the disintegration of the Soviet armed forces, and Russian military reform; but in essence the Russian order of battle remains concentrated west of the Urals, even though the eventuality of its deployment in war is now a distant prospect.[32]

Second, European states account for a sizeable proportion of Russian foreign trade and this share has increased during the 1990s as Russia has re-oriented its trade away from less profitable markets in the successor states. The fact, moreover, that the east Europeans have simultaneously shifted their trade patterns away from Russia means that the European direction of Russian trade has been increasingly concentrated on transactions with EU member states.

Third, Russia's pretensions toward preserving its role as a great power requires an active engagement in European affairs. While it could be argued that Russian influence is more easily demonstrated among the successor states, such a position is problematic on two counts: the region is as much a burden as an asset in economic and military terms; and Russia's sense of status cannot be sufficiently realized by a reliance on its own periphery. A great power views itself in a global context, and Europe remains in geopolitical terms a still pivotal region which demands engagement.[33]

Cooperation

The fact that Russia is demonstrably part of Europe does not in itself suggest that its relationship with the other states of the continent will be harmonious. Indeed, the history of the continent could well suggest the opposite; the frequent visitations of war indicate that being part of Europe actually increases the likelihood that a state will experience antagonistic relations with its neighbours. In this light, if one is to argue that

cooperation is a durable condition of the Russian–European relationship then it needs to be shown that the whole context of international
politics on the continent has altered; altered that is, in a manner
favourable to amity among states and, in particular, among those states
who, during the Cold War period, had regarded one another as potential
adversaries. To suggest that this is the case need not be recklessly optimistic. It is a view that recognizes the insecurities that still bedevil Europe
(of which the conflicts in the former Yugoslavia are the most obvious
examples) and that the Russian–European relationship itself is not free
of periodic tension. Equally, however, it highlights a crucial fact – namely,
that the likelihood of great power war on the continent has been reduced
to negligible levels and thus cooperation among those same powers is,
consequently, that much more likely.[34]

What accounts for the emergence of this state of affairs? First, is the
end of the Cold War itself. Although arguably a source of stability in
some respects (see above), its existence did amount, to use Lawrence
Freedman's phrase, to an 'obvious precondition for another Great War'
in that the likely adversaries and the *casus belli* of such a war could easily
be identified.[35] From the perspective of the western states, the Soviet
military presence coupled with the political subjugation of ECE permitted
no confidence that Moscow's intentions toward Europe as a whole were
benign.[36] This, moreover, reflected not simply military calculation. The
Cold War was, after all, a conflict between two ideologically divergent
and seemingly irreconcilable systems of social organization. Until one
was removed the international and regional system they both occupied
would inevitably be characterized by enmity.[37] Such removal occurred
by virtue of the dramatic political transitions of 1989 in ECE and the
subsequent collapse of the Soviet Union itself in 1991.

Second, the post-communist states which have emerged from this
process pose no large-scale threat to European security. Much of ECE
actually aspires to alliance with the west European states. As for Russia,
its internal political and economic upheavals, the dismal condition of
the Russian military (amply illustrated by the war in Chechnya) and the
absence of any conceivable objectives it might want to satisfy through
military confrontation make the waging of war against western Europe
inconceivable and against ECE highly improbable.[38] This, of course,
begs the question of whether the west European states are perceived as a
threat in Russia, a not entirely academic point in view of NATO enlargement and the show of force on the part of the Alliance during the 1999
air-war against Serbia/Yugoslavia. This issue will, in fact, be addressed in
a number of the chapters in the present volume. Suffice it to say here

that while NATO activities can be construed as antithetical to Russia's security interests, some of their more damaging consequences have been cushioned by the existence of a 'contextual environment' that continues to favour cooperation between Russia and Europe.[39]

In straightforward military terms, this environment equates with what Michael Mandelbaum has described as the 'common security order' in Europe which arose at the end of the Cold War. Initiatives such as the 1987 Intermediate Nuclear Forces Treaty, the 1990 CFE Treaty and the series of Confidence Building Measures agreed between 1986 and 1992 have transformed the European strategic landscape. The former adversaries of the Cold War, rather than being poised at the point of aggression, have embraced transparency, arms reductions and the renunciation of offensive military postures.[40] NATO enlargement may be at odds with the principles of mutual confidence building inherent in this order[41] and, along with NATO military action during the 1999 Kosovo crisis, has prompted Russia to question some of the assumptions upon which it rests. Yet, as will become clear in the remaining chapters, NATO's growing ascendancy in European security affairs has not occasioned a Russian withdrawal from that order. What is more, the European states (both east and west) themselves appear to recognize that it is very much in their own interests that Russia remain within a cooperative framework. Russian participation is seen as indispensable in addressing a whole range of security issues, be this border control, conventional disarmament, nuclear non-proliferation, and the preservation of political and civil order in ECE and the Balkans.[42]

These security arrangements, moreover, are supplemented by other complementarities between Russia and Europe which favour cooperation. In political terms this relates, in part, to the acceptance of certain principles of inter-state relations. The states of Europe, and most importantly its major powers (Russia included), hold no desire to subvert the international order out of ideological or power-related motives. The post-Cold War settlement of a unified Germany and an ECE removed from a Soviet/ Russian sphere of influence is, in other words, considered legitimate and, therefore, no longer a cause of conflict.[43] Domestic politics are also relevant. One might question the validity of defining Europe in terms of the political orientation of its various states. However, as a factor in explaining cooperation between states, political complexion is of some importance. The standard contention in this respect is that democratic states are more predisposed toward cooperation than are non-democracies.[44] With regard to Russia this suggests a qualified optimism. Russia is hardly a stable, consolidated democracy and the very fact of its transition may spell danger – the political dynamics of democratizing states can induce a propensity toward bellicose foreign policies.[45] Yet neither is Russia any longer a communist state, and hence one major ideological impediment to its cooperation with the democracies of Europe has been removed. Furthermore, its emerging political order does exhibit some democratic features that constrain aggressive foreign policy impulses[46] and a good proportion of its political élite does subscribe, albeit in a modified form, to democratic principles.[47]

Economic complementarities are also apparent. Russia's post-communist transition has, of course, been littered with grave economic consequences domestically and its development as a capitalist market may have external consequences as likely to lead to competition with Europe. What is important, however, is that the demise of the communist state-controlled economy has removed a major obstacle to Russia's greater interaction with the west European economies. This refers to trade (noted above), but also to other activities of potential mutual benefit such as the provision of investment funding and economic assistance by European companies, governments and organizations such as the EU and the European Bank for Reconstruction and Development (EBRD).

Russia and Europe: the role of multilateral institutions

Assuming that conditions in Europe now provide a favourable setting for a greater level of interaction with Russia, the issue of how such interaction is carried out – its organization and scope – still needs to be addressed. There are several ways of analysing the relationship. A first focus might be that of bilateral relations. Russia has, for historical reasons, important connections to certain states; Germany in western Europe, Poland in ECE and Serbia/Yugoslavia in the Balkans. These have continued to have some significance in the post-Cold War period. Germany is pivotal to Russia's economic links with western Europe, Poland's traditional strategic importance has been reconfigured in view of NATO enlargement, and Serbia has remained a conduit of Russian policy in relation to the wars and the post-conflict settlement in the former Yugoslavia. Other relations too have assumed a new importance. France, for instance, is regarded with some sympathy in Moscow owing to its semi-detached position in NATO and the understanding it has shown to Russian proposals regarding the OSCE. Turkey also is keenly regarded, albeit in this case rather suspiciously, the perception being in Moscow that Ankara constitutes a rival for influence in the Transcaucasus and Central Asia.

There is also an important sub-regional dimension to Russia's relationship with Europe. In very broad terms one might draw a distinction between Russia's relations with states in the western and eastern halves of the continent. The former is quite clearly a distinct political and economic entity and through organizations such as the EU and NATO seeks to speak with a common voice with regard to Russia. The eastern half, by contrast, is far less homogeneous and relates to Russia in a number of different ways. Here Russia is concerned with up to six separate sub-regions: its Slavic neighbourhood made up of Belarus and Ukraine; the Baltic states of Estonia, Latvia and Lithuania; those former Warsaw Pact states now inside NATO (the Czech Republic, Hungary and Poland formally acceded to the Alliance in March 1999); those former Warsaw Pact states still outside NATO but who have declared a desire to join (Bulgaria, Slovakia and Romania); the Balkans and surrounding areas; and the Transcaucasus (Armenia, Azerbaijan and Georgia).[48]

The bilateral or regional bases of Russia's relations with Europe are then obviously important. The present volume, however, is not concerned primarily with either. Its frame of reference is instead the multilateral and institutional setting of those relations.[49] This is considered fruitful for two main reasons.

First, it is an appropriate means for consideration of the volume's central theme, the balance between conflict and cooperation. Fundamental issues of controversy between Russia and European states have concerned the design and purpose of multilateral arrangements in Europe. Divisions have emerged over the proper role of international organizations, something explored by Caroline Kennedy-Pipe in Chapter 3 on Russia's relations with NATO and by Dov Lynch in Chapter 5 which concerns itself with the OSCE. Michael Andersen's chapter on Russia and the former Yugoslavia also touches upon these issues. Certain multilateral treaty obligations are a further source of controversy, and the interpretation and implementation of the CFE Treaty (perhaps the most important of these) are considered in some detail by Derek Averre's chapter on issues of demilitarization. Disagreement is not always the order of the day and important areas of cooperation have meant an engagement with Europe through multilateral mediums. This is clearly apparent in Jackie Gower's discussion of Russia's relations with the EU in Chapter 4 and to some degree in the analysis of the COE by the editor in Chapter 6. Moreover, as the chapters on NATO, demilitarization and the former Yugoslavia make clear, even over otherwise vexed issues, compromise and a certain degree of cooperation have been in evidence.

Second, multilateral institutions have loomed increasingly large in the shaping of Europe as whole. Again, the end of the Cold War is of some significance here, in that the military, political and economic barriers it once erected in Europe have, to some extent, disappeared. Having once been a continent of two mutually exclusive parts with very low levels of interaction, Europe is being transformed into an increasingly interdependent whole. Interdependence is not always to be welcomed and in some settings can give rise to feelings of vulnerability and threat among states. Equally, however, it can lead states to perceive that they share interests in common. It is in such circumstances that institutions loom large by providing the means to formalize and facilitate cooperation; and while not all institutions are effectual in this respect some notably are, a good number of them being situated in Europe.[50] True, the nature of this institutional activity has not been without problems or controversy. As already noted, with the exception of the OSCE, the institutions which have come to define Europe's post-Cold War organization are western in political origin and focus. This has, of course, meant certain tensions with Russia. It has also meant that in claiming a role in wider European affairs, these organizations have had to restructure, redefine their activities and confront serious regional challenges, some of which (notably the war in the former Yugoslavia) have tested them to the limit.[51] However, the states of Europe have invested considerable amounts of effort and resources in institutionalized activities. In the western half of the continent, institutional density is high and has a determining effect on foreign policies and inter-state cooperation. This has been less the case in its eastern half, where the end of the Cold War witnessed the demise of institutions such as the Warsaw Pact and the Council for Mutual Economic Assistance. Many states of the region have sought in consequence to embrace 'western' organizations. Most have now joined the COE, most want to join the EU and three, as noted above, have recently joined NATO. Such an embrace has been less obvious in the case of Russia. However, it too has recognized the efficacy of institutional engagement and in certain cases (the COE, the OSCE and, to some degree, the EU) has been an active suitor of international organizations.

What then do international institutions provide? To begin with, one ought to recognize that they are of little use when states hold security interests that are totally at odds; for instance, in situations in which an expansionist power is present, there are competing claims to territory, and the use of force is perceived as low cost and effective. Here, a reliance upon power and unilateral measures is the norm.[52] Such a state of affairs, however, approximates only particular parts of Europe (the former Yugoslavia and the Transcaucasus), and is far from typical of the continent as a whole. That said, states may still view institutions from a distinctly instrumental position. Involvement with them may occur because it holds out the prospect of international respectability, influence or access to material rewards. This can mean that institutions end up weakened as a consequence of becoming the arenas of inter-state competition and/or the repository of the particular interests of powerful states. However, this need not be the only outcome. While state interest may be the starting point for engagement, incorporation into multilateral institutional arrangements can have moderating effects. This occurs partly because institutions lay down procedures which generate trust between states – they facilitate reciprocity (the assumption that one state will meet its commitments to ensure that others do so also); and because they reduce uncertainties (through monitoring, the provision of information, the fixing of agendas and the laying down of rules).[53] In this manner, institutions offer a framework for bargaining, negotiation and the channelling of disputes, and thus, ultimately, offer the possibility of compromise and agreement. In fact, institutional arrangements may create habits of contact that lead states to recognize that their interests are neither zero-sum nor immutable. States may redefine their own interests either in light of the norms, rules and practices of the institutions with which they are engaged or by virtue of exposure within those same institutions to the state preferences of others. By such means differences can be overcome and cooperation enhanced.[54] Institutional efficacy is not, of course, pre-ordained. Success will depend upon the nature of the issue at hand (some being more impervious to resolution than others), the organizational strengths and weaknesses of the institution itself and the perceived usefulness of a recourse to unilateral and bilateral rather than multilateral channels.

These institutionalist assumptions have clear implications in understanding the manner of Russia's engagement with Europe: its at times obviously self-interested character, the fashion in which grievances have been aired, the scope for bargaining and compromise, and the possibilities for cooperation. Overall, it permits a relatively balanced perspective. Chapter 2 by Mike Bowker does suggest that Russian policy has been far from unchanging in its relationship with Europe. However, while the 'honeymoon' period in relations ended fairly swiftly after the Soviet Union's demise in 1991 this has not meant a lurch back into the animosity and stalemate of the Cold War. While it is the case that from the mid-1990s, Russia's relations with Europe's western half became much more conditional and fraught, as the chapters in this volume illustrate, a cooperative trend has not disappeared. Such a state of affairs has many explanations, some of which have been touched upon in the previous sections. Of clear importance, however, is the development of a multilateral basis of the relationship. This, the following chapters will seek to demonstrate, has provided both an anchor and compass for Russia in Europe.

Notes

1. In so far as this volume is an exercise in a foreign policy analysis of Russia, what the Introduction attempts is to set Russian foreign policy in its external and, to some extent, its domestic setting, leaving aside for the moment the actual content of the policy and the manner in which it is formulated.
2. B. Buzan, M. Kelstrup, Pierre Lemaitre, Elzbieta Tromer and Ole Waever, *The European Security Order Recast. Scenarios for the Post-Cold War Era* (London and New York: Pinter, 1990), pp. 45–6.
3. N. Davies, *Europe. A History* (London: Pimlico, 1997), pp. 39–40.
4. S. Lehne, *The CSCE in the 1990s. Common European House or Potemkin Village?* (Wien: Braumüller, 1991), pp. 23–4, 30. The Charter is reprinted in full in *NATO Review*, Vol. 38, No. 6, 1990, pp. 27–31.
5. America's European credentials in this scheme of things rest on its wartime contributions in Europe, its security and political engagement with the continent during the Cold War and the commonality of principles of political and economic organization.
6. R. Ullman, *Securing Europe* (Twickenham: Adamantine Press, 1991), pp. 145–6.
7. A. Zagorski, 'Russia and the CIS', in H. Miall (ed.), *Redefining Europe. New Patterns of Conflict and Cooperation* (London: Pinter/Royal Institute of International Affairs, 1994), p. 73.
8. I. B. Neumann, 'Russia as Europe's Other', *Journal of Area Studies*, No. 12, 1998, pp. 26–73.
9. S. Huntington, *The Clash of Civilizations and the Remaking of World Order* (London: Simon and Schuster, 1997), pp. 139–40; S. N. Macfarlane, 'Russian Conceptions of Europe', *Post-Soviet Affairs*, Vol. 10, No. 3, 1994, pp. 237–40; H. Mikkeli, *Europe as an Idea and an Identity* (London: Macmillan, 1998), pp. 162–76.
10. Buzan et al., *op. cit.*, pp. 46–7; J. P. Arnason, *The Future that Failed. Origins and Destinies of the Soviet Model* (London and New York: Routledge, 1993), p. 97.
11. E. Ponarin, 'Security Implications of the Russian Identity Crisis' (Programme on New Approaches to Security, Harvard University), Memo No. 64, June 1999, <http://www.fas.harvard.edu/~ponars/POLICYMEMOS/Ponarin64.html>.
12. O. Tunander, 'Post-Cold War Europe: Synthesis of a Bipolar Friend-Foe Structure and a Hierarchic Cosmos-Chaos Structure?', in O. Tunander, P. Baev and V. I. Einagel (eds.), *Geopolitics in Post-Wall Europe. Security, Territory and Identity* (London etc.: Sage Publications, 1997), p. 37.

13. M. Light, 'Security Implications of Russia's Foreign Policy for Europe', *European Foreign Affairs Review*, Vol. 3, No. 1, 1998, p. 58.
14. D. R. Kinder and J. A. Weiss, 'In Lieu of Rationality. Psychological Perspectives on Foreign Policy Decision Making', *Journal of Conflict Resolution*, Vol. 22, No. 4, 1978, p. 710; J. A. Rosati, 'A Cognitive Approach to the Study of Foreign Policy', in L. Neack, J. A. K. Hey and P. J. Haney (eds.), *Foreign Policy Analysis. Continuity and Change in its Second Generation* (Englewood Cliffs, New Jersey: Prentice-Hall, 1995), pp. 63–4.
15. J. H. Wyllie, *European Security in the New Political Environment* (London and New York: Longman, 1997), p. vii.
16. J. J. Meirsheimer, 'Back to the Future. Instability in Europe after the Cold War', *International Security*, Vol. 15, No. 1, 1990, pp. 11–13.
17. C. L. Ball, 'Nattering NATO Negativism? Reasons Why Expansion May be a Good Thing', *Review of International Studies*, Vol. 24, No. 1, 1998, p. 53.
18. T. Taylor, 'Security for Europe', in Miall (ed.), *op. cit.*, p. 179; Wyllie, *op. cit.*, pp. 76–7; F. Carr, 'Structure and Change in International Order', in F. Carr (ed.), *Europe: The Cold Divide* (Houndmills: Macmillan, 1998), pp. 28–9.
19. W. Odom, 'Russia's Several Seats at the Table', *International Affairs*, Vol. 74, No. 4, 1998, p. 820.
20. W. Park, 'A New Russia in a New Europe: Still Back to the Future', in G. W. Rees and W. Park (eds.), *Rethinking Security in Post-Cold War Europe* (London and New York: Longman, 1998), p. 98.
21. N. Malcolm, 'Preface', in N. Malcolm (ed.), *Russia and Europe: An End to Confrontation?* (London and New York: Pinter Publishers/London: Royal Institute of International Affairs, 1993), p. x.
22. Davies, *op. cit.*, pp. 9–15.
23. M. Mazower, *Dark Continent: Europe's Twentieth Century* (London: Penguin, 1998), pp. xii–xiii.
24. Davies, *op. cit.*, p. 28; J. Mayall and H. Miall, 'Conclusion: Towards a Redefinition of European Order', in Miall (ed.), *op. cit.*, p. 263.
25. Mazower, *op. cit.*, pp. 409–10; A. D. Smith, 'A Europe of Nations – Or the Nation of Europe?', *Journal of Peace Research*, Vol. 30, No. 2, 1993, pp. 129–35.
26. Neumann, *op. cit.*, p. 67.
27. P. H. Morgan, 'Multilateralism and Security: Prospects in Europe', in J. G. Ruggie (ed.), *Multilateralism Matters. The Theory and Praxis of an Institutional Form* (New York: Columbia University Press, 1993), pp. 330–1, 360–1 note 17.
28. A. Brown, M. Kaser and G. S. Smith (eds.), *The Cambridge Encyclopedia of Russia and the former Soviet Union* (Cambridge: Cambridge University Press, 1994), pp. 150–266.
29. Tunander, *op. cit.*, p. 35.
30. G. A. Fondahl, 'Siberia: Native Peoples and Newcomers in Collision', in I. Bremmer and R. Taras (eds.), *Nations and Politics in the Soviet Successor States* (Cambridge: Cambridge University Press, 1993), pp. 477–510.
31. V. Shlapentokh, '"Old", "New" and "Post" Liberal Attitudes Toward the West: From Love to Hate', *Communist and Post-Communist Studies*, Vol. 31, No. 3, 1998, p. 200. On a related point, the demographic and confessional make-up of Chechnya and Russia's north Caucasus more generally suggests that this area in some ways constitutes Russia's more Asiatic part. Being situated west of the Urals means it also qualifies the character of that part of Russia

geographically speaking regarded as part of continental Europe. However, the north Caucasus, for all its strategic significance and ethnic diversity, has effectively been quarantined in Russia. It has at times impinged upon relations with Europe (Russia's military operation soured relations with the EU and the COE) but its geopolitical importance lies more in terms of policy with regard to the Transcaucausus and, to some degree, Turkey.

32. A. Duncan, 'Russian Forces in Decline – Part 1', *Jane's Intelligence Review*, September 1996, pp. 404–7; A. Duncan, 'Time of Consolidation for Russia's Military', *Jane's Intelligence Review*, October 1997, pp. 453–6. This orientation is slightly skewed in that the region west of the Urals embraces Russia's north Caucasus (including Chechnya and surrounding areas) and the Transcaucasus (Russian forces in Armenia, Georgia), where military contingencies relate to domestic operations and those in the successor states. Nonetheless, even when these districts are excluded, the west of the Urals region still accounts for a far greater proportion of military deployments than the Far Eastern Military District east of the Urals.

33. O. Waever, 'Imperial Metaphors: Emerging European Analogies to Pre-Nation-State Imperial Systems', in Tunander et al. (eds), *op. cit.*, p. 75.

34. M. Mandelbaum, *The Dawn of Peace in Europe* (New York: The Twentieth Century Fund Press, 1996), p. 171.

35. L. Freedman, 'Military Power and Political Influence', *International Affairs*, Vol. 74, No. 4, 1998, p. 763.

36. Mandelbaum, *op. cit.*, p. 119. The Soviets, of course, argued that they had no intentions toward the western half of Europe and, objectively speaking, this claim seems credible. However, what mattered in creating an air of mistrust was perceptions of threat rather than whether the threat itself had any foundation in reality.

37. W. Loth, 'The East–West Conflict in Historical Perspective – An Attempt at a Balanced View', *Contemporary European History*, Vol. 3, No. 2, 1994, p. 193.

38. Light, *op. cit.*, pp. 60–1; C. Bluth, 'The View from the East', in C. Bluth, E. Kirchner and J. Sperling (eds.), *The Future of European Security* (Aldershot: Dartmouth, 1995), pp. 205–6.

39. J. Sperling and E. Kirchner, *Recasting the European Order* (Manchester and New York: Manchester University Press, 1997), p. 5.

40. Mandelbaum, *op. cit.*, pp. 81–109. See also Sperling and Kirchner, *op. cit.*, pp. 8–9.

41. M. MccGwire, 'NATO Expansion: "A Policy Error of Historic Importance"', *Review of International Studies*, Vol. 24, No. 1, 1998, p. 39.

42. See 'Action Plan for Russia', *Bulletin of the European Union*, No. 5, 1996; 'Common Strategy of the European Union on Russia', May 1999, <http://ue.eu.int/pesc/article/asp?lang=en&id=99908199>; 'Founding Act on Mutual Relations, Cooperation and Security between NATO and the Russian Federation', *NATO Review*, Vol. 45, No. 4, 1997 (special insert, pp. 7–10); 'WEU's Relations with Russia' (Document 1603 of the Assembly of the Western European Union, 28 April 1998); L. Pastusiak (special rapporteur), 'Poland and Neighbours – Military Cooperation' (North Atlantic Assembly, Sub-Committee on Transatlantic and European Relations, 9 April 1998), pp. 1–2; V. Havel, 'NATO and the Czech Republic: a Common Destiny', *NATO Review*, Vol. 45, No. 5, 1997, p. 8; L. Kovács, 'Hungary's Contribution to European Security', *NATO Review*, Vol. 45, No. 5, 1997, pp. 9–11.

43. Morgan, *op. cit.*, pp. 330–2.
44. T. Risse-Kappen, 'Collective Identity in a Democratic Community: the Case of NATO', in P. J. Katzenstein (ed.), *The Culture of National Security. Norms and Identity in World Politics* (New York: Columbia University Press, 1996), pp. 368–9.
45. E. Mansfield and J. Snyder, 'Democratization and the Danger of War', *International Security*, Vol. 20, No. 1, 1995, pp. 26–31.
46. Thus, Neil Malcolm and Alex Pravda have challenged the contention that democratization results in aggressive foreign policies. In the Russian case, while the rhetoric of assertive nationalism has often been in evidence among certain political groups, public opinion, the mass media and the particular balance of influence amongst political and economic élites have served to impede its translation into policy. See their, 'Democratization and Russian Foreign Policy', *International Affairs*, Vol. 72, No. 3, 1996, pp. 537–52.
47. Shlapentokh, *op. cit.*, pp. 199–216; B. F. Braumoeller, 'Deadly Doves: Liberal Nationalism and the Democratic Peace in the Soviet Successor States', *International Studies Quarterly*, Vol. 41, 1997, pp. 375–402.
48. This categorization is adapted from A. Arbatov, V. Baranovsky, P. Hassner, R. Levgold, J. Roper and A. D. Rotfeld, 'Introduction', in V. Baranovsky (ed.), *Russia and Europe. the Emerging Security Agenda* (Oxford: Oxford University Press/Frösunda, Sweden: Stockholm International Peace Research Institute, 1997), pp. 10–12.
49. By multilateralism is meant situations involving more than two states usually in an institutionalized format that entails one or more of the following: a formal international organization, a treaty-based arrangement, and a set of informal rules and understandings. See R. W. Cox, 'Multilateralism and World Order', *Review of International Studies*, Vol. 18, No. 2, 1992, pp. 161–80. J. G. Ruggie, 'Multilateralism: the Anatomy of an Institution', *International Organization*, Vol. 46, No. 3, 1992, pp. 561–81. By 'institution' is meant 'sets of rules that stipulate the ways in which states should cooperate and compete with each other . . . These rules are typically formalized in international agreements and are usually embodied in organizations . . . ' See J. J. Meirsheimer, 'The False Promise of International Institutions', *International Security*, Vol. 19, No. 3, 1994/95, pp. 8–9.
50. Largely ineffective institutions include the Organization of African Unity, the Arab League, and the United Nations Industrial Development Organization. The institutions considered in this volume are generally regarded as effective, indeed in comparative terms the EU, NATO and the COE are amongst the most effective. The OSCE has attracted mixed opinion, although it is rarely condemned as an outright failure, while the CFE Treaty regime (an 'institution' in the broad sense of the word) has usually attracted plaudits as a crucial cornerstone of post-Cold War disarmament efforts.
51. S. Croft, J. Redmond, G. W. Rees and M. Webber, *The Enlargement of Europe* (Manchester and New York: Manchester University Press, 1999), passim.
52. C. A. Wallander, *Mortal Friends, Best Enemies. German–Russian Cooperation after the Cold War* (Ithaca and London: Cornell University Press, 1999), p. 20.
53. R. O. Keohane and L. L. Martin, 'The Promise of Institutionalist Theory', *International Security*, Vol. 20, No. 1, 1995, pp. 41–2; R. O. Keohane, 'International Institutions: Can Interdependence Work?', *Foreign Policy*, No. 110, 1998, p. 86.

54. Sperling and Kirchner, *op. cit.*, pp. 16–17; R. O. Keohane and J. S. Nye, 'Introduction: the End of the Cold War in Europe', in R. O. Keohane, J. Nye and S. Hoffmann (eds.), *After the Cold War. International Institutions and State Strategies in Europe, 1989–91* (Cambridge, Mass.: Harvard University Press, 1993), pp. 8–9.

2
The Place of Europe in Russian Foreign Policy

Mike Bowker

Lenin and Stalin

Russians have always held ambivalent attitudes toward Europe. This is so, at least in part, for the obvious reason that their country traverses the two continents of Europe and Asia. Russia is a part of Europe but not wholly a European state. Such ambivalence has been reflected in debates throughout Russian history – between the Slavophiles and the westernizers during the nineteenth century and the Eurasianists and Atlanticists in the post-Soviet period. These debates relate to the problems of Russian identity and the country's relative backwardness, and have obvious policy ramifications. They are complicated, moreover, by the difficulties of trying to define what it is to be European. There is insufficient space in this chapter to pursue this point (but see Chapter 1). Suffice it to say, that race, religion, history, culture are only ever partial explanations of what it means to be European; even the geographic borders of Europe are vague and contentious.

During the nineteenth century, Slavophiles emphasized Russia's difference from the West. They rejected the western path of development, which they saw as ill-suited to Russian culture. They did not look outward, but inward for inspiration. Slavophiles gloried in the simplicity of peasant culture and the spirituality of peasant life and they pointed to a Russian culture, which emphasized the collective over the individual. They argued that Russia was, in a sense, unique and could escape the brutality of industrialization and the decadence of the West. Russia could create an alternative society based around the Orthodox Church and the peasant commune. westernizers rejected such a view. Russia, they said, could not isolate itself from the main currents of European culture and history, nor should it attempt to do so. Russia needed to modernize, and to modernize according to the western model. It needed to look outward, toward the West, in order to develop as a modern state and a great power in Europe. In the context of this general debate, élite attitudes and policy toward Europe can be characterized as veering between isolationism and engagement. On the one hand, there was a clear sense that Russia could only affirm its identity and greatness through imperial expansion and territorial consolidation. This was a process, in part, with a European focus through possession of Poland, but one which was mainly concentrated on outposts of Europe such as Ukraine and the Transcaucasus and, indeed, outside of Europe altogether in Central Asia. On the other hand, Russia's status, it was felt, required being an active participant in the affairs of Europe. Hence, its decisive role in the Napoleonic wars, the concert of the great powers and the diplomatic manoeuvrings that preceded World War One.

The Russian Revolution of 1917 marked an obvious political break with the Tsarist period. It did not, however, resolve the issue of Russia's relationship with Europe. Lenin, in many ways, epitomized the continuing ambivalence.[1] The Russian leader sought the destruction of the capitalist form of development which had emerged first in the West, but he wanted to use the ideas of a German philosopher to do it. Yet Lenin adapted Marx to perceive a unique role for Russia in the coming international communist revolution. Capitalism would be first overthrown, not in the most developed states as Marx had predicted, but in the weakest like Russia. As revolution came to Russia it would disrupt the highly interdependent international capitalist system and set off revolutions throughout the western world. Lenin recognized that Russia was too backward to move directly from semi-feudalism to socialism without help and aid from the more developed countries of the West. For the revolution to succeed in Russia there had to be an international revolution. The Bolsheviks were indeed successful in overthrowing the weak Provisional Government in November 1917 but sadly, from Lenin's perspective, the workers of the world did not rise up in support. The international socialist revolution simply did not happen. Nationalism proved stronger than working-class solidarity. As a result, instead of Russia being surrounded by friendly socialist states after the revolution, as Lenin had envisaged, it became an isolated Marxist-Leninist state on the eastern fringe of Europe. During the civil war of 1918–20, western powers invaded in support of counter-revolutionary forces in a rather half-hearted attempt to overthrow the Bolsheviks. By the time the Red Army emerged victorious from the civil war, a *cordon sanitaire* around Russia's western border had already been set up by the western powers by virtue of the provisions of the 1919 Treaty of Versailles. This was not so much an attempt to contain the military threat of Bolshevism (the threat at this time was minimal in any case), but rather to contain the spread of Bolshevik ideas. Lenin, however, never gave up on the idea of international revolution, but in the absence of any socialist uprising in Europe, he began to revive relations with the West to improve trade and encourage foreign investment in the new Soviet state. The 1922 Rapallo Agreement can be seen as the first example of what would become characteristic features of Soviet foreign policy toward Europe: the forging of a special relationship with Germany and the manipulation of differences between the European powers.

A decisive break in policy followed Lenin's death in 1924. Few believed the Soviet Union could survive alone as a Marxist-Leninist state, but Lenin's successor, Joseph Stalin, offered an alternative to surrender. He argued for 'socialism in one country'. He turned away from the West (which had been rather slow to invest in the new socialist state in any case) and declared that the Soviet Union had both the strength and the political will to create a socialist state on its own. According to Stalin, Moscow no longer required the aid and support of states in Europe. He never abandoned international revolution as the ultimate goal of Soviet foreign policy but, he said, the Communist Party of the Soviet Union (CPSU) could create socialism at home on the back of the Soviet Union's huge reserves of labour and natural resources, coupled with the commitment of the Soviet people. Stalin went on to create a siege mentality during the inter-war years. He effectively cut the Soviet Union off from the rest of Europe – economically, politically and socially. He created an autarkic state whose development was based on the theory of import substitution. Stalin refused to allow the Soviet Union to become dependent on the West, which, he believed, would always seek to undermine and weaken socialism. He used the image of an isolated and besieged country to call for enormous personal sacrifice from the Soviet people. The Soviet Union, he declared in 1931, is 'fifty or a hundred years behind the advanced countries. We must make good this lag in ten years. Either we do it or they will crush us.'[2] Thus, Stalin used fear of the West as a justification for the mass terror, which he unleashed during the 1930s. Former communists were falsely exposed as British spies or Gestapo agents and millions were killed as the outside world was portrayed as an unremittingly evil and threatening place.

The rise of Hitler in Germany (and the attendant ascendancy of a Nazi ideology that was both anti-communist and anti-Slav) presented a threat to the very survival of the Soviet state. This threat was only temporarily deflected by the 1939 Nazi–Soviet pact and in 1941 Germany invaded the Soviet Union. At a time of great peril, Moscow was once again forced to turn westward, and by the end of the year the Grand Alliance was formed. Britain, the United States (US) and the Soviet Union – the so-called Big Three – were united in a military effort to defeat the fascist threat in Europe. Stalin closed down the Comintern (the international organization run by Moscow whose aim was to subvert foreign capitalist states) during the war as an act of goodwill towards the West. The alliance was a strange and often tense one. It was certainly constrained by suspicion and mistrust, but western aid was vital to Moscow's early war effort. There was no doubt, however, that the Soviet victory on the eastern front was decisive in the overall war against the Nazis. The Soviets also paid the heaviest price: 20–25 million Soviet people lost their lives as a direct result of the war. However, the spoils of battle for Moscow were also great. As the Soviet Union drove the Nazi army back, it occupied the small and politically weak states of east-central Europe (ECE). The West could accept the idea of a Soviet buffer zone given the sacrifices the Soviet Union had made. It was, however, shocked by the brutality with which Moscow imposed Stalinist-style dictatorships throughout ECE. Stalin's actions seemed to contravene both the letter and the spirit of the 1945 Yalta agreement which guaranteed free and fair elections in post-war Europe.

The Soviet Union had always been a potential ideological threat to the West ever since the Bolsheviks seized power in 1917. However, it emerged after World War Two, for the first time, as a military threat as well. This threat seemed magnified after 1945 by the fact that the Soviet Union had, in a sense, become more of a European power as Moscow extended its influence westward. This presence had an ideological as well as a military purpose. Stalin wanted to keep western ideas out and thus was eager to keep the Soviet bloc as isolated as possible. The aim was to create an alternative world system, one which could ultimately challenge international capitalism. Stalin replaced the Comintern with the Cominform after the war and renewed his efforts to subvert western states through propaganda, communist infiltration of state institutions, and financial backing for west European communist parties. The strength of the Communist Party, particularly in France and Italy, did appear to pose a potential threat to the stability of liberal democracy in those countries in the immediate post-war period.

Furthermore, Moscow built up its military presence in ECE, to a point that clearly went beyond simple defensive needs. In the initial post-war period Soviet conventional military dominance in Europe could be justified as a counterweight to America's nuclear monopoly. However, when the Soviet Union tested its own nuclear device in 1949, four years after

Washington, this argument was fatally weakened. The North Atlantic Treaty Organization (NATO) was formed the same year, committing the US to the defence of Europe, but the Soviet Union never gave up its conventional superiority over western Europe. Although there is little evidence to suggest that Moscow seriously considered an invasion of western Europe (the fear of a US response was too great), the manner in which troops and military equipment was deployed in ECE did indicate that, at a minimum, Moscow had the potential to use the region as an offensive bridgehead against the West.[3] Both sides felt threatened by the other. Europe had been divided ideologically since the Bolshevik Revolution, and now that division was becoming militarized in an emerging bipolar world. The Soviet Union had stretched its influence into the continent's eastern half – socialism in one country had become socialism in one zone – and the US now dominated western Europe through its position in NATO and its ground troops deployed in West Germany and a number of other countries. Europe had become the most militarized continent on the planet. The stand off between East and West seemed complete. There were now two Europes in the Cold War period, East and West.

Khrushchev and Brezhnev

After Stalin's death in 1953, the Soviet leadership attempted to consolidate its position in ECE in two main ways: first, through seeking greater political support from the people in the region; and second, through improving relations with the West. To increase the legitimacy of the communist system, the brutality of the Stalinist period came to an end under Nikita Khrushchev and the exploitative economic relationship between the Soviet Union and its allies in ECE began to change. It was estimated that Stalin took from ECE in the period 1945–53 roughly the equivalent of what the US put into western Europe in the form of Marshall Aid.[4] But by the 1970s this relationship had been reversed. Between 1971 and 1980 Soviet aid to the region (in the shape of hard currency loans, trade subsidies etc.) amounted to a staggering $133.8 billion.[5] Yet, even such a dramatic shift in the terms of policy failed to gain Moscow much in the way of public support in the region. Soviet military interventions in Hungary in 1956, in Czechoslovakia in 1968 and the proxy invasion of Poland in 1981 (the declaration of martial law by the ruling Polish communists) clearly showed that Moscow's position in ECE still rested ultimately on force or the threat of force. Moscow had been unable to transform its relationship with ECE states from one of dominance to one of hegemony.

However, relations with the West began to improve. By the 1960s at the latest, both sides accepted the reality of the divided Europe. A balance of power had developed which, it was generally agreed, could not be disturbed short of a major superpower conflict. To reduce the risk of such a war, the division of Europe was formalized through the years of Leonid Brezhnev's rule (1964–82) in a raft of international agreements. These included, most importantly, a series of bilateral agreements in the early 1970s between West Germany and the communist states of Poland, Czechoslovakia, East Germany and the Soviet Union (which recognized the post-war reality of a divided Germany), and the Helsinki Final Act of the Conference on Security and Cooperation in Europe (CSCE), signed in August 1975. This latter document, in many ways, represented a multi-lateral agreement on the status quo in Europe, albeit in a form open to differing interpretations.[6] It contained three sections, or 'baskets' as they became known. The first was mainly concerned with security issues, the second with trade, and the third with human rights. For many, Helsinki represented the high point of European *détente*. All of Europe (with the exception of the ultra-isolationist Albania) and the US and Canada (as members of NATO) took part in the discussions leading up to the final document. Although the third basket on human rights was a potential threat to communist regimes, Brezhnev was desperate for an agreement. He saw the promise of increased trade in basket two as a way of consolidating the economies of the Soviet bloc, and most importantly of all, he believed basket one offered formal western acceptance of Moscow's wartime gains in Europe. Although this interpretation was disputed by some in the West, the apparent concession to Moscow was certainly the basis of much criticism levelled against the Helsinki Final Act at the time. It was seen by some as the Western equivalent of the Brezhnev Doctrine which had been used to justify the Soviet invasion of Czechoslovakia. It appeared to be asking the people of ECE to accept communist dictatorship, the repression of human rights and Soviet occupation for the perceived greater benefit of stability in Europe. West Europeans could be happy in the knowledge that the threat of war had gone and that they could concentrate less on security concerns and rather more on making money and getting rich.[7] As things turned out, European *détente* proved to be a rather more subversive process than it might have appeared at the time. ECE became increasingly dependent on the West for aid and credit, whilst the Final Act's focus on human rights played a part in gradually undermining the legitimacy of communism.

In the short term, however, *détente* improved state-to-state relations in the 1970s across the political divide in Europe. West Germany, in particular, became a major trading partner with the Soviet Union and ECE. Student, scientific and cultural exchanges became a common feature of the European landscape, whilst politicians from the two blocs met on a fairly regular basis. Nevertheless, there were limits to the development of European *détente*. Although the US and the Soviet Union were able to reach agreement to limit the growth of strategic nuclear missiles in the two Strategic Arms Limitation Treaty (SALT) agreements of 1972 and 1979, there were no parallel arms agreements for Europe. The Mutual and Balanced Force Reduction talks on conventional forces in Europe, initiated in 1973, rambled on inconsequentially for years before they were abandoned and replaced in January 1989 by the Conventional Forces in Europe (CFE) framework. Even in economic terms, there were problems. Stalin's fears of dependency came back to haunt his successors. Western investment in the communist half of Europe was reduced after the oil shocks of 1970s, and as repayments on loans were called in, Poland and some other countries in the region faced economic collapse. The Soviet Union itself was far less dependent on the West than many of its European allies, but its economy too was facing problems, with a general and persistent slowdown in growth a particular concern.

Human rights also returned as an issue on the international agenda in the early 1980s. In part, this was due to a revival of the anti-communist right in the West and the election of Ronald Reagan as US President. Reagan had always been critical of *détente* and favoured a more robust policy toward Moscow. *Détente*, it was argued, had not delivered the long-term benefits expected by the West. The Soviet Union continued to build up its military forces; it continued to intervene in regional conflicts in the third world; and it had made no effort to reform the political system or improve human rights in Europe in line with the Final Act. The most dramatic example of the latter was the imposition of martial law in Poland in December 1981.[8] The CSCE review conferences at Belgrade (1977–80) and Madrid (1980–83) were, consequently, dominated by the issue of human rights, much to the embarrassment of the Soviet bloc.[9]

Gorbachev

Mikhail Gorbachev was a more convinced westernizer than any of his predecessors as CPSU General Secretary. He wanted to modernize the Soviet Union, whilst maintaining the integrity of the Soviet state and the ideological credentials of communism (albeit in a much revised form). Brezhnev had sought to improve relations with western Europe on the basis of getting western acceptance for the division between the two blocs and establishing a secure balance of power. Gorbachev, on the other hand, sought to transform relations through the mutual acceptance of ideological diversity. 'Ideological differences', he wrote, 'should not be transferred to the sphere of interstate relations, nor should foreign policy be subordinate to them.'[10] He preached the virtues of tolerance. The Cold War, he argued, was the result of a drive by both sides to impose their own view of history on the world. If a more tolerant view of ideological difference was adopted, Europe could live without the constant threat of nuclear Armageddon. Let history judge, he proclaimed, whether capitalism or communism is the superior social system. In the meantime, let the countries of different social systems live together peacefully in an atmosphere of mutual respect.[11]

In this context, Gorbachev reinterpreted the concept of a 'common European home' which had first been used by Brezhnev in 1981.[12] In Gorbachev's vision, it was a home with many rooms in which different nations, races and ideologies could all coexist and cooperate. Gorbachev acknowledged the problem of using such a metaphor when the continent was still divided by concrete, barbed wire and mines. In his book, *Perestroika*, Gorbachev recorded a conversation with President Richard von Weizsäcker of West Germany who asked him how it could be possible to construct a common European home when there was a trench running through the living room.[13] Whilst Gorbachev was reluctant to reopen the German issue at that early stage in the reform process, he clearly hoped that his new ideas would lead to a lessening of political divisions in Europe.

Arms control was a central part of his long-term goal of ending the Cold War. The agreements, which most directly concerned Europe, were the Intermediate Nuclear Forces (INF) and CFE Treaties. The INF Treaty of 1987, which abolished all land-based intermediate nuclear forces, was the first significant arms control treaty signed in the Gorbachev years. In terms of number of weapons destroyed, the treaty was not significant (only about 4 per cent of the total nuclear arsenals of the two superpowers was affected), but symbolically it was vitally important. It showed it was possible to reach agreement to cut the number of missiles rather than just limit their growth – as had happened in the case of the two Strategic Arms Limitation Treaties of the 1970s. It also opened the way toward on-site verification and greater transparency on all sides in military affairs. The CFE Treaty, signed in 1990, was far more complex. However, in essence, it created a rough parity in all of the most important conventional weaponry between NATO and the Warsaw Pact. The fear of a surprise conventional attack from the East, it was hoped, would disappear after the treaty was implemented. It might well have been seen as a landmark treaty, but it was overtaken by events as communism collapsed in ECE in 1989. By the end of 1991, the Warsaw Pact had ceased to exist and the Soviet Union itself had disappeared. Since the treaty was based on the premise of rough parity between the Warsaw Pact and NATO, this inevitably led to a weakening of Russia's position. From a position of a rough 3:1 conventional advantage over NATO forces by the end of the Cold War, Moscow found itself facing a 4:1 disadvantage in the 1990s. This represented a remarkable turn around in fortunes, which unsurprisingly has worried many military strategists in Russia (see Chapter 7).

In ECE, Gorbachev's foreign policies were the most radical and the most unexpected. As noted above, the region had always been seen as an area of vital strategic interest to Moscow. Yet, as soon as Gorbachev came to power in 1985, he abandoned the Brezhnev Doctrine. Gorbachev privately told ECE leaders in March 1985 that the principle of equality and respect for sovereignty would henceforth govern relations between the Soviet Union and its allies. Outside interference in their affairs, he said, would no longer be tolerated.[14] At a November 1986 meeting of the CPSU politburo, it was formally agreed that the Brezhnev Doctrine would be abandoned.[15] Thus, the Soviet Union was no longer committed to intervening with force to uphold communist governments in ECE. However, this did not mean that Gorbachev was abandoning communism – far from it. Gorbachev seemed to believe these new initiatives would not weaken communism and Soviet influence in the region. On the contrary, he argued that the end of the Brezhnev Doctrine would encourage communist regimes to be more accountable and responsive to the demands and desires of their home publics and, thus, would render them that much more legitimate. The sudden collapse of communism in the region in 1989–90 was, therefore, a surprise and a disappointment. Although Gorbachev made no attempt to forcibly defend communism or Soviet interests in ECE when the Berlin Wall came down in November 1989, in reality the events spelled the end of a strategy based on the mutual acceptance of ideological difference.

The political establishment in the Soviet Union gave up control over ECE surprisingly easily. The Council for Mutual Economic Assistance (CMEA) was dissolved in June 1991 without much of a struggle, although it was hoped in Moscow that economic links between the Soviet Union and ECE would continue in some form. A leaked document from the CPSU International Department argued that the region was highly dependent on the Soviet Union both as a market for consumer goods and as a source of energy and natural resources. The document estimated that as much as 80 per cent of the region's oil and almost all of its gas came from the Soviet Union. It was hoped, therefore, to use such dependency to defend Soviet interests in the area.[16] Although sanguine on economic matters, considerable concern was expressed in the Soviet Union during 1990–91, however, over the winding down of the Warsaw Pact. Both political and military leaders were worried at the prospect of losing the pro-Soviet buffer zone in ECE. Chief of the General Staff, Mikhail Moiseyev, argued that Soviet troops should remain in ECE as long as there were US troops on the continent.[17] However, by the spring of 1990, Moscow had agreed to start the process of withdrawal. Why was this? First, the cost of maintaining a Soviet presence at a time when the Soviet economy was in a state of disintegration was becoming more and more insupportable; and second, the continued presence of Soviet troops without the support of the new regimes in the region could have sparked armed revolt in many countries. Better to withdraw peacefully with some dignity, rather than be forced out by popular revolution.

Gorbachev, to his credit, showed no inclination to stay and fight and soon came to accept the voice of the people, a decision no doubt, in part, the result of his own domestic preoccupations at this juncture (a mounting economic crisis, an increasingly divided CPSU and growing ethnic tensions). This acceptance greatly improved the Soviet Union's image abroad and allowed Moscow to quickly rebuild relations with ECE in a peaceful and friendly way. However, the issue of East Germany was always likely to be the most difficult to resolve. The central rationale of Soviet post-war policy in Europe had been to prevent the re-emergence of a strong, militarized Germany allied to the West, which could again threaten the Soviet Union. A divided Germany had been the practical means of achieving this. Yet in January 1990, some two months after the Berlin Wall came down, Hans Modrow, the then leader of East Germany, convinced Gorbachev that the German people would accept nothing less than full political reunification.[18] In the circumstances, Gorbachev bowed to the inevitable and telephoned German Chancellor Helmut Kohl on 10 February to say that Moscow would accept reunification.[19] This had the effect, which was very beneficial to Soviet finances, of immediately transferring the cost of transition from Moscow to Bonn.

The timing and terms of unification, however, required several patient months of negotiation to formalize. A central point of dispute in these talks was the position of a reunited Germany in NATO. Although resisted by powerful factions within the political and military establishments in Moscow, by mid-1990 Gorbachev was able to convince his colleagues that membership was a realistic way of containing the potential military power of Germany in the centre of Europe. In July Gorbachev and Kohl formally agreed to German membership of NATO and this was re-affirmed in an agreement signed by the two Germanys and the four occupying powers (the Soviet Union, France, the US and the United Kingdom) the following September (the so-called 'Two-Plus-Four' treaty). As such, this was a major concession by Moscow and in return it was agreed that the army of the reunified Germany should not exceed 370 000 troops. Bonn also agreed not to permit the stationing of nuclear weapons on the territory of the former East Germany.[20] The three NATO states for their part pledged not to station foreign troops there and gave a verbal commitment (seemingly later ignored) that the Alliance would not seek to expand into ECE.[21]

The analogy of the common European home was suggestive not just of the geographic focus of Soviet foreign policy but also its multilateral character. In this light, Gorbachev was initially critical of earlier Soviet policy (personified by Andrei Gromyko, the dour Soviet Foreign Minister from 1957 to 1985) which had emphasized the relationship with the US at the expense of all others. Although Gorbachev found the relationship with Washington an inevitable priority, he nonetheless showed a greater interest than his predecessors in western Europe as a political bloc. Thus, while Brezhnev and his short-lived successors Yuri Andropov and Konstantin Chernenko had all been hostile toward the process of European integration, fearing its potential power as a united political entity, Gorbachev held a much more positive view of the European Community (EC). He saw the EC as a useful counter-balance to US power and he recognized also that dealing with one institution rather than innumerable nation-states would greatly simplify negotiations with Europe over such issues as trade and investment. In February 1989, Moscow appointed an ambassador to the EC and by December a ten-year cooperation treaty had been signed which was very wide-ranging and included such things as trade, energy and the environment. Gorbachev also recognized the reality of other European and Euro-Atlantic bodies. He made speeches in which he called for the transformation of NATO and the Warsaw Pact into purely political organizations and for the elevation of the CSCE, as the only pan-European organization, to a role similar to that of the United Nations (UN) on a regional basis. However, the response from the West, and indeed his fellow East Europeans, was lukewarm.

In line with this emphasis on multilateralism, Gorbachev envisaged the Soviet Union as very much a part of Europe, and he wanted the Soviet Union to integrate with western Europe as far as possible. However, as the Soviet Union began to disintegrate, he found his hopes for a reformed Soviet bloc within a common European home being frustrated. He was left in his last months in office, rushing around western capitals seeking economic aid. To an extent, he was successful. Gorbachev received about DM 15 billion from Bonn in return for the acceptance of German unification and its full membership of NATO.[22] The European Bank for Reconstruction and Development (EBRD) was set up in May 1990 to provide much-needed capital for transitional economies. Other initiatives were introduced to try to support Gorbachev's reform process. But it was never going to be enough. The US gave approximately $10 million in Marshall Aid to the countries of western Europe between 1948 and 1950, which amounted to about 2 per cent of the receiving nations' gross national product. This would have required annual injections into the Soviet Union of at least $50 billion at 1990–91 values. This was a lot of money, particularly at a time of deepening recession in Europe and the commitment of German resources to unification. Overall, the West Europeans and the US proved reluctant to embark upon the equivalent of the Marshall Plan for Gorbachev's Soviet Union. On the one hand, it could be argued this parsimony showed a lack of appreciation of the need to spend money to secure the long-term benefit of reform in the Soviet Union. On the other, the West feared the money would be wasted due to political and economic instability and general doubts in financial circles over the viability of Gorbachev's economic reform proposals. In sum, Gorbachev's domestic reforms failed to impress the western banks and finance ministries. Indeed, relying on Gorbachev as the guardian of Soviet stability and reform was proving increasingly problematic. By 1991 he was facing opposition from several assertive Union Republics, from factions within the CPSU and from the Soviet military. On his left he also had to contend with Boris Yeltsin elected President in June of the, still then, Union Republic of Russia. By the end of the year Gorbachev had been forced out of office as the Soviet Union collapsed. The newly independent state of Russia looked to more radical reform to restore its position in the world.

Yeltsin

Yeltsin finally abandoned Gorbachev's notion of creating stability and cooperation in Europe through the tolerance of ideological difference. The Russian leader wanted to end all differences and move beyond tolerance to acceptance and partnership. In effect, this meant the end of communism as an ideology and the end of the Soviet Union as an empire. Partnership with the West could only be possible, it was argued, if Russia fully accepted the western concept of capitalism and liberal democracy. The Soviet Union, as a communist empire, would never integrate into the world community. Therefore, according to this scenario, Gorbachev's reforms were never going to be sufficient. Russia needed the equivalent of a bourgeois revolution. Only then would the West be willing to give plentiful economic aid to Russia and, more to the point, only then would Russia be able to benefit from this aid. Why should the West help buttress the failed communist system? Why should it give money to corrupt *apparatchiki*? As a result of such thinking, Yeltsin in 1991 embarked upon a policy of full-blooded westernization.

To this end, Yeltsin was instrumental in the dissolution of the Soviet Union (and thus the affirmation of full Russian statehood), in the setting up of the Commonwealth of Independent States (CIS) and in the launch of radical economic reform (known as 'shock therapy') in Russia in January 1992. Russia had also to find a new national identity for itself. Marxism-Leninism had been abandoned, and the country now found itself within new and unfamiliar borders. For the first time in centuries, Russia was an independent nation-state rather than the dominant part of a Tsarist or Soviet empire. Russia, moreover, had to work through the challenge of this new position while simultaneously addressing the issue of what its role should be in the post-Cold War world. The position of post-Soviet Russia had been diminished as a consequence of the Soviet collapse. Although Russia inherited the Soviet Union's elevated diplomatic status[23] and nuclear arsenal, the Soviet dissolution overlapped with a process of profound decline in Soviet Russia's military and economic capabilities and a geographic relocation of historical Russia away from the European continent (see Chapter 1). Inevitably, there were disputes over the direction of Russian foreign policy. In the period since 1991 this has coalesced into a debate between three general viewpoints: the reformist westernizers (or Atlanticists) led by Andrei Kozyrev; the centrists (state realists or Eurasianists) led by Yevgeni Primakov; and the anti-western authoritarians led by figures such as the ultra-nationalist Vladimir Zhirinovsky, Gennadi Zyuganov (the leader of the Communist Party of the Russian Federation) and Colonel-General (retired) Aleksandr Lebed.[24]

Reformist westernizers dominated the debate in the early months of the Yeltsin administration. Andrei Kozyrev, post-Soviet Russia's first Foreign Minister, was the leading figure in this group, and he gained support from the key presidential adviser, Gennadi Burbulis, and the acting Prime Minister, Yegor Gaidar. Westernizers supported the radical reforms introduced by Yeltsin and argued that foreign policy should aim to create the best international environment possible to promote their success. The Cold War was over. The ideological rivalry between East and West had also come to an end. Thus, according to Kozyrev, no basic conflict of interest existed. As such, the two sides could cooperate on all the major international issues and become partners and allies in the struggle for peace and stability in Europe and beyond. Russia would, it was hoped, become an equal of the major western powers in a 'community of civilized states'.[25]

Kozyrev's policies were highly controversial, but relations between Russia and the West did approve markedly during this 'honeymoon' period. For example, important arms control agreements were signed. Yeltsin signed the Strategic Arms Reduction Treaty (START) II in January 1993, which outlined a 50 per cent cut in strategic weapons on top of the 30 per cent agreed in the earlier START I Treaty of 1991. The CFE Treaty was amended and extended in 1992 to take account of the changes which had taken place in Europe since 1989, and to allow for the reallocation of troops and military equipment to several of the Soviet successor states (see Chapter 7). Russia also continued to withdraw militarily from ECE and the third world (Vietnam, Cuba) such that no Russian troops were deployed outside the former Soviet Union by August 1994. In terms of other cooperative initiatives, Moscow backed sanctions against Iraq when Saddam Hussein continued to defy the UN peace terms after the Gulf War in 1991 and Yeltsin also agreed to deploy peacekeepers in Krajina (Croatia) in January 1992 as part of a UN Protection Force (UNPROFOR). In Bosnia, in the crucial first year of the conflict, Moscow supported all the main UN initiatives, including sanctions against Belgrade in May 1992, humanitarian aid in September and even a NATO-backed no-fly zone in October (see Chapter 8). The West, in return for such cooperation, set up various multilateral, national and private schemes to promote aid and investment in Russia.

Within Russia, opposition to Kozyrev and reformist westernism became increasingly apparent during 1992–93. Why was this? Most important of all, Kozyrev's policies were seen not to be working. Some kind of economic decline had been expected after the introduction of shock therapy in January 1992, but nothing on the scale witnessed in its first few months. Moreover, the Yeltsin government was wholly unable (for whatever reason) to halt the economic collapse and external conditions offered only a partial solution. Trade with ECE was halved between 1991 and 1993,[26] and western economic assistance, although provided on a seemingly generous scale (in July 1992 the Group of Seven announced a package of measures to the sum of $24 billion) was never likely to be enough to kick-start an economy the size of Russia and with its depth of problems.

Elsewhere, Kozyrev was not having the success he might have hoped for. During the latter half of 1992 the successor states became a contentious issue for the Yeltsin administration. Initially, Kozyrev had favoured a policy of benign neglect but such an approach soon became the target of sustained criticism within Russia. Some 25 million Russians lived in these states and their interests were increasingly seen as in need of support. Some faced discrimination (as in Estonia and Latvia), while others were caught in the line of fire of civil wars (as in Moldova, Tajikistan, Georgia and Azerbaijan). Trade links were disrupted and migration to Russia from these trouble spots increased markedly. There were fears also that the political vacuums which had opened up in the successor states as a result of the collapse of the Soviet Union would be filled by foreign powers. Turkey and Iran vied for influence amongst the Muslim states in Central Asia and the Transcaucasus, whilst influential figures in the US such as Zbigniew Brzezinski and Henry Kissinger called on the West to strengthen Ukraine as a means of balancing Russian power. After the concessions over arms control and ECE, few in Moscow were willing to tolerate a loss of influence in the Soviet successor states as well.

Further afield, Kozyrev's initiatives were also berated for not having brought any significant gains to Russia. The war in Bosnia showed no sign of ending in 1992–93 despite Russia's cooperation with the West; Saddam Hussein was still in power in Iraq, and Moscow's support for the sanctions imposed on its former allies, such as Iraq, Libya and Serbia/Yugoslavia, had cost Russia as much as $30 billion in lost contracts.[27] But perhaps most damaging of all for Kozyrev was the appearance that Russia was still being excluded from security matters in Europe despite all of its concessions to the West. The Warsaw Pact and the CMEA had been abolished in 1991, but the EC and NATO were still extant. Kozyrev had adopted Gorbachev's earlier proposals and promoted the idea of replacing existing Cold War institutions with the pan-European CSCE, the one significant organization in Europe of which Russia was a full member. However, although a process of restructuring the organization had been launched as early as 1990 and its role extended to include conflict mediation and the monitoring of elections and minority rights, the CSCE was not perceived in the rest of Europe as a serious alternative to NATO. It appeared to Kozyrev's critics that Russia was being taken for granted and its interests ignored. It was increasingly felt that a foreign policy more independent of the West would better serve Russian interests.

Among the more influential alternatives to the early Yeltsin/Kozyrev line in foreign policy was that of Eurasianism. Sergei Stankevich, an adviser to Yeltsin, first put forward the Eurasianist case in an article published in

Russia in March 1992.[28] Stankevich was not anti-western like many nationalists and communists, but he did call for a more balanced foreign policy, one which recognized Russia's Asian as well as its European roots. Stankevich acknowledged that western and Russian interests could converge on a number of issues – for example, on nuclear proliferation and nuclear safety – but argued that for Russia, relations with the Soviet successor states should take priority. He also argued for a revival of ties with former allies beyond, including China and India, as well as some countries in the Middle East. More broadly, Stankevich argued that Russia's future role in international relations should be to act as a bridge between Asia and Europe. Although there were doubts over Russia's suitability to play this role, unquestionably Eurasianist ideas held a certain attraction in Russia. They offered Russia a meaningful mission in the post-Cold War world, whilst also seeming to take more account of Russia's history, culture and geopolitical position. Importantly, it also implied an end to Russia's subservience to the West. Prominent figures, such as the economist Grigori Yavlinsky and then head of the Russian Foreign Intelligence Service, Yevgeni Primakov, began to shift towards this more centrist position. Since they were committed to reform, their objections to Kozyrev's 'naive westernism' were harder for the government to refute.

The authoritarians were even more dismissive. They were also, as their title suggests, strongly anti-western in their views and they had no compunction in blaming the West for the state of their country. It was argued that economic assistance had led to an intolerable level of external dependency. Although this analysis was greatly exaggerated, it was certainly true that much assistance from the West was ill conceived, inappropriate, and often blatantly self-interested. Reports, however unfair, of the EBRD spending more money in its first year on the decoration of its premises than aid to ECE only reinforced this unfortunate image. The nationalists and communists sought to manipulate the growing constituency in Russia that was feeling increasingly resentful toward the West. Their approach could be seen simply as 'scapegoatism' and these groups tended to have few positive and realistic proposals on domestic reform and Russia's external orientation. What proposals existed were rather vague and non-specific and general agreement could be found only on the notion that Russia should become great again. Views on how this was to be achieved differed according to taste but usually involved calls to increase defence spending and to reintegrate the old Soviet Union or Tsarist empire, preferably by voluntary means but, if necessary, through coercion.

Alongside these voices of the political opposition, Kozyrev and the Foreign Ministry also increasingly faced challenges from institutional interests. The Foreign Ministry, having experienced a fairly free run in early 1992, soon had to coordinate its activities with two, more conservative, institutions – the Ministry of Defence (established in March), and the Security Council (established in May). Under the leadership of Pavel Grachev and Yuri Skokov respectively, these two organs began to challenge the views of Kozyrev. The Russian Parliament (the Congress of People's Deputies), moreover, was also a repository of Eurasianist and anti-western thinking, and the parliamentary committees proved particularly adept in influencing government policy.[29] Kozyrev (and, indeed, Yeltsin), in the face of such pressure began to adopt a more centrist line. In this context, a speech of Yeltsin's in February 1993 proved to be important. This was not so much because it affirmed a commitment to the integration of CIS (much the same had been said throughout 1992), but because of its unambiguous assertion that Russia's vital interests lay in the successor states and that Russia should take upon itself a 'special responsibility' to ensure stability in the region.[30] The Foreign Policy Concept, which was published in January 1993, and the new Military Doctrine which came out later that year, moreover confirmed the policy shift. Both documents were more anti-western in tone, and, as well as emphasizing the importance of policy towards the successor states, also reasserted Russia's claims to be a great power.[31] In putting the successor states at the top of the Russian foreign policy agenda, this alteration of policy suggested that the Eurasianists had achieved a decisive influence over the Yeltsin administration. The strong showing of Vladimir Zhirinovsky's ultra-nationalist Liberal Democratic Party of Russia in the December 1993 elections to the new Parliament (the State Duma), furthermore, also reaffirmed the need, in Yeltsin's mind, for a foreign policy which was more assertive in pushing Russian national interests.

In line with its policy shift, Moscow took a more assertive position *vis-à-vis* policy issues involving western states. This did not mean an end to cooperation, but it did signal a more qualified position toward it. Thus, Russia began to compete more vigorously with the West for arms sales; it argued for a partial lifting of economic sanctions on Iraq; rhetorically, at least, it became more supportive of the Serbs in Bosnia; and in December 1994, oblivious to western criticism, launched the brutal, and ultimately unsuccessful, assault on the secessionist Russian republic of Chechnya. This period of lengthening disagreement was capped by a communiqué issued by a meeting of NATO's North Atlantic Council in December 1994 in which the Alliance gave its clearest statement to date in favour of enlargement. In response, Yeltsin declared that there was a danger of the Cold War being replaced by a 'cold peace'.[32]

The domestic position of the reformists appeared to weaken further as communists performed well in the 1995 parliamentary elections, and Yevgeni Primakov replaced Kozyrev as the new Foreign Minister in January 1996. The West was generally rather unhappy about his appointment at the time. Primakov was a man who had been a prominent official in Gorbachev's administration, most prominently during the Gulf War of 1990–91. During that conflict, many had viewed Primakov, rather simplistically, as a man whose main aim had been to protect Saddam Hussein's interests.[33] Yet, the West's suspicions were quickly cast aside as Primakov proved himself to be an adept administrator. The new Foreign Minister was able to bring a greater clarity to Russian foreign policy-making after certain confusions of policy formulation during the Kozyrev era. This was so for a number of reasons. First, he benefited from the new 1993 Russian Constitution, which established executive primacy over the legislature in foreign matters. Second, he was able to reassert the pre-eminence of the Foreign Ministry in executive decision-making, with the support of Yeltsin who was re-elected President in the summer of 1996. Thirdly, and unlike his predecessor, Primakov enjoyed some support within the Russian Parliament. In this respect, Primakov's centrist viewpoint undoubtedly helped. His views were closer to those of the mainstream in Russia, and he was able to forge a new consensus in foreign policy on that basis. Redolent, in part, of Eurasianism, it was, however, free of that policy's more messianic aspects. More accurately it has been characterized as 'statist' or 'multipolar' in outlook.[34] This is a policy that has given priority to the successor states, extended relations with regional powers such as India, Iran and China and yet, at the same time, has also aimed at maintaining decent relations with the West.[35]

In essence, then, Primakov's tenure as Foreign Minister (and, indeed, that of his successor Igor Ivanov appointed in September 1998),[36] while not fixated with Europe or the West more generally, ought not to be regarded as anti-western. Primakov played a subtle game of sounding like a Russian nationalist, whilst in practice remaining rather more pragmatic in his dealings with the West. Simply put, he recognized the realities of Russia's position in the post-Cold War world. The US had to be respected as the sole world power, and Moscow had to deal with Washington on those terms. However, in economic terms, the US was nowhere near as important as Europe, and more specifically the European Union (EU) (see Chapter 4). Moscow, moreover, has become aware of the risk of isolation. Russia remains outside of certain key institutions in Europe, most notably the EU and NATO. This has meant that Russia has been unable to play the pivotal role it wishes to on the continent.

Yet, there is little chance of Russia joining such institutions in the foreseeable future. Full membership of NATO would bring the Alliance to the borders of China, and require a commitment on behalf of its members to defend Russia against a putative attack by the world's most populous state. Such a development would be just as unacceptable in Brussels as in Beijing. Membership of the EU may be less difficult to imagine, but Russia's sheer size would threaten to destabilize its structures and institutions, even supposing that Moscow is capable of fulfilling the stringent criteria of membership and willing to come to terms with the partial loss of sovereignty that membership entails.

Russia may be too large (and too different) to be easily absorbed into all of Europe's institutions, but it is also too important to ignore. Thus, a compromise of sorts has been reached with West European states that maintains cooperative interactions but which falls short of full integration. The various aspects of this state of affairs are covered in detail in the following chapters, but it is instructive to note some of the more significant measures here. A partnership agreement was signed between Russia and the EU in 1994, in 1996 Russia joined the Council of Europe and one year later it signed the NATO–Russia Founding Act. All in all, it seems clear that Moscow has rejected isolationism as an option in foreign policy. Although Russia will never be an easy partner to deal with, its participation in Europe has, in the main, been a positive one.

Conclusion

In conclusion, how can we summarize Russian foreign policy? What are its central dynamics? In both its Soviet and post-Soviet guises Russia has felt that it deserves to play a pivotal role in international affairs. This, at one time, was partly born of an ideological imperative, but has also been sustained by an appreciation of geographic size, historical and cultural importance, and economic and military potential. Proceeding from these features, there has been an almost uncanny resemblance between the claims of Soviet leaders and their successors in post-Soviet Russia. Simply put, these amount to a demand that the Soviet Union/Russia be accorded its due: a recognition of its influence and a willingness on the part of other powers to involve it in important regional and global affairs.[37]

In this light, some of the twists and turns of Russian foreign policy can be more easily understood. The early Atlanticist phase, for instance, was premised on an assumption that Russia would be treated as an equal of the western states and that it would, therefore, play an influential role in the post-Cold War reconfiguration of Euro-Atlantic institutions, and linked security, economic and political relations. The eclipse of Kozyrev as Russian Foreign Minister was a consequence partly of feeling amongst a wide circle of Russia's political élite that this assumption was seemingly not shared in western capitals and that Russia needed to be that much more muscular in defence of its own national interests. The subsequent turn toward a more qualified form of cooperation with the West under Foreign Ministers Primakov and then Ivanov has, in turn, been based on a growing realism regarding the manner and prospects of beneficial interaction with Europe and the US. The key for Russia in this regard boils down to what Primakov in 1997 referred to as the establishment of a 'reliable foundation' of relations which allows Russia to play a full part in Europe.[38] Such a construct cannot, it is argued, be simply based on NATO, but requires a more comprehensive multilateral basis, which offers Russia some scope for influence. Hence Russia's insistence (apparent most authoritatively in the 1997 'National Security Concept') on 'a model of general and all-embracing security for Europe' centred on the OSCE and, to some degree, the UN.[39] Hence also its quest for membership and association with previously neglected bodies such as the Council of Europe and the EU.

What this stance suggests, is that Russia is not *per se* opposed to cooperation in Europe. What it seeks is forms that advance it concrete benefits. Significantly, this is the case even when the benefits are shared with fellow European states. Russia, in other words, does not measure the utility of cooperation in zero-sum terms.[40] Initiatives that are seen to disadvantage Russia are, however, scorned. This is particularly so when western-led policies seemingly marginalize Russian participation in European affairs. Hence, as detailed in Chapters 3 and 8, Moscow's ire at NATO enlargement and Alliance-led actions in relation to Kosovo.

The demand for external recognition, while a constant in both Soviet and Russian foreign policy, has become especially insistent during the 1990s. Indeed, the invocation of a claim to great power status and the demand for a commensurate weight in international affairs have become almost a mantra of Russian foreign policy discourse. As Hans Adomeit has pointed out, however, states which enjoy such credentials do not need to advertise, their very acts are sufficient proof of their influence.[41] Russia has clearly declined as a global power. Its weight as a regional power has also been challenged and not just in Europe. Russia has seen its influence diminish among the successor states, and can hardly claim to be a major actor in the affairs of proximate regions such as the Indian sub-continent or the Asia-Pacific. The domestic bases of its regeneration (political stability, economic growth and military coherence) meanwhile remain underdeveloped. In this light, Russian foreign policy (and to some extent that of the Soviet Union under Gorbachev) can usefully be interpreted as a policy of weakness, one preoccupied with the management of decline and the promotion of external conditions favourable to internal recovery.[42] Russia consequently has often a small voice in international affairs. European states may listen to Russian protestations, but they need not act upon them. The Czech Republic, Hungary and Poland formally joined NATO in March 1999 in the face of sustained criticism in Moscow, and the Alliance carried out air-raids against Serbia/Yugoslavia shortly after, despite all manner of dire warnings of the consequences from Yeltsin, Ivanov and others.

Yet it is precisely such weakness that helps to sustain in Russian foreign policy a desire for constructive relations with Europe. This no longer has the political basis once provided by the pro-westernism of the early Yeltsin–Kozyrev axis and may reflect little other than the absence of reasonable alternatives: without a European direction Russia cannot hope to revive either internally or internationally. Despite its unbalanced nature, however, Russia's ties with Europe still present opportunities for productive interaction. In broad historical terms, moreover, these are opportunities that have been largely missing for most of the last 80 years. The Soviet/Russian relationship with Europe has moved through estrangement, temporary alliance and division (Lenin and Stalin) to a competitive consolidation of spheres of influence (Khrushchev and Brezhnev), to courtship and partnership (Gorbachev and Yeltsin), and thence to its present situation of pragmatic engagement. Admittedly, the end-point has resulted in a situation in which Russia is incorporated but not integrated in Europe.[43] This is a state of affairs characterized by arrangements that are often obscure and sometimes controversial, but it may well be the best way of managing what has been and still remains a complex and ambivalent relationship.

Notes

1. See J. F. Hough, *Russia and the West: Gorbachev and the Politics of Reform* (New York and London: Simon and Schuster, 1988), pp. 44–8, for an interesting discussion of Lenin's 'Slavophile' influences.
2. L. Kochan, *The Making of Modern Russia* (Harmondsworth: Penguin, 1971), p. 282.
3. M. MccGwire, *Perestroika and Soviet National Security* (Washington D.C.: Brookings Institution, 1991), Chapter 2.
4. T. Garton Ash, *In Europe's Name: Germany and the Divided Continent* (London: Vintage, 1994), p. 91.

5. V. Bunce, 'The Empire Strikes Back: the Evolution of the Eastern Bloc from a Soviet Asset to a Soviet Liability', *International Organization*, Vol. 39, No. 1, 1985, p. 20.
6. See M. Bowker and P. Williams, 'Helsinki and West European Security', *International Affairs*, Vol. 61, No. 4, 1985, pp. 607–18.
7. For detailed discussion of this view, see Garton Ash, *op. cit.*, pp. 258–65.
8. See M. Bowker and P. Williams, *Superpower Détente: a Reappraisal* (London: Sage, 1988), Chapter 7.
9. C. O'Halloran, 'Human Rights as Realpolitik: the United States in the CSCE', in *Defence Yearbook 1991* (London: Brasseys, 1991), pp. 63–84.
10. M. S. Gorbachev, *Perestroika: New Thinking for our Country and the World* (London: Collins, 1987), p. 143.
11. *Ibid.*, p. 151.
12. *Ibid.*, pp. 194–5.
13. *Ibid.*, p. 199.
14. Mikhail S. Gorbachev, *Zhizn' i reformy*, Vol. 2 (Moscow: Novosti, 1995), pp. 311–12; and Anatoly Chernayev, 'Gorbachev and the Reunification of Germany: Personal Perspectives', in G. Gorodetsky (ed.), *Soviet Foreign Policy, 1917–1991: a Retrospective* (London: Frank Cass, 1994), p. 158.
15. R. L. Garthoff, *The Great Transition: American-Soviet Relations and the End of the Cold War* (Washington D.C.: Brookings Institution, 1994), p. 573; J. Gedmin, *The Hidden Hand: Gorbachev and the Collapse of Eastern Germany* (Washington D.C.: AEI Press, 1992), p. 19.
16. *Frankfurter Allgemeine Zeitung*, 7 June 1991.
17. *New Times*, No. 12/13, 1991.
18. *Pravda*, 31 January 1990.
19. Chernayev, *op. cit.*, p. 167.
20. G. Gornig, 'The Contractual Settlement of the External Problems of German Unification', *Aussenpolitik*, Vol. 42, No. 1, 1991, pp. 3–12.
21. Many Russians speak of this oral agreement, and I have spoken to some of them. Western officials, however, continue to deny that any such undertaking was given. See also Chapter 3.
22. F. Oldenburg, 'The Settlement in Germany', in N. Malcolm (ed.), *Russia and Europe: An End to Confrontation?* (London and New York: Pinter Publishers/ London: Royal Institute of International Affairs, 1994), p. 110.
23. Russia was recognized as the 'continuing' state and thus assumed the Soviet Union's permanent seat on the UN Security Council.
24. These viewpoints have been divided up in rather different ways, and sometimes given different titles. See, for example, A. Pravda, 'The Politics of Foreign Policy', in S. White, A. Pravda and Z. Gitelman (eds.), *Developments in Russian Politics 4* (Houndmills: Macmillan, 1997), pp. 211–17; and A. Arbatov, 'Russia's Foreign Policy Alternatives', *International Security*, Vol. 18, No. 2, 1993, pp. 8–14, for detailed summaries of different schools of thought in regard to Russian foreign policy.
25. A. Kozyrev, 'Russia: A Chance for Survival', *Foreign Affairs*, Vol. 71, No. 2, 1992, pp. 8–10.
26. *Rossiiskie vesti*, 16 February 1993.
27. H. Adomeit, 'Russia as a "Great Power" in World Affairs: Images and Reality', *International Affairs*, Vol. 71, No. 1, 1995, p. 57.

28. *Nezavisimaya gazeta*, 28 March 1992.
29. J. Checkel, 'Russian Foreign Policy: Back to the Future', *Radio Free Europe/ Radio Liberty (RFE/RL) Research Report*, Vol. 1, No. 41, pp. 15–29; J. S. Adams, 'Legislature Asserts its Role in Russian Foreign Policy', *RFE/RL Research Report*, Vol. 2, No. 4, 1993, pp. 32–6, and S. Crow, 'Ambartsumov's Influence on Russian Foreign Policy', *RFE/RL Research Report*, Vol. 2, No. 19, 1993, pp. 36–41.
30. J. Lough, 'Defining Russia's Relations with Neighbouring States', *RFE/RL Research Report*, Vol. 2, No. 20, 1993, p. 58.
31. *Diplomaticheskii vestnik* (supplement), No. 1, 1993 and *Rossiiskie vesti*, 18 November 1993 contain the Foreign Policy Concept and Military Doctrine respectively.
32. *International Herald Tribune*, 6 December 1994.
33. M. Bowker, *Russian Foreign Policy after the Cold War* (Aldershot: Dartmouth, 1998), p. 148.
34. C. A. Wallander, 'The Russian National Security Concept: A Liberal-Statist Synthesis' (Programme on New Approaches to Russian Security, Harvard University), Memo No. 30, July 1998, <http://www.fas.harvard.edu/~ponars/ POLICYMEMOS/Wallander30.html>.
35. 'Russia in the Multi-Polar World' (interview with Yevgenni Primakov), *Russia*, No. 3, 1997, p. 6; L. Klepatskii (Deputy Director of the Department of Foreign Economic Planning, Russian Foreign Ministry), 'Russia's Foreign Policy Landmarks', *International Affairs* (Moscow), Vol. 45, No. 2, 1999, electronic edition, <http://home.mosinfo.ru/news/int-aff/1999/data/0021epat.htm>.
36. At this juncture Primakov was appointed Russian Prime Minister, hence enjoying a continued influence on foreign policy.
37. Soviet Foreign Minister Andrei Gromyko's boast in 1971 that 'there is not a single important question today which could be settled without the Soviet Union or in opposition to it' is echoed in Russian Foreign Minister Igor Ivanov's claim in 1999 that '[m]ost countries recognize [that] they cannot resolve today's major problems without Russia's direct participation'. See respectively, *Pravda*, 4 April 1971 and 'Russia Claims Progress in Search for World Role', Reuters, 25 January 1999, as carried on *Johnson's Russia List* (davidjohnson@erols.com), 26 January 1999.
38. 'Russia in the Multi-Polar World', *op. cit.*, p. 6. See also I. Ivanov, 'Europe on the Threshold of the 21st Century', *International Affairs* (Moscow), Vol. 45, No. 1, 1999, electronic edition, <http://home.mosinfo.ru/news/int-aff/1999/ data/019901.htm>.
39. *Diplomaticheskii vestnik*, No. 2, 1998, p. 4.
40. Celeste Wallander points to Russian involvement in CFE implementation and treaty adaptation, the withdrawal of former Soviet troops from East Germany, membership of the Paris Club of creditor nations and partnership with the EU as examples of mutually beneficial cooperation. See her 'International Institutions and Russian Security Cooperation' (Programme on New Approaches to Russian Security, Harvard University), Memo No. 48, November 1998, <http://www.fas.harvard.edu/~ponars/POLICYMEMOS/ wallander48.html>.
41. Adomeit, *op. cit.*, p. 35.
42. The 1997 National Security Concept thus states '[t]he main aim of safeguarding the Russian Federation's national security is the creation and

maintenance of an economic, political, international, and military-strategic position for the country which creates favourable conditions for the development of the individual, society and the state and [which] rules out the danger of a weakening of the Russian Federation's role and importance as a subject of international law and an undermining of the state's ability to implement its national interests in the international arena'. *Diplomaticheskii vestnik*, No. 2, 1998, p. 10.

43. O. Schuett, 'Russia and Europe: Balancing Cooperation with Integration', Discussion Papers in German Studies, No. IGS98/1 (University of Birmingham, Institute for German Studies, 1998), p. 29.

3
Russia and the North Atlantic Treaty Organization

Caroline Kennedy-Pipe

Introduction

The admission of the Czech Republic, Hungary and Poland into the North Atlantic Treaty Organization (NATO) in March 1999 represented a failure for Russian foreign policy. Opposition to the enlargement of the Atlantic Alliance had been prevalent throughout Russia's ruling circles from 1993. Russian antagonism to NATO enlargement centred not just around the question of the strategic orientation of the states of east-central Europe (ECE) but arose also from a desire not to be excluded from new security arrangements in Europe. The Russians attempted through a variety of tactics to prevent their former allies joining the western military alliance but also tried to persuade the western powers to consider pan-European security frameworks in preference to a larger NATO.

This chapter investigates Moscow's views of NATO following the end of the Cold War. After an initial, but short period, which was known as the 'honeymoon' in East–West relations, Moscow began to express its objections to the prospect of an enlargement of NATO's membership. Partly in response to Russian concerns, in 1994 NATO initiated the Partnership for Peace (PfP) programme. Western moves, however, did little to ameliorate Russian sensibilities and as this chapter demonstrates, Moscow remained deeply suspicious of enlargement. Indeed, it affected Russian attitudes toward the western powers, especially the United States (US), on a number of different issues, most notably the developing 'security architecture' in Europe, the conflicts in Bosnia and Kosovo, and Anglo-American military action in the Gulf region.

However, as this chapter also makes clear, Russia's internal problems (not least its economic weakness and continued political instability) have meant that it has had few options other than a pragmatic acceptance of an enlarged NATO and the adoption of a strategy to secure a special position for Russia in new NATO-related arrangements. Furthermore, since the mid-1990s, Russian foreign policy has sought to emphasize the possibility of a distinct Europe–Russia dimension (to the exclusion of the US) and has also stressed the possibility of a strategic alliance with either China, India or Iran to balance an enlarged NATO.

The 'honeymoon' period

Yeltsin's initial strategy in foreign policy was characterized by a determination to develop positive relations with the West and a pro-western and a pro-American stance was apparent in the Kremlin's relations with the outside world. In a manner reminiscent of the policies of Mikhail Gorbachev, Yeltsin appeared to believe that the maintenance of positive relations with the West would result in economic benefits. Contact with western leaders was evident in Yeltsin's priorities. At the turn of the year 1991–92 he paid visits to all the Group of Seven (G7) states apart from Japan (Russo-Japanese relations were still marred by an outstanding dispute over the Kurile Islands).

This orientation toward the West was facilitated by a drive for democratization. Some within the Russian leadership favoured a form of rapid integration with the West to help political liberalization at home. Yeltsin's advisers at this stage were markedly pro-western. This was true especially of Andrei Kozyrev, the Foreign Minister who had, in the past, been an unstinting supporter of Gorbachev's 'new political thinking' in foreign affairs. Under Yeltsin, he was, at least initially, given wide-ranging powers to oversee and coordinate foreign policy issues.

In early 1992, Kozyrev asked the European Community (EC) to assist Russia in becoming a 'normal' state and in June 1992, at a summit in Washington, Kozyrev promised greater collaboration between Russia and the US.[1] The thinking of the Foreign Minister was inspired by the belief that many of the problems which had dogged the Soviet Union, both economically and politically, had actually arisen from 'being on the wrong side of the Cold War'. He argued that Russia had to join its natural home which, he claimed, lay with the developed nations of the West.[2]

During this period, Yeltsin implemented a series of measures designed to reassure the West of benign Russian intent. Amidst the better known (the signing of the Strategic Arms Reduction Treaty (START) II in January 1993 and Russian support for sanctions against Yugoslavia) some notable steps were also taken with specific regard to NATO. In late December

1991, Yeltsin made the surprising and highly symbolic suggestion that membership of the Alliance was 'a long-term policy aim' of Russia.[3] At this juncture Russia also joined the North Atlantic Cooperation Council (NACC), a consultative forum embracing the NATO members, the former Warsaw Pact states and the Soviet successor states. During 1992 NACC played an important part in facilitating talks on an adjustment of the Conventional Forces in Europe (CFE) Treaty in the former Soviet zone of application, and was a useful forum for discussions involving Mosow on Russian troop withdrawals from the Baltic states and conflict resolution in the former Soviet Union (FSU) (in Georgia, Moldova and Nagorno-Karabakh).[4] Military-to-military contacts were also pursued and in January 1993 John Shalikashvili, the Supreme Allied Commander in Europe, visited Moscow to discuss future cooperation between Russia and NATO.[5]

The basis of this cooperative policy was, however, under strain from an early stage and there were indications during 1992 that the honeymoon in relations between East and West might not last for a variety of reasons. One of the most compelling was the emergence of opposition within Russian ruling circles to what might be termed the Kozyrev strategy. Indeed, the pro-western stance in foreign policy became immersed in the developing struggle between Yeltsin and his parliamentary opponents over the future of the reform process. During December 1992, Yeltsin suffered a notable setback when he yielded to pressure and replaced his liberal leaning Prime Minster, Yegor Gaidor with Viktor Chernomyrdin, a politician from the centre of the political spectrum.

During a speech to a Conference on Security and Cooperation in Europe (CSCE) meeting of Foreign Ministers in Stockholm in December 1992, Kozyrev, influenced by events at home, warned his audience that if the opposition to the Yeltsin government was successful, a far less cooperative line would be taken in foreign policy. This might, he indicated, include less support for the western position over the conflict in the former Yugoslavia and the adoption of a more assertive line toward the other former Soviet republics.[6] Despite Kozyrev's assertion that this was only a warning shot to alert the West to what might happen if Yeltsin's opponents took power, it also indicated a struggle over the future course of Russian foreign policy. Indeed, at this point it was not clear where, institutionally, foreign policy was being determined. Changes during 1991–92 had shaken up the distribution of decision-making power among the Foreign Ministry, the security services and the Ministry of Defence. The disintegration of the Communist Party apparatus had also deprived the foreign policy system of its central information processing and decision-making agency.

By early 1993, movement within and amongst Russian institutions signalled a resurgence of more conservative institutions such as the military. In January, the role of the Ministry of Defence was formalized in the making of foreign policy but this development was overshadowed by the struggle between Yeltsin and his opponents in the Parliament. All aspects of foreign policy were affected by the prolonged power struggle within Russian politics. The violent suppression of the Parliament (the Russian Congress of People's Deputies) in October 1993 had actually eradicated the most visible opposition to Yeltsin but its successor, the Federal Assembly (and particularly the lower chamber of this new body, the Duma) continued to put pressure on the President. The formation of Duma committees on foreign policy issues seemed to signal an attempt by the new Parliament to influence the conduct of external strategies. The Head of the Geopolitics Committee, Viktor Ustinov, and his Vice Chair, Mikhail Sidorov, were actually members of the aggressively nationalist Liberal Democratic Party of Russia and had visibly demonstrated their dissatisfaction with the Kozyrev line in foreign policy. In addition, the International Affairs Committee was chaired by Vladimir Lukin, a former ambassador to the US, and a man renowned for his tendency to stress Russia's position as a great power and its important role among the successor states. Not only was Lukin reputed to have developed a strained relationship with Kozyrev but he had been openly critical of what he termed the 'romantic infantile pro-Americanism' of the early post-Cold War period.[7] These committees were accordingly markedly less pro-western in their outlooks than the Ministry of Foreign Affairs. Their composition undoubtedly helped to weaken the overall position of the Foreign Minister.

Kozyrev was further undermined by the growth of the military as a direct participant in political affairs. During the Soviet period the military had avoided crossing into direct involvement in political struggles and even during the coup of 1991 had remained largely neutral in the moves made against Gorbachev. During the political crisis of 1993, Yeltsin's decision to order the army against those who threatened to unseat him signalled a break with the past. However, the Yeltsin-inspired storming of the Parliament meant that the military as an institution was now a powerful factor in politics. Indeed, the military doctrine of November 1993 provided for the army to become involved in internal politics in order to tackle internal social, ecological and other upheavals.[8] Senior military officers became increasingly outspoken on all political issues. The general dissatisfaction with the orientation of Kozyrev's foreign policy as well as the lack of resources for the armed forces accounted for the strong support given by the military to the ultra-nationalist Liberal Democratic Party of Vladimir Zhirinovsky during the December 1993 Duma elections.

Continued economic decline within Russia was at this stage a significant influence on external policies. It undermined those such as Kozyrev who argued that closer integration with the West would result in positive economic linkages. In particular, resentment was expressed at the terms under which Yeltsin had allowed the International Monetary Fund (IMF) to exact high interest rates from Russia in return for credit.[9] Moreover, there was great resentment that early western promises of substantial economic assistance, private investment and quick benefits for Russia had never really materialized. This resulted, by 1993, in an increasing backlash against the idea of a 'strategic friendship and partnership' between Russia and the West.

The formal adoption of a more assertive line in Russian foreign policy came in the autumn of 1993. The 'Main Provisions of the Military Doctrine of the Russian Federation' of November 1993 allowed for the use of force on the territory of the successor states and abandoned the Soviet pledge of 'no first use' of nuclear weapons.[10] NATO and the issue of western military expansion quickly became another area in which the Russians attempted to exercise influence.

The problem of NATO enlargement

Kozyrev had, during his tenure as Foreign Minister, outlined a distinct vision for the future security architecture of Europe. He had envisaged a partnership with the US which would manage the affairs of the continent. In the new Europe, he hoped that NATO would, over time, be regarded as a relic of the Cold War and that pan-European security structures would take precedence over bloc politics.[11] However, as became clear throughout 1993 and 1994, NATO proved to be far more resilient than Kozyrev had anticipated. Part, at least, of this vigour was derived from the enthusiasm of certain of the former Warsaw Pact states to join the Alliance.

As early as February 1990, Hungary, for example, had intimated that it wished to become a member of NATO. This ambition was not at first subject to any hard scrutiny in the West. In the main this was because western politicians feared that any such discussion might boost anti-democratic forces within Russia, but also because it was believed that such a debate might delay the withdrawal of Soviet troops from ECE. The western powers were also reluctant to open such a controversial dialogue when Moscow was providing valuable support to the anti-Iraq coalition which was waging war against Saddam Hussein.

Yet throughout 1991 the so-called Visegrad three of the then Czecho-slovakia, Poland and Hungary continued to press their case for admission to NATO. The Visegrad states put forward a triple rationale for admission: to be relieved of their position as part of the historic *cordon sanitaire* between Russia and western Europe, to achieve the benefits of collective security, and to promote the westernization of their region. On the latter point, they cited the importance of NATO to the development of a vibrant community of democratic states. Indeed, ECE leaders were keenly aware of the important role played by the Alliance in supporting democracy in Spain, Portugal and Greece after periods of dictatorship. The western powers, however, made it clear that it was unlikely that Hungary or any of the other ECE states would be admitted to either the then EC or NATO, both of which remained committed, at this point, in Jacques Delors' words, to a 'deepening not a broadening' of their organizational bases.[12] Such statements did little to dampen the ardour of the Visegrad three; and their insistence that their destinies lay with western institutions continued to engender Russian opposition to the idea of an enlarged NATO.

The Russians argued that the expansion of NATO posed several security-related problems. One was that it represented the creation of a new dividing line separating Russia politically and economically from Europe. The Russians also argued that enlargement was a betrayal of the terms on which the Cold War had ended in Europe. Western leaders, it was asserted, had promised not to enlarge the Alliance, during the 'two-plus-four' talks, which had taken place over German unification in 1990. Russia claimed that it had agreed to the incorporation of East Germany into NATO but that in return for this concession, the western powers had agreed not to extend NATO beyond into ECE.[13] Furthermore, Kozyrev was, by 1993, concerned at the ramifications of the extension of NATO for Russian domestic politics. In particular, he was anxious that it might feed support for radical nationalist sentiment. Kozyrev attempted some diplomatic subtlety and argued that the idea of NATO enlargement 'smelt of mothballs'. Rather, he called for a new and 'creative' solution to escape the old bloc mentalities, which had sustained the Cold War. In particular, he returned to the idea of a reinvigorated CSCE as the primary agent for security in Europe. This meant the development of a security structure in which Russia would be a major participant and rebuffed any notion that the US could operate a unipolar foreign policy or a Pax Americana.[14]

While opposition to the extension of NATO ran through practically all the ruling élite in Moscow, it took different forms. The most dramatic scenario was that NATO expansion was an aggressive move that threatened

Russia's security and demanded a response. The 1993 military doctrine, for instance, referred to the 'expansion of military blocs and alliances' as a main source of military threat to Russia, while Alexi Arbartov, the Director of the Centre for Geopolitical and Military Forecasts, argued that 'if NATO is moving eastward for no apparent reason, it is Russia's duty to push its defensive lines as far westward as possible'.[15]

From Partnership for Peace to the Founding Act

Russian foreign policy in Europe was, during 1993–94, a not terribly well coordinated mixture of new initiatives and rather familiar sounding threats of military reaction. Yeltsin, for example, urged the West not to expand NATO and exclude Russia, yet almost simultaneously, Moscow requested that the restrictions imposed by the CFE Treaty on combat equipment in the Russian Caucasus be lifted. Moscow appeared likely to try and counter-balance any enlargement of NATO with a build up of forces in the area of the Caucasus bordering on Georgia, Armenia and Azerbaijan.[16]

In deference to Russian objections, a compromise agreement was put forward at a NATO summit in January 1994. This was the PfP programme. It arose from an idea that had been discussed at a meeting of NATO Defence Ministers in Trevemune in Germany in October 1993. PfP was a halfway house that allowed the ECE states (plus the Soviet successor states and Russia itself) to move closer to NATO but stopped short of their formal incorporation as full members of the Alliance. In this light, and rather cynically, PfP became known as the 'partnership for postponement'. One senior American diplomat described it as a 'very skilful compromise between people who said we should do nothing to offend the Russians and people who said we should let the east Europeans in now'.[17] Aspirant new members, rather than being offered admission to the Alliance were, through PfP, permitted individual cooperation agreements that involved activities such as military training, and aid in the strengthening of civilian control over their armed forces.[18]

Although in ECE, the PfP programme was regarded as a waiting room through which NATO membership could eventually be secured, officially, Moscow claimed PfP represented a success for Russia for it showed that western capitals had taken into account Russian objections to the expansion of NATO. Kozyrev suggested that PfP could be seen as an initiative which would facilitate movement toward a pan-European security system involving not only NATO but also the CSCE.[19] Yet some in Moscow continued to object publicly to PfP, and the Duma was especially vocal in its criticisms. Even advisers close to Yeltsin accepted that Russian acquiescence to PfP had given a seal of approval to NATO's widening ambitions in European security.[20] Yet, after a great deal of backroom diplomacy, Yeltsin succeeded in over-riding the objections of the Duma and negotiated Russia's own membership of the scheme. In June 1994, Kozyrev signed the PfP general framework agreement in Brussels, which, in deference to Russian sensitivities, was accompanied by a special Russia–NATO protocol that acknowledged Russia's 'unique and important contribution [...] as a major European, world and nuclear power'.[21] This satisfied, at least in part, the Russian desire to have its status as a great power recognized. Russia's decision to join PfP appeared motivated by the fear that if it did not join, NATO would proceed with enlargement anyway. A second motive was also apparent, namely to exploit PfP to Russia's advantage. Moscow, however, despite its hopes, received no veto over NATO's decisions nor special privileges in any of NATO's formal mechanisms.[22]

Despite signing up to PfP, the Russians continued to advocate alternative schemes for security in Europe. In particular, Moscow remained a proponent of a broadly based security structure centred on the CSCE. Such a scheme would, of course, have secured a leading role for Russia, as the CSCE was the one security organization in Europe of which Russia had full membership. During 1994, Russian diplomats espoused the idea for a radically reformulated CSCE. The Russian idea was that over a period of time, this organization would subsume NATO. The initiative was, however, rejected at the preparatory meeting for the CSCE summit in Budapest. Yet despite this lukewarm reception, Russian spokesmen continued to advocate the notion that pan-European security arrangements could be seen as viable alternatives to an expansion of NATO (see Chapter 5).

Both PfP and Russia's pan-European vision failed to meet either the security concerns or the political ambitions of the ECE states, many of whom continued to press for full admission to NATO. The Polish President, Lech Walesa, was open in his criticism that PfP was a timid response and utterly inadequate to meet the security aspirations of his country. The Czech President, Vaclav Havel was equally adamant that the Visegrad countries should be admitted to NATO immediately as a reassurance against Russian revanchism and in particular the possibility that totalitarian forces could once again take power in Moscow.[23] The brutal Russian military attack on Chechnya later in 1994, demonstrated for many in ECE that Yeltsin had succumbed to an alliance with chauvinistic nationalist forces.

In response to ECE demands, as early as the autumn of 1994, the US administration of Bill Clinton acknowledged that PfP had limitations and began to explore avenues through which the Visegrad states might become full members of NATO. The Americans presented their views in December 1994 to a meeting of NATO's North Atlantic Council in Brussels. This discussion sparked a furious Russian reaction. Kozyrev, who had been due to sign Russia's individual PfP cooperation agreement demurred,[24] while Yeltsin warned at the CSCE's Budapest summit of the onset of a 'cold peace' should NATO enlarge (see also Chapter 2). The Russian Defence Minister, Pavel Grachev, meanwhile warned that Russia would have to take additional security measures; some commentators in Moscow suggested that this might even take the form of the redeployment of tactical nuclear missiles.[25] Kozyrev delivered a speech before the assembly of the Western European Union (WEU) in which he accused the ECE states of capriciousness and suggested that the US was trying to force the enlargement of NATO on its allies. In tones reminiscent of Mikhail Gorbachev's call for a 'common European home' during the late 1980s, he suggested that the Europeans should look after themselves and intimated that the WEU in conjunction with Russia could provide adequate security measures.[26]

The Russian propaganda offensive against the enlargement of NATO continued over the following months. In November 1995, for example, Grachev, during a visit to NATO headquarters, argued that the goal for NATO should be its transformation into an instrument of pan-European security. Grachev, however, as well as putting forward new initiatives continued to mix ideas with threats. Failure to recognize Russia's concern over NATO expansion would, he warned, mean that Russia's military doctrine would have to be revised toward mounting a stout defence. The preference though continued to be a genuine pan-European security organization (which need not be NATO) to secure Russia's position in Europe. It was thus suggested that Russia could, given the opportunity, became a natural partner in the East for both the European Union (EU) and the WEU.[27]

Russia, however, failed to appreciate that for many of the major European powers European security institutions were seen as complementary to, but certainly not replacements for NATO. In particular, the British under both Conservative and Labour governments were adamant that the US should continue to play an important part in the new European security architecture. As Tony Blair told the House of Commons in 1997, one of the purposes of NATO was to bind the Americans and the Europeans more closely together.[28]

On 5 January 1996, Kozyrev was replaced as Foreign Minister. This event appeared directly related to the issues of NATO and the broader problems of European security. In particular, Kozyrev was accused by the influential Russian commentator Sergi Karaganov of having mishandled the problem of NATO expansion. Karaganov had earlier warned that the Russian people were experiencing what he termed 'a Versailles syndrome' after the collapse of the Soviet Union and the corresponding growth in the power of the West. He argued that rather than inhibiting NATO expansion, Kozyrev's strategies had in fact led to its acceleration.[29] Kozyrev was replaced by Yevgeny Primakov, a former head of Russia's Foreign Intelligence Service. This appointment was read by many as yet more evidence of the decision in Moscow to take a more assertive line in relations with the West.

These observers were seemingly not disappointed. Primakov suggested that his appointment was inspired by the need to 'strengthen the Foreign Ministry's efforts to protect Russia's national interests' and that Russia was a great power and needed to protect its status.[30] At his first press conference as Foreign Minister Primakov argued that Russia held a 'negative attitude' toward NATO expansion and that such a move was 'counter-productive for the stabilization of the situation in Europe and would undoubtedly create a new geopolitical situation for Russia'.[31] Primakov made it clear that Russian opposition to enlargement was premised on a belief that it would re-divide Europe. Russian objections were further elaborated upon when, in December 1996, Grachev's successor as Defence Minister Igor Rodionov outlined the grounds on which the Russian military opposed expansion. In particular, he stressed that in its push eastwards, the military-political equilibrium in Europe would be upset by NATO as its air and ground forces would increase in potential by approximately 15–20 per cent. He also argued that the 'buffer zone' would disappear and that NATO might deploy nuclear weapons in ECE.[32] NATO attempted to allay Russian fears by outlining the so-called 'three no's' formulation. The final communiqué of the North Atlantic Council meeting in December 1996 stated that NATO had 'no intention, no plan and no reason' to deploy nuclear weapons on the territory of any new members. While this might have provided a modicum of reassurance for Russia, NATO also announced that it would agree on a timetable for enlargement by July 1997.[33]

Opposition within Russian ruling circles to the expansion of NATO was also articulated by Aleksandr Lebed, Secretary of the Security Council for a few months after Yeltsin's re-election in July 1996. Lebed, a veteran of the Afghan war, argued that the expansion of NATO could provide the grounds for a third world war that would bury everyone under the rubble. Less dramatically and perhaps more accurately, Lebed pointed out that NATO was a military alliance, by its very nature it needed a foe and in the context of Europe that enemy was obviously Russia. Lebed however seemed to understand that there was little that Russia could do to prohibit the entry of the ECE states into NATO. Instead, Lebed turned to pointing out that the costs of expansion for the West European states might very well outweigh the benefits. He argued that NATO leaders would soon see their error especially as he promised that Moscow would find ways of bringing the costs of NATO expansion home to the attention of British and American taxpayers.[34] However, Lebed's pragmatism was not shared by others. In January 1997 statements from the Russian leadership made it clear that Moscow objected to the long-term presence of NATO troops in south ECE in support of the peacekeeping mission in Bosnia; and the following month Lebed's successor Ivan Rybkin argued that Russia should be prepared to be the first to use nuclear weapons if attacked.[35]

The Russian Duma, meanwhile, linked the process of NATO expansion to Russian compliance on other security issues, withholding, for example, ratification of the START II Treaty. A link between nuclear disarmament and NATO plans for enlargement was also explicitly made by Gennadi Zyuganov, the leader of the Russian Communist Party. He argued that as NATO expansion would disrupt the balance of power in Europe, Russia would have to find means to offset its new more disadvantaged position.[36] Parliamentary opposition in Moscow to NATO expansion intensified during the spring of 1997 when it became apparent that Yeltsin and Primakov were negotiating a special security charter with the Secretary General of NATO, Javier Solana. These negotiations implied an acceptance that NATO would expand eastwards. In the course of the Yeltsin–Clinton summit at Helsinki in March, Yeltsin, despite criticism at home, acknowledged that reality. In this light, the Russian position had undergone a significant shift. This boiled down to continued public opposition to enlargement, coupled with a recognition, often unspoken, that the process was inevitable and that Russia should seek to exact as many concessions as possible from the Alliance. These included putting the Russian–NATO relationship on some sort of legal footing[37] and demands that NATO make no plans for either the construction of new bases or for the deployment of foreign troops and nuclear weapons on the territory of new NATO members.[38]

Russian policy, then, had struck a balance between cooperation and confrontation. Throughout early 1997 rhetoric in Russia was highly charged. Yeltsin, for instance, compared the political climate between Moscow and Washington to that of the period of the Cuban missile crisis of 1962.[39] Yet in May, Yeltsin agreed a deal with NATO. Through this, the way was paved for the expansion of the Alliance into ECE. 'The Founding Act on Mutual Relations, Cooperation and Security' between NATO and Russia, signed in Paris in May 1997, enshrined several key provisions. NATO affirmed its stance on nuclear weapons policy toward new members and suggested also that in the foreseeable future it had no intention of deploying any significant combat forces on a permanent basis in ECE, although the Alliance did reserve the right to deploy additional forces 'in the event of defence against a threat of aggression'. One further feature of the Founding Act was the establishment of the NATO–Russia Permanent Joint Council (PJC), which was designed as the principal mechanism for consultation with Moscow. This body was tasked with the resolution of future disagreements. Although, once again it should be noted that, despite the creation of the new body, the Russians would not actually be able to veto NATO decisions. It was also agreed that Moscow would establish a mission to NATO headed by an ambassador. Specific areas for consultation and cooperation were also agreed across areas such as theatre missile defence forces, regional air traffic safety and increasing transparency in the size of the conventional forces of both NATO member states and Russia.[40]

One of the most significant features of the western attitude toward enlargement in this period was that the criteria for admission to NATO contained an explicit connection between democratic government and the evolution of comprehensive security regimes in Europe. In particular, agreement was demanded from aspiring members that principles of democracy, pluralism, the rule of law and respect for human rights and free market economics had central roles to play in future security arrangements. The idea that security could only really flourish amongst and between democratic states was stressed at a NATO summit in Madrid in July 1997. This emphasis on the requirement for members to have fostered successful democracies and market economics made it less likely that Russia (if it still harboured the hope) could or would be admitted to the Alliance at any point in the near future.

At Madrid, NATO invited Poland, the Czech Republic and Hungary to open talks for accession. Discussions over this so-called 'first wave' of membership were, however, dogged by disagreements amongst NATO members over exactly which states should be admitted. Dispute centred in particular around the French insistence that Romania be accepted. The Americans were adamant that Romania did not yet conform to the conditions of membership. This disagreement was studied avidly on the Russian side, which interpreted the row as clear evidence of tension between American and European visions of the future. The resolution of the issue was an American victory: Romania was denied immediate access to membership. This was interpreted in Moscow as a substantial blow not just for the French but for the unity of the Alliance. Not least, it was correctly perceived as postponing the full reintegration of France into NATO, President Jacques Chirac having made his view clear that France would be prepared to rejoin NATO's integrated military structures, only if and when the organization became less dominated by America.[41]

During these debates, the Russians appeared to become aware of what might be termed the 'Europeanization' of defence, a process which had been slowly evolving within NATO since the end of the Cold War. The French in particular had taken the lead in initiating debate and suggesting the practical steps which might be taken on the road to a more assertive and specifically European dimension to security on the continent. The EU had began to move toward the notion that it should possess a credible set of policies and priority was attached to developing forces to address this contingency, albeit in a manner that would complement, not replace, NATO. A new defence agreement was actually signed between the UK and France at St Malo in December 1998, which provided for joint military and diplomatic actions in response to international crises.[42] This was taken a step further by the EU's European Council meeting in Cologne in June 1999. Here the EU agreed to appoint a supremo to oversee the organization's Common Foreign and Security Policy and to develop military capabilities (through a formal absorption of the WEU by the end of 2000) in order to undertake conflict prevention and management tasks.[43] NATO itself, moreover, had, at its 50th anniversary summit in April, facilitated this process by indicating a willingness to permit the EU access to its collective military facilities.[44]

Russia was keen to see in which direction the Europeanization of defence would move. In particular, at this point, there were signs that the Russians believed that Germany could yet take the initiative in promoting discussion over a new security regime on the continent. The Russian press was intrigued in late 1998 when German Foreign Minister Joschka Fischer floated the idea that NATO renounce its nuclear first strike option. Once it was obvious that the Americans were upset by this idea, the German government was quick to assure the US Secretary of Defence, William Cohen, that it supported a policy of first strike and would not subject NATO to a rupture on the issue.[45] Nevertheless, the discussion in Germany was noted with interest in Russia as a sign, along with developments in Britain and France, that 'today's Europe [. . .] has grown tired of American monopolism'.[46] Indeed, since at least 1997 a trend has been apparent in Russian diplomacy which seeks to find and exploit contradictory trends within NATO. During the Cold War, analysts often claimed that Soviet foreign policy-makers sought to manipulate contradictions within the West, especially those between the US and its European allies. It used, indeed, to be fashionable to discuss the ability of the Soviet leadership to create special relations with western states such as France to perhaps 'dilute' American influence on the continent.[47] There is a certain resonance between Soviet tactics and those of contemporary Russia. There is little doubt that both Primakov and his successor as Foreign Minister, Igor Ivanov, have tried to create a sense of a European destiny that is separate from that of the US. In part this has arisen from a desire to promote pan-European security arrangements in preference to NATO, but Russian diplomacy was also inspired by the distinct downturn in its relations with the second Clinton administration.

The new 'cool war'

During 1998–99, although elements of cooperation were still evident (notably, Russian participation in S-For in Bosnia and, until March 1999, activities under the auspices of the PfP and the PJC[48]), the relationship between Russia and the NATO states deteriorated markedly. One commentator quipped that by the autumn of 1998 a new 'cool war' had broken out.[49] In part, this can be attributed to western (and specifically American) unease at economic and political developments in Russia following the financial crash of August 1998 and the formation the following month of a left-leaning government under newly appointed Prime Minister Primakov. Yet the downturn was also caused by a growing Russian resentment at NATO actions. In the first place, Moscow remained concerned – even fixated – on the enlargement issue. The accession talks with the Czech Republic, Hungary and Poland during 1998 resulted in continual warnings from Yeltsin, Primakov and Ivanov at the dangers of enlargement and that the process should not cross a 'red line' and embrace any of the Soviet successor states, specifically those of the Baltics.[50]

In this light, US and NATO overtures toward Estonia, Latvia and Lithuania were particularly unwelcome. In January 1998, President Clinton signed a formal document with his Baltic counterparts. Although the document – known as the 'Charter of Partnership' – did not make a definite promise of Alliance membership, it did display a formal commitment to the preservation of the independence of the Baltic nations and suggested that NATO membership remained 'open to all European democracies [. . .] as each aspirant proves itself able and willing to assume the responsibilities and obligations of membership'.[51] NATO's 50th anniversary summit in April 1999 reiterated this pledge, while welcoming the 'continuing efforts and progress of Estonia, Latvia and Lithuania' toward meeting the standards of membership.[52]

Russia has objected not only to the prospect of the Baltic states joining NATO but to the relationship which has developed between Ukraine and the Alliance. This has raised, for Moscow, the spectre of western influence in the strategic area of the Black Sea. Russia vigorously objected to American-led naval exercises ('Operation Sea Breeze 97') off the Crimean coast in August 1997. US warships, the first to visit the Crimea since the USSR collapsed in 1991, joined naval vessels from Turkey, Romania, Bulgaria and Georgia in manoeuvres just offshore of the Ukrainian naval base at Donuzlav, which lies north of Sevastopol. The decision to hold the manoeuvres had been taken by Kiev, a move interpreted as provocative by Moscow as Russia and Ukraine still remained at loggerheads over the sovereignty of Sevastopol and ownership of the Black Sea Fleet. Russian sensitivities over the region had already been aroused, when they discovered that during the naval exercises NATO forces were to enact an invasion of the Crimea to help Ukraine put down a separatist uprising.[53] There has also been discussion between Kiev and NATO that the Alliance might lease the Yavorov military training ground.[54]

Despite Russian objections, there is little that it can do to prevent NATO playing a more active role *vis-à-vis* Ukraine or indeed elsewhere. When, in April 1999 NATO adopted its new 'Strategic Concept' with references to the Alliance's role in the provision of 'security and stability' in the entire 'Euro-Atlantic area', Defence Minister Igor Sergeyev threatened that Russia would be forced to 'reconsider many provisions for ensuring its own security'.[55] Similarly, the NATO air attacks against Serbia/Yugoslavia during the Kosovo crisis in the spring of 1999 provoked Yeltsin to threaten military intervention and the possibility of 'a European war or even a world war'.[56] Russian consternation on this latter issue had a number of causes, but foremost amongst them was a disillusionment at NATO's ability to execute military action without any prior consultation with Moscow and without any regard for those diplomatic fora, such as the United Nations Security Council and the Organization for Security and Cooperation in Europe (OSCE), which would have permitted Russia a key role in conflict resolution efforts. As such, this seemed to make a mockery of the spirit of consultation that imbued the NATO–Russia Founding Act. As Colonel-General Leonid Ivashov, head of the Defence Ministry's Main Directorate for International Military Cooperation, argued shortly after air-strikes were launched, 'NATO ha[d] negated the fundamental principles upon which Russia's relations with this bloc were based.' NATO, he continued, had 'spat' upon the Founding Act and it was difficult to foresee how Moscow could trust any future agreements entered into with the Alliance. In this light, it was 'hard to say when a constructive period in relations with NATO [... could] be resumed'.[57]

Despite the diplomatic atmospherics, however, the actual measures that Russia has taken in response to NATO actions have been largely symbolic. Moscow's protestations during the Kosovo crisis led it during March–April 1999 to suspend Russian participation in the PfP, to remove staff officers from the Russian contingent in S-For, to recall its chief military representative at NATO headquarters in Brussels, to postpone negotiations on opening a NATO military mission in Moscow and to withdraw from the PJC. As such, these were hardly likely to dissuade NATO from its air campaign. Russian restraint can be seen as, in part, premised on a desire not to jeopardize ongoing areas of cooperation essential to its own material interests. Tellingly, at the same time that Yeltsin was warning of an escalation of tension with NATO and alluding to a muscular Russian response, the Primakov government was negotiating with the IMF for further loans and taking delivery of food assistance from the EU. As Lebed had explained shortly before the Kosovo crisis, 'it's hard to make threats and bear your chest when your stomach hurts from lack of food'.[58]

Yet whatever the weakness of the Russian response, it was clear that Moscow harboured some deeply felt grievances at the increasing assertiveness of NATO. This did not mean a complete termination of links with the Alliance;[59] it did, however, suggest that the balance between confrontation and cooperation had shifted toward the former.

Conclusion: toward a new realism?

Jonathon Haslam has made the point that since the end of the Cold War, Russia has been treated as a defeated power.[60] While there is some substance to this claim, it is only truly accurate, if contemporary Russian interests are equated with Soviet ones. Although it is undoubtedly the case that the shrinkage of the Soviet sphere of influence in ECE has been a painful process for Moscow, the new Russia has extracted certain concessions from the West to sustain its position in a reconfigured Europe. To this extent at least, Russia has argued forcibly, and in many senses successfully, that it has an important and considerable role to play in the future security architecture of the European continent. The profile of the OSCE has been raised and although many western powers were never realistically going to accept what might be termed Russia's 'either NATO or OSCE' strategy, there is now a serious and sensible discussion of the relationship between the two. During December 1998, Ivanov visited Sweden, Norway, Belgium and Spain in a bid to promote debate about the new European security architecture for Europe. While Moscow has continued to pursue the notion of the OSCE as a parallel organization to NATO,[61] it has also stressed that Moscow would attempt to use the Founding Act to exercise influence over NATO activities. The 1999 Kosovo crisis may have disabused Russia of the value of these channels, but it has not made them redundant. The European neutrals remain as committed to the OSCE as ever and the organization retains some credibility in the Balkans as a neutral arena of diplomacy and post-conflict settlement efforts. As for NATO, while Russia was aggrieved at the absence of prior notification of air-strikes in relation to Kosovo, once these had been launched NATO was keen to keep Moscow abreast of developments and to solicit its assistance in communicating and negotiating with the Milosevic regime in Belgrade (see Chapter 8).

There are also signs that the Russians have accepted the enlargement process (outside of the FSU at least) and the fact that little can be done to prevent the closer integration, both militarily and politically, of the former Warsaw Pact states with western Europe. Indeed, Moscow has, since the signing of the Founding Act, displayed elements of what might be termed a new realism in its foreign policy. It has accepted that many of the ECE states will indeed go their own way and that Moscow's most constructive path is to build positive relationships with its former Soviet allies.

Moscow has, furthermore, benefited from indirect pressure placed upon the ECE states to normalize their relations with Russia. NATO has made it clear that before any 'second wave' of enlargement can begin, potential new members must prove that they are stabilizing factors in regional politics.[62] For Russia this has positive benefits, for it suggests that states such as Romania, Bulgaria and the Slovak Republic must have resolved outstanding political and territorial problems (often stemming from the Soviet period) with Moscow before their admission. Thus in the autumn of 1998, for example, Russia held talks with the Romanians to tackle historical disputes such as those relating to the treatment of Bessarabia and Northern Bukovina in 1940.[63]

Within the region of the FSU, Russia is far more jealous of NATO activities and there are signs that Moscow will continue to resist the

Alliance here. Its options, however, are not plentiful. Russia is at present economically and militarily too weak to offer comprehensive military assistance to its neighbours that would undermine PfP activities, and the prospect of a counter-alliance against NATO, either within the Commonwealth of Independent States or alongside say China and Iran, is questionable (a point taken up in the book's concluding chapter). NATO is, however, very sensitive to Russia's claims to influence in the region and is aware of the strategic challenges of incorporating states along Russia's borders. In this light, the loudness of Russian protests alone may prove sufficient to deter NATO from deepening its engagement in this area.

Notes

1. *Pravda*, 13 May 1992.
2. Cited in D. Simes, 'The Return of Russian History', *Foreign Affairs*, Vol. 73, No. 1, 1994, p. 78.
3. BBC, Summary of World Broadcasts, SU/1262 A1/1, 23 December 1991.
4. S. Croft, J. Redmond, G. Wyn Rees and M. Webber, *The Enlargement of Europe* (Manchester and New York: Manchester University Press, 1999), p. 28; A. de Franchis, 'The CFE Treaty – the Role of the High Level Working Group', *NATO Review*, Vol. 40, No. 5, 1992, pp. 12–16.
5. *Nezavisimaya gazeta*, 30 January 1993.
6. *The Independent*, 15 December 1992.
7. *Nezavisimaya gazeta*, 20 October 1992, cited in A. A. Bouchkin, 'Russia's Far Eastern Policy in the 1990s', in A. Dawisha and K. Dawisha (eds.), *The Making of Foreign Policy in Russia and the New States of Eurasia* (New York: Sharpe, 1995), p. 69.
8. D. R. Herspring, *Russian Civil-Military Relations* (Bloomington and Indianapolis: Indiana University Press,1996), p. 168.
9. *Pravda*, 13 May 1992.
10. 'Osnovnye polozheniya voennoy doktriny Russiyskoy Federatsii', *Krasnaya zvezda*, 19 November 1993.
11. A. Kozyrev, 'The Lagging Partnership', *Foreign Affairs*, Vol. 73, No. 3, 1994, pp. 58–71.
12. Delors was speaking specifically about the EC but his message had a broad relevance, namely that the development of any new security structures following the collapse of the Cold War order should not derail the West European integration process. See his 'European Integration and Security', *Survival*, Vol. 32, No. 2, 1991, pp. 99–110.
13. *Frankfurter Allgemeine Zietung*, 8 May 1995, cited in C. Bluth, 'The Post-Soviet Space and Europe', in R. Allison and C. Bluth (eds.), *Security Dilemmas in Russia and Eurasia* (London: Royal Institute of International Affairs 1998), p. 335.
14. *Sevodnya*, 9 September 1993.
15. *Nezavisimaya gazeta*, 1 October 1993.
16. *Izvestiya*, 8 October 1993.

17. *The New York Times*, 4 January 1994, quoted in J. Haslam, 'Russia's Seat at the Table: a Place Denied or a Place Delayed?', *International Affairs*, Vol. 74, No. 1, 1998, pp. 119–30.
18. M. Mihalka, 'European–Russian Security and NATO's Partnership for Peace', *Radio Free Europe/Radio Liberty Research Report*, Vol. 3, No. 33, 1994, pp. 34–45.
19. *Ibid.*, p. 37.
20. *Nezavisimaya gazeta*, 15 May 1994.
21. 'Protocol on the Results of Discussions between Russian Foreign Minister Andrei Kozyrev and the NATO Council', reprinted in Mihalka, *op. cit.*, p. 44.
22. See B. Kazantsev, 'Pervye shagi k partnerstvu Rossii s NATO', *Mezhdunarodnaya zhizn'*, No. 10, 1994, pp. 22–9 quoted in M. Kramer, 'NATO, Russia, and East European Security', in U. Ra'anan and K. Martin (eds.), *Russia – a Return to Imperialism?* (New York: St Martin's Press, 1995), pp. 124–5.
23. On Polish and Czech ambitions to join NATO, see *ibid.*, p. 124.
24. The agreement was later signed in May 1995.
25. *Nezavisimaya gazeta*, 7 December 1994. See also Chapter 7.
26. *Nezavisimaya gazeta*, 2 December 1994.
27. *Nezavisimaya gazeta*, 27 December 1995.
28. *Hansard*, No. 1760, col. 941 (1997), cited in Haslam, *op. cit.*, p. 123.
29. *Nezavisimaya gazeta*, 18 January 1996.
30. *Nezavisimaya gazeta*, 1 March 1996.
31. *The Guardian*, 13 January 1996.
32. *Krasnya zvezda*, 20 December 1996.
33. 'Ministerial Meeting of the North Atlantic Council. Final Communiqué – Brussels, 10 December 1996', *NATO Review*, Vol. 45, No. 1, 1997, p. 31.
34. Itar-Tass, World Service, Moscow, 18 June 1996; *The Guardian*, 8 October 1996.
35. *Nezavisimaya gazeta*, 17 January 1997; *Rossiskaya gazeta*, 11 February 1997 (Rybkin's position was, in fact, consistent with the abandonment of the concept of 'no first use' in the 1993 military doctrine).
36. *Sevodnya*, 31 January 1996.
37. Hence the phrase in the Yeltsin–Clinton joint statement that '[w]hile they continue to disagree on the issue of NATO enlargement, in order to minimize the consequence of this disagreement [Presidents Yeltsin and Clinton . . .] agreed to work, together with others, on a document to establish a cooperative relationship between NATO and Russia as an important part of a new European security system'. Cited in A. D. Rotfeld, 'Europe: the Transition to Inclusive Security', in *SIPRI Yearbook 1998. Armaments, Disarmament and International Security* (Oxford: Oxford University Press/Frösunda, Sweden: Stockholm International Peace Research Institute, 1998), p. 143, note 3.
38. *The Guardian*, 16 April 1997.
39. Associated Press, 'Yeltsin Warns on NATO Expansion', as carried by *Johnson's Russia List* (davidjohnson@erols.com), 8 May 1997.
40. 'Founding Act on Mutual Relations, Cooperation and Security between NATO and the Russian Federation', *NATO Review*, Vol. 45, No. 4, 1997.
41. *The Times*, 18 June 1997.
42. *The Guardian*, 3 December 1998.
43. Presidency Conclusions, Cologne European Council, 3–4 June 1999, Annex III 'European Council Declaration on Strengthening the Common European

Policy on Security and Defence', <http://www.europa.eu.int/council/off/conclu/june99/annexe_htm#a3>.

44. 'An Alliance for the 21st Century' (Washington Summit Communiqué issued by the heads of state and government, NATO – North Atlantic Council, Washington D.C., 24 April 1999), *NATO Review*, Vol. 47, No. 2, 1999, pp. D3–D7, paragraph 10.
45. *The Washington Post*, 4 December 1998.
46. *Sevodnya*, 28 November 1998.
47. R. F. Laird and S. L. Clark (eds.), *The USSR and the Western Alliance* (Boston: Unwin Hyman, 1990).
48. In May 1998 a platoon of Russian troops joined Operation Cooperative Jaguar – a NATO peacekeeping exercise in Denmark. This marked the first time that Moscow had sent ground troops to a NATO exercise conducted within the PfP framework. Shortly after in September military exercises named 'Central Asia Battalion 98' took place in Uzbekistan as part of the PfP. Over 700 troops took part including some from Russia and the US.
49. *Obshchaya gazeta*, 5–11 November 1998.
50. Yeltsin cited in *The Guardian*, 15 May 1998; Primakov cited in *Rossiiskaya gazeta*, 12 May 1998; Ivanov cited in *Nezavisimaya gazeta*, 30 September 1998.
51. Cited in Rotfeld, *op. cit.*, p. 148.
52. 'An Alliance for the 21st Century', *op. cit.*, paragraph 7.
53. *Kommersant-daily*, 8 August 1997.
54. *Nezavisimaya gazeta*, 25 September 1998.
55. *Moscow Times*, 28 April 1999.
56. *The Guardian*, 10 April 1999.
57. Itar-Tass, 3 April 1999, as carried by *Johnson's Russia List* (david-johnson@erols.com), 4 April 1999.
58. *The Sunday Times*, 13 September 1998.
59. Russian participation in S-For continued throughout the Kosovo crisis and in June–July arrangements were finalized for Russian involvement in K-For in Kosovo. The PJC, having not met since before the NATO bombing campaign, convened in late July, albeit with an agenda limited to the Kosovo issue.
60. Haslam, *op. cit.*, pp. 119–30.
61. Rather mischievously, Defence Minister Igor Sergeyev suggested in October 1998 that Russia would have an interest in joining NATO if the Alliance were to integrate with the OSCE. See Itar-Tass, 8 October 1998 as carried by *Johnson's Russia List* (davidjohnson@erols.com), 10 October 1998.
62. 'Madrid Declaration on Euro-Atlantic Security and Cooperation. Issued by the Heads of State and Government Participating in the Meeting of the North Atlantic Council in Madrid on 8 July 1997', paragraph 8, *NATO Review*, Vol. 45, No. 4, 1997.
63. *Nezavisimaya gazeta*, 5 November 1998.

4
Russia and the European Union
Jackie Gower

Introduction

The European Union (EU) has so far occupied a much less prominent place in Russian foreign policy than other European institutions and there has been little of the public debate and controversy that has surrounded relations with the North Atlantic Treaty Organization (NATO), or indeed the Council of Europe (COE). The EU has been perceived primarily as an economic organization and its aspirations to play a leading political and security role in the 'new Europe' have only gradually come to be recognized, let alone accepted, by the Russian authorities. Certainly, Russia does not appear to share the EU's own perception of itself as the other major power on the continent and has continued to regard bilateral relations with the traditional 'great European powers' such as Germany and France as the normal way of conducting relations with the EU member states.[1] Although access to the EU's market has been seen as an important objective by Moscow, the potential benefits of a closer political relationship are only gradually being appreciated. The other major reason for the relatively low profile of the EU in Russian foreign policy has been that membership does not seem to be a serious policy option, despite occasional press statements to the contrary. Russia's huge size, Eurasian geopolitical position, global interests and the continuing perception of itself as a great power would make it very difficult to accept the constraints of EU membership. Whether this might change some time in the future will be discussed later, but so far it has meant that priority has been given to relations with those western institutions to which Russia has sought membership (the COE, the Group of Seven and the World Trade Organization (WTO)).

The rather slow development of Russian–EU relations over the past decade should not be attributed solely to their relatively low position in Russia's foreign policy agenda. The EU has also been partly to blame for the neglect. It has been preoccupied with its own internal agenda (Maastricht, economic and monetary union, and the accession of the three European Free Trade Area states) and more recently with the prospect of enlargement to the countries of east-central Europe (ECE). Furthermore, the political and economic situation in Russia has often seemed unstable and the prospect for the reforms less certain than in most of the ECE states.[2] Officials in Brussels have, therefore, found it difficult to know how to deal with Russia, and have been confused and frustrated by frequent inconsistencies in the positions adopted by different ministries and departments. The EU's response to the collapse of communism and the break-up of the Soviet Union has been essentially reactive, with no evidence of a clear strategy or vision as to the way in which Russia and indeed the other successor states, with the noticeable exception of the Baltics, might fit into the grand European integration project. It seems to have been assumed that Russia has no aspiration for EU membership, but precisely what kind of relationship Moscow might have with an enlarged EU of perhaps 27 states has not been clear.

The publication of the EU's 'Agenda 2000' in July 1997[3] and the decision in December to open negotiations with the leading five applicants (including Estonia), seem to have given a new impetus to the development of Russian–EU relations as both parties have taken stock of the potential consequences of EU enlargement to the east. On the EU side there is a clear desire 'not to create another fault line in Europe'[4] and, therefore, a determination to find ways of engaging Russia in a constructive relationship across a broad range of policy areas. Russia, while having no fundamental objection to EU enlargement (in marked contrast to its position in relation to that of NATO), is nevertheless anxious to avoid any possible negative repercussions for itself. In particular, the emergence of the EU as Russia's largest trading partner makes Moscow determined to ensure that the integration of the ECE states into the EU's internal market should not be detrimental to its own trading position.[5]

Historic decisions in relation to the EU's enlargement have coincidentally taken place at the same time as the Partnership and Cooperation Agreement (PCA) finally came into force which is intended to provide the legal and institutional framework for the development of future relations between Russia and the EU.[6] The inaugural meetings of the new Russia–EU Cooperation Council and Parliamentary Cooperation

Committee have set ambitious agendas for future cooperation in economic, environmental, scientific and societal security areas. There is clear recognition of the potential advantages of working together to try to solve pan-European and regional problems and evidence of a greater degree of political commitment to the relationship by both parties than in the past.

This chapter will examine the institutional bases for the development of a more constructive and multifaceted relationship between Russia and the EU and assess whether these will prove adequate to meet the needs and objectives of the respective partners. The key question is whether an alternative model of European integration can be developed that can include states such as Russia as equal partners but not necessarily on the basis of their accession to the EU.

The development of Russia's policy toward the EU

Throughout most of the Cold War period, Soviet attitudes toward European integration in general and the European Community (EC)[7] in particular were both sceptical and hostile.[8] The EC was seen as an integral part of the western alliance against the communist bloc and no clear policy distinction was made between it and NATO. Although during periods of *détente* the Soviet government expressed some interest in establishing relations with the EC, its main objective was to secure international recognition of the Council for Mutual Economic Assistance (CMEA) as a comparable economic organization. As the EC member states were not prepared to afford it such a status, there was virtually no relationship between the two organizations for nearly 30 years.[9] It was only in 1986, on Mikhail Gorbachev's initiative, that negotiations were finally opened leading to a Joint Declaration two years later and the conclusion of a Trade and Cooperation Agreement (TCA) in 1989.[10]

The change in policy was clearly in line with Gorbachev's 'new political thinking' and in particular the concept of the 'common European home' that led to a reassessment of the nature and potential of all European institutions. In the case of the EC, economic motives were undoubtedly the most important as access to West European markets and technical cooperation were seen as key elements of the Soviet domestic reform strategy. Baranovsky also suggests that internal developments in the EC itself, in particular the Single European Act and a commitment to complete the internal market by December 1992, contributed to a more serious appraisal of the agreement on the part of both Soviet academics and officials.[11] However, it was clear from the relatively few references to the EC in official Soviet foreign policy statements that it was still regarded as only one of many international institutions with which the Soviet Union wished to establish cooperative relations. It was not, in other words, afforded a very high priority.

Since the break-up of the Soviet Union, the Russian leadership has continued to pursue a positive, but rather low-key, policy toward the EU. The EU's status as a European rather than a Euro-Atlantic institution has increasingly been seen as one of its more attractive features and there has been a clear differentiation in Russian attitudes toward the EU and NATO, especially with regards to enlargement.[12] Although since the mid-1990s Russian attitudes toward the West have generally cooled, policy toward the EU has been relatively unaffected. One of the strategic goals of Yeltsin's foreign policy has been the encouragement of a multi-polar world order and the EU is now regarded as at least having the potential to act as a counter-balance to American hegemony.[13] One leading Russian academic has claimed that 'both Russia and the EU are striving to oppose American mono-centrism with the strategy of a multi-polar world. The traditional chain of Europe–United States–Russia must be transformed into a triangle by closer Russian–EU relations.'[14] Another suggested that the launch of the EU currency unit, the 'Euro', could challenge the dominance of the American dollar and lead to the development of a more balanced structure in world financial markets.[15] This kind of analysis has contributed to a generally favourable image of the EU in Russia but there are no illusions about its current political, as opposed to economic, weight. The crises in both the former Yugoslavia and the Gulf have only served to highlight the limited capacity of the EU to act as an effective international actor, and the US and NATO understandably continue to be regarded as the main players on security issues.

However, the EU's contribution to 'soft' security is both acknowledged and valued. Borko claims that within Russia, government officials, senior administrators and intellectuals have tended to regard European integration as a positive development and in Russia's national interest.[16] The main reason for such an assessment is that European integration is seen as 'one of the cornerstones of stability in Europe'.[17] Russia's own history makes it acutely conscious of the significance of Franco-German rapprochement and German unification could only have been accepted within the framework of European integration. In the aftermath of the break-up of the Soviet Union, Russia has been deeply concerned about actual or potential instability on its borders and, therefore, stability to the west is a welcome factor. From this perspective, EU enlargement to the potentially rather volatile ECE states is of some benefit to Russia. The

EU has insisted that applicant states must resolve all outstanding issues such as border disputes with their neighbours before they can be considered eligible for accession. It has also made respect for the human rights of minorities one of the accession criteria; it thus exercises significant political leverage in respect of the treatment of the large Russian minorities in the Baltic states.[18]

These potential benefits aside, Russia does have some anxieties. Its main concern is that it will find itself shut out from an enlarging zone of stability and prosperity in Europe and marginalized from the mainstream of European political and economic life. This is a concern particularly apposite in relation to the European single market. Over the past decade there has been a dramatic shift in the pattern of Soviet/Russian trade. Whereas prior to 1991, the CMEA area was the most important region for Soviet trade, the EU has emerged during the 1990s as post-Soviet Russia's largest trading partner. As can be seen in Figure 4.1, the EU's share of both Russia's imports and exports is significantly greater than that of either the Commonwealth of Independent States (CIS) or ECE. Before the financial crisis in the summer of 1998, the expectation had been that trade with the EU would continue to grow and that with the accession of at least some of the ECE states would come to exceed 50 per cent of Russia's total trade. By comparison, the US is a much less significant trading partner and thus, from an economic perspective, its central place in Russia's foreign policy seems incongruous. Although political factors will undoubtedly mean that relations with the US will continue to take precedence, economic considerations are likely to lead to a greater appreciation of the importance of good relations with the EU.

Although Russia enjoys a significant surplus in its trade with the EU (amounting to some ECU 3 billion in 1996),[19] there are a number of aspects of the economic relationship which have given rise to concern in Moscow. The relationship is seen to be asymmetric in two senses: firstly, whereas by 1995 the EU accounted for 35 per cent of Russia's trade, Russia was responsible for only 3.5 per cent of the EU's trade.[20] In fact, this understates the real significance of the trading relationship on the EU side because Russia supplies 36 per cent of the EU's total imported gas and 10 per cent of its oil. However, the apparent imbalance in the relationship is a worry for the Russian side, especially as there is a widespread perception that Russia's potential volume of exports to the EU is being deliberately suppressed by discriminatory trade policies.[21] Secondly, the relationship is seen to be asymmetric due to the preponderance of raw materials, especially energy, in Russia's exports to the EU. The fact that Russia is exchanging raw materials for manufactured goods is

Imports by main geographical area, 1996

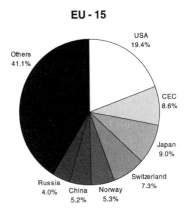

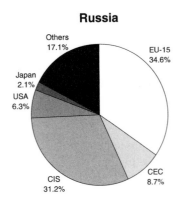

Exports by main geographical area, 1996

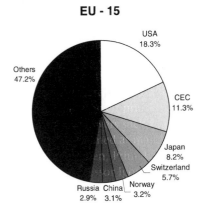

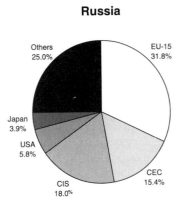

Figure 4.1   Trade of Russia and the EU.
Note: CEC – Central European Countries; CIS – Commonwealth of Independent States.
Source: TACIS, *Russia and the EU Member States Statistical Comparison 1990–96* (Luxembourg: OOPEC, 1998).

perceived as placing it in a 'colonial' position in relation to western Europe and does not reflect the normal exchange of goods between developed economies.[22] The depressed price of oil throughout much of the 1990s has also demonstrated the dangers of relying too heavily on a limited range of products for hard currency earnings. In this light, Russia's economic objectives have been geared not only to increasing the total volume of exports to the EU but also to changing their composition to include more manufactured goods. Again, however, this has fallen foul of EU protectionism. There is a widespread perception in Moscow that EU member states are only interested in securing an expansion of energy imports while continuing to impose barriers to Russian exports of other goods. There has, therefore, been both frustration and anger at the reluctance of the EU to revise Russia's economic status from that of a 'transitional economy' to a 'market economy' and thereby end anti-dumping measures and quotas.[23] Consequently, in the negotiations leading to the signing of the PCA in June 1994 and in the subsequent meetings of its related institutions, a number of real or perceived conflicts of interest have arisen.

The Partnership and Cooperation Agreement

The TCA signed by the Soviet Union and the EC in 1989 was very similar to agreements reached by the EC with Poland and Hungary, and served only to normalize trading relations on the basis of granting most-favoured nation treatment in accordance with rules under the General Agreement on Tariffs and Trade (GATT). However, by 1992 it was clear that the EU was pursuing a policy of differentiation between the former CMEA states. This involved negotiating association agreements known as 'Europe Agreements' with the ECE states (including the three Baltic states), but separate PCAs with Russia and the other CIS states.[24] The political significance of the different types of agreement offered by the EU became apparent at the EU's Copenhagen Council in June 1993 when it was announced that 'the associated countries of central and eastern Europe that so desire shall become members of the Union. Accession will take place as soon as a country is able to assume the obligations of membership by satisfying the economic and political conditions.'[25] Although never explicitly stated, the PCAs have, therefore, been widely interpreted as being 'for countries such as Russia for which membership of the EU is not on the agenda for the foreseeable future'.[26] This distinction does not seem to have been a deliberate act of discrimination against Russia but merely a recognition on the part of the EU that, whereas the ECE states have pressed strongly for a commitment to eventual accession to the Union, there has been no evidence that Russia has had a similar goal.[27]

The objectives of the PCA

In the preamble to the PCA there is no mention of future EU membership for Russia even as a long-term goal, only a reference to the agreement 'favouring a gradual rapprochement between Russia and a wider area of cooperation in Europe and neighbouring regions and Russia's progressive integration into the open trading system'.[28] However, it is clear from the scope of the proposed cooperation, the overtly political nature of the institutions it creates and the provision for future evolution to a free trade area, that the PCA marks a significant upgrading of relations from the earlier TCA. Indeed, Borko regards it as 'the broadest and most comprehensive agreement concluded so far between Russia and any Western country or organisation'.[29] Although the original draft of the agreement was written by the Commission on the basis of negotiating guidelines agreed by the EU member states, the Russian delegation pressed hard for amendments and the final text can legitimately be regarded as a reflection of shared values and goals. It was ratified by the Duma almost unanimously in November 1996 indicating a high degree of consensus within the Russian political élite on policy towards the EU.[30]

Article 1 lists the objectives of the partnership:

- to provide an appropriate framework for political dialogue between the Parties allowing the development of close relations between them in this field;
- to promote trade and investment and harmonious economic relations between the Parties based on the principles of market economy and so to foster sustainable development in the Parties;
- to strengthen political and economic freedoms;
- to support Russian efforts to consolidate its democracy and to develop its economy and to complete the transition to a market economy;
- to provide a basis for economic, social, financial and cultural cooperation founded on the principles of mutual advantage, mutual responsibility and support;
- to promote activities of joint interest;
- to provide an appropriate framework for the gradual integration between Russia and a wider area of cooperation in Europe;
- to create the necessary conditions for the future establishment of a free trade area between the Community and Russia covering substantially all trade in goods between them, as well as conditions for bringing about freedom of establishment of companies, of cross-border trade in services and of capital movements.

Political conditionality

One of the clearest indications of the much greater political character of the 'partnership' envisaged in the agreement is the emphasis on the importance of 'common values' shared by Russia and the EU. These values include a commitment to political and economic freedoms, the promotion of international peace and security, and respect for democratic principles and human rights as defined in the Helsinki Final Act and the 1990 Charter of Paris for a New Europe.[31] Despite objections by the Russian negotiators, the agreement also contains provision for unilateral action by one party if it believes that the other has failed to fulfil its treaty obligations (Article 107). A Joint Declaration appended to the PCA explicitly states that 'respect for human rights constitutes an essential element of the Agreement'. It is assumed, therefore, that if there is evidence of a serious violation of human rights or democratic principles in Russia then the EU could, and probably would, suspend the agreement. The action by the European Parliament in suspending the ratification of the PCA for several months in 1995 owing to its concern about the violation of human rights in Chechnya demonstrated that political conditionality is no empty threat. The future of Russian–EU relations is undoubtedly dependent on the domestic political situation in Russia remaining stable.

Economic provisions

Although most of the articles in the PCA cover economic and commercial matters, they are actually only a modest extension of the 1989 TCA[32] and are much less generous than the provisions of the Europe Agreements which govern trade between the EU and the states of ECE. Whereas in the Europe Agreements a ten-year timetable is established for the progressive movement towards free trade in industrial goods,[33] in the PCA there is only the rather weak commitment 'to examine together in the year 1998 whether circumstances allow the beginning of negotiations on the establishment of a free trade area' (Article 3). Initially, the EU had been reluctant to include even this reference and Moscow was very displeased to find itself being treated so much less generously than its former CMEA partners.[34] In 1993, under pressure to speed up the negotiations and bolster President Yeltsin's domestic position, the EU Council amended its negotiating mandate to allow for the possibility of the development of a free trade area.[35]

The Russian leadership has continued to regard the evolution to a free trade area as the most important objective of the PCA and secured a commitment at the first Cooperation Council in January 1998 that studies would be undertaken in preparation for consideration later in the year as to whether 'circumstances allow the beginning of negotiations'.[36] In view of the Russian economic crisis later that summer, however, the question had to be postponed and it seems increasingly unlikely that any real progress will be made toward the achievement of a free trade area in the foreseeable future. That certainly is the assumption in Brussels and even on Russia's side there seems to be some doubt about the desirability of securing a free trade area at the present stage of economic transition. Apart from the danger of exposing Russian manufacturing industries to the full blast of western competition, customs duties provide a significant proportion of the federal budget in a society where the payment of taxes is not yet widely accepted.[37] The potentially evolutionary nature of the PCA is, therefore, still valued by both parties, but it is recognized that it is dependent on the achievement of a much greater degree of economic stability in Russia.

In practice, tariffs are not really at present a significant barrier to Russian exports to the EU since raw materials and energy, which account for most of its trade, are already zero rated. However, as noted above, Russia is very keen to diversify the composition of its trade with the EU, so tariffs might prove a problem in the future, particularly if the ECE states enjoy a more advantageous trading position either as a result of the Europe Agreements or their accession to the EU. In the immediate future, though, the main concern is that the PCA permits the continuation of quantitative restrictions on the export of designated 'sensitive' goods and the use of contingent protection such as anti-dumping measures.[38] Furthermore, some of the most sensitive goods, namely textiles, steel and nuclear materials, are subject to separate agreements that include provisions for quotas. The EU generally receives scant mention in the Russian press, but invariably the stories that do appear concern the EU's alleged discrimination against Russian industries struggling to survive in a supposedly 'free market' world.[39] There are a number of long-running trade disputes, particularly in relation to coal, steel, aluminium, chemicals, nuclear materials, textiles and carpets, which have soured relations and dominated the agenda of the Cooperation Councils and Committees.[40]

The underlying problem is that although the PCA recognized that 'Russia is no longer a state trading country – it is now a country with an economy in transition', the EU, as noted above, has been reluctant to take the next step and concede market-economy status to Russia. From Russia's perspective, this has meant that some of its most competitively priced goods have been subject to quotas or prohibitively high tariffs. It has been claimed that the loss to the Russian economy as a result of EU anti-dumping measures amounts to some 300 million dollars a year.[41] The EU Commission decided in December 1997 to recommend that Russia should be removed from its list of 'non-market economies' before the first meeting of the Cooperation Council in order to ensure a good start to the PCA. However, the EU's Council of Ministers did not approve the proposal, allegedly because the Belgium government used its veto in retaliation for Russia's imposition of quotas on imports of carpets.[42] EU Foreign Ministers finally agreed in April 1998 to remove Russia from its official list of 'non-market economies' and to judge each case of alleged anti-dumping on its own merits.[43] As the onus is on the exporter to demonstrate that market economy conditions prevail in the relevant sector, there are likely to be continuing disputes.

When Russia gains admission to the WTO, the trade liberalization provisions of the PCA will be largely superseded so in a sense they are only transitional arrangements. In the longer term, therefore, the PCA's most significant contribution to the integration of the Russian economy into the wider European economic space could potentially be the provision for legislative harmonization to remove non-tariff barriers to trade. In Article 55 of the PCA, Russia commits itself to 'endeavour to ensure that its legislation shall be gradually made compatible with that of the Community' in respect of company law, banking law, company accounts and taxes, health and safety, competition, consumer protection, the environment, technical rules and standards. If Russia really was to achieve this degree of legislative harmonization, something very close to the European Economic Area (but excluding free movement of people) might be created covering virtually the whole continent. The ECE states are, of course, currently undertaking just such an endeavour as a crucial part of their pre-accession strategy. However, in the absence of the incentive of EU membership, it is uncertain whether Russia will in practice be willing or able to adopt so much of the EU's *acquis*. At the moment its market economy is so fragile that adherence to the legislative norms of the mature economies of the EU could be very damaging. However, on paper at least, it remains one of the shared goals in the development of the partnership.

The institutional framework for political dialogue

One of the potentially most significant consequences of the PCA is the establishment of a set of high-level joint institutions that provide opportunities for regular political dialogue on a very wide range of issues of common concern. Summit-level meetings between the Presidents of the EU Commission and Council and the Russian President were instituted as early as November 1993, partly to offer public support for President Yeltsin and his government. These are scheduled to be held twice a year[44] and continue to perform an important political function.

Their symbolic role in demonstrating western support for the Russian government during the financial crisis of 1998 was an important stabilizing factor. In addition, the PCA strengthened the institutional framework of Russian–EU relations by creating a number of new bodies:

- The Cooperation Council composed of senior ministers from Russia and the EU member states (usually the Foreign Ministers) plus members of the Commission. It is scheduled to meet at least once a year and is charged with the responsibility of 'monitoring' the PCA and examining 'any other bilateral or international issues of mutual interest'.
- The Cooperation Committee composed of senior officials from the EU member states, the Commission and the Russian government. The PCA envisaged that it would meet more frequently than the Cooperation Council, providing continuity and undertaking preparatory work for the ministerial meetings.
- The Parliamentary Cooperation Committee composed of members of the European Parliament and the Duma. It may make recommendations to the Cooperation Council.

These institutions are very similar to those created under the Europe Agreements but hopefully might have a better chance of proving mutually useful. The ECE states have generally been critical of both the style and results of political dialogue and have seen meetings under the aegis of the Europe Agreements as a poor substitute for actual involvement in the decision-making process of the EU as full members. However, given that in Russia's case, the institutions for political dialogue are not temporary measures pending EU accession but rather constitute a permanent framework for cooperation and discussion, there is a much greater incentive for both parties to make them work. Certainly, from the EU's perspective, dialogue with Russia as the largest state on the continent is potentially much more important than dialogue with the generally rather small ECE applicants. Both parties frequently refer to the well-established institutionalized dialogue between the EU and the US as the model for the development of what is now widely described as 'privileged' relations or partnership between Russia and the EU.[45]

That said, it is too early to give an assessment of the contribution the new institutions will make to the development of a genuine partnership between the EU and Russia. Due to the long delay before the PCA came into force, the first Parliamentary Committee did not meet until December 1997 and the Cooperation Council until January 1998. The official press statement claimed that the latter marked 'a very important milestone in the relations between the European Union and the Russian Federation as equal partners' and gave a rare insight into how both parties view the relationship. It reported that the two sides 'emphasized that the European Union and Russia are strategic partners for peace, stability, freedom and prosperity in Europe and that they share a responsibility for the future of the continent and beyond'. They affirmed their commitment to 'intensify their relations' and adopted an ambitious work programme for 1998 covering cooperation in a wide range of areas including the fight against international crime, customs and borders procedures, transport, space, science and technology, and technical standards. A number of sub-committees and working groups were also established with the intention of institutionalizing relations further at the official and expert levels.[46] The political and economic uncertainty in Russia during 1998–99, not surprisingly, had a deleterious effect on the implementation of the planned work programme and there was some disappointment on the EU side that more progress had not been made. Hans van den Broek, the Commissioner responsible for EU relations with Russia, told the third meeting of the Parlimentary Cooperation Committee in September 1998 that 'we feel that we lack very much a coordinating and driving force on the Russian side. We need someone at sufficiently senior ministerial level who can coordinate PCA related activities on the Russian side and ensure that the necessary work is done.'[47] The appointment the following month of just such a senior minister with responsibility for Russia's relations with the EU in the context of the PCA may have been an indication of the increasing importance Moscow afforded the relationship.[48] At the second meeting of the Cooperation Council in May 1999 the official communiqué was much more positive and 'welcomed the momentum which has been created in developing relations between the European Union and Russia, particularly over the past six months'. It reported 'intensive work' through the official PCA institutions and sub-committees and 'continued day-to-day work on both sides'.[49] Clearly the PCA has had a major impact on the frequency and breadth of official contacts between the EU and Russia, and laid the basis for more effective cooperation on a wide range of policy areas.

The Parliamentary Cooperation Committee has been particularly active and has undoubtedly influenced opinion in the European Parliament. It has pressed the Commission and Council to grant Russia market-economy status and generally helped to mobilize support for Russia's reform process. The regular formal and informal contacts between members of the European Parliament and their counterparts in the Duma have contributed to a more informed debate on the situation in Russia in the European Parliament and have helped to dispel some of the prejudices of the past. Although the European Parliament took a very firm line in condemning the violation of human rights in Chechnya, its general position on Russia has been supportive and in many ways more far-sighted than that of the Commission or Council. In a report prepared by its Committee on Foreign Affairs on future relations between Russia and the EU, it demonstrated a greater sense of vision of the place Russia should occupy in the new European order and even revived the concept of the 'common European home' in order to integrate Russia into the 'great family of European peoples'.[50] The resolution on the report called on the EU to 'develop special links with a democratic Russia going beyond the partnership and cooperation agreement [. . .] to consolidate and guarantee peace and security worldwide'.[51]

Generally, therefore, the value of the partnership institutions is first and foremost that they provide regular channels for communication and that they should help to increase mutual trust and understanding. The agendas so far have been dominated by trade disputes but that is also often true of meetings within the framework of the trans-Atlantic partnership (e.g. the Helms Burton amendment and squabbles over beef and bananas). What is important is that there are institutionalized opportunities for resolving them. It has also been extremely valuable to have scheduled as opposed to crisis meetings at which Russia's economic and political problems could be discussed on the basis of a shared interest in minimizing their impact on the overall Russian–EU relationship. The structures are now in place and working, but ultimately the test will be whether they are judged by both parties to produce tangible results and not just joint press statements.

The 1996 Action Plan for Russia

Although the PCA contains some strong political rhetoric and provision for regular political dialogue with Russia, it is much less specific about how the political dimension of the relationship might be developed than it is about the economic. This is probably because most of the negotiations took place prior to the coming into force of the (Maastricht) Treaty on European Union (TEU) in November 1993 with its new procedures for the EU's Common Foreign and Security Policy (CFSP). One of the EU's first CFSP objectives was the development of stronger political relations with Russia, particularly as it became an immediate neighbour following Finland's accession in 1995. In November 1995 the EU adopted one of its first 'common positions' under Article J2 of the TEU on a 'strategy for future EU–Russia relations' which went some way to balancing the economic focus of the PCA. It stressed that 'good relations between the EU and a democratic Russia are essential to stability in Europe' and identified five policy areas as particularly important for future relations. It is significant that four of them were explicitly political: contribution to Russia's democratic reforms, cooperation on justice and home affairs, security issues and foreign policy (the fifth was economic cooperation).[52]

The next step was to identify a package of specific proposals for developing 'a substantial partnership with Russia' and incorporate them into an Action Plan which would supplement the PCA by identifying priorities and providing a work programme in a wide range of policy areas. Adopted in May 1996, its objectives were to 'promote the democratic and economic reform process, to enhance respect for human rights, to consolidate peace, stability and security in order to avoid new dividing lines in Europe and to achieve the full integration of Russia into the community of free and democratic nations'.[53] It was recognized that these ambitious goals could only be achieved by the EU working closely with other institutions and individual member states. One of the main criticisms that could be made of the Action Plan is that it has failed to identify a distinctive contribution the EU might make to these very ambitious and broad policy goals. The Plan, therefore, ran the risk of duplicating the efforts made by other institutions and of dissipating its work so widely that its impact would be difficult to evaluate.

The main purpose of the Action Plan, however, was to send a strong political message of commitment and support to the reformers in Russia in the run-up to the 1996 presidential election and to inject renewed dynamism into the relationship during the frustratingly long period while the PCA was still being ratified in the EU. It therefore identified a large number of possible initiatives for specific action under the five policy objectives agreed in the 1995 common strategy. These were, however, only indicative and translating good intentions into concrete action proved more difficult as the Plan itself did not have legal force, nor any policy instruments or budget of its own. It is mainly through TACIS, the EU's technical assistance programme and its related Democracy Programme, that some of its proposals have been put into practice (see below).

A follow-up report prepared by the Commission after the Action Plan's first six months gave examples of some of its achievements.[54] These included EU monitoring of the 1996 Russian presidential elections, the convening of an international conference on combating organized crime in the EU and Russia, progress on negotiating new agreements for textiles and steel, and the establishment of a Security Working Group. The report described these as 'among the most visible elements of the Plan to have already been implemented'; but, of course, they would only actually have been 'visible' to a relatively small group of officials which perhaps explains why the EU continued to have such a low profile in Russia itself. It is clear, however, from the rest of the report that one of the most tangible results of the Action Plan has been the growth of regular contacts at both official and ministerial levels. In particular, it has provided the impetus to establish a large number of regular meetings to discuss foreign policy and security issues and to exchange views prior to meetings of other international bodies such as the United Nations (UN) General Assembly and the Organization for Security and Cooperation in Europe (OSCE).

The Action Plan has undoubtedly contributed to the development in recent years of much deeper and wider cooperation with Russia on a broad spectrum of both bilateral and pan-European issues. Its most important role has been to provide the broad policy framework of objectives and goals for EU policy toward Russia, including the TACIS programme considered in the section that follows. Although not formally rescinded, both the 1995 strategy and the Action Plan have been *de facto* superseded by the Common Strategy adopted in June 1999 which seeks to develop cooperation further (see below).

TACIS

The successful development of a genuine partnership between the EU and Russia as envisaged in the PCA and the Action Plan is dependent on the continuation and consolidation of political and economic reform. TACIS[55] is the main financial and policy instrument through which the EU has tried to influence the reform process in Russia by giving practical support to the development of stable democratic institutions and a functioning market economy. A total of ECU 1060.79 million was allocated from 1991 to 1997 to projects ranging from nuclear safety to public administration reforms (see Table 4.1).[56] Although this makes the EU the leading donor of non-repayable aid to Russia, it still falls far short of the level of support the Russian authorities seem to have expected and has thus led to a growing disillusionment in Moscow with the West. A TACIS evaluation report acknowledged that EU aid is 'almost negligible in GNP terms', representing less than 0.05 per cent of Russia's GNP and amounting to just 1.5 Euros per capita a year.[57] There is also quite a widespread perception in Russia that most of the money ends up in the hands of

Table 4.1   TACIS funds allocated to Russia by sector, 1991–97

Funds allocated by sector, 1991–97 (in ECU million)	1991	1992	1993	1994	1995	1996	1997	Total
Nuclear safety and environment	12.89	0	0	0	0	5.5	5	23.39
Restructuring state enterprises and private sector development	27.2	29.76	54.5	43.4	40.6	31.3	28.7	255.46
Public administration reform, social services and education	46.64	24.57	44	18.85	52.8	33.8	27	247.66
Agriculture	50.85	21.44	12.5	16.3	17	10.6	13	141.74
Energy	41.5	16	21.1	19.5	18	11.5	13	40.6
Transport	32.87	14.25	13.55	13.9	12.6	8.5	7	102.67
Policy advice	0	0	0	18.95	0	26	31	75.95
Telecommunications	0	4.93	5.1	4.1	5.4	3	4	26.53
Others	0	0	10	15	14.79	2.8	4.2	46.79
Total	211.95	111	160.75	150	161.19	133	132.9	1060.79

Source: European Commission, *The TACIS Programme. Annual Report 1997* (Brussels: July 1998).

western consultants rather than going to the people most in need.[58] Again, this perception is not entirely unfounded as the same report found that 60 per cent of TACIS funds goes to pay the fees of EU experts.[59]

Part of the reason for the rather negative assessment of the TACIS programme in Russia is a misunderstanding of its purpose. Although there have been periods when humanitarian aid has been appropriate,[60] the general EU strategy has been to facilitate the transfer of 'know-how' and expertise in order to assist in the development of the institutions, legal and administrative systems, and management skills necessary for a functioning market economy and stable democracy. It is believed that the potential multiplier effect of such technical assistance on economic growth is larger than the likely impact of similar amounts of investment inflows.[61] TACIS therefore finances projects involving a wide range of public and private organizations with the objective of combining western expertise and experience with local knowledge and skills.

The 1996–99 Indicative Programme

An Indicative Programme has provided the policy framework for TACIS projects for the period 1996–99 and was drawn up after extensive consultations with the Russian authorities. It was based on the objectives agreed in the 1996 Action Plan discussed above and identified eight priority areas for support:

- Enterprise support: advice and training for sectoral and enterprise restructuring and development; advice on ways to improve the business and investment climate through the development of a clear legal framework; support for small and medium enterprises; consolidation of the reforms of the financial sector.
- Human resources: training and education; reform of the educational system; improvement of legal training; reform of public administration.
- Social protection: policy advice and training on the development of a new social security system including pensions, unemployment benefits, health insurance and the management of health services.
- Food and agriculture: policy and legislative advice on farm restructuring and the development of dealer and wholesale networks; promotion of better access to finance for farms and distribution networks.
- Energy: advice on the development of a legal and regulatory framework; management retraining; promotion of energy savings and environmental protection.
- Transport and telecommunications: policy and legal advice on privatization, regulation and restructuring; specific projects linked to the development of trans-European networks.
- Environment: advice on the strengthening of institutions, the development of environmental law and the training of enforcement officers; the inclusion of environmental objectives in projects in other sectors wherever possible.
- Nuclear safety: technical and policy advice.

This long list of priorities is an indication of the ambitious scope of EU policy toward Russia and certainly provides a large number of opportunities for practical cooperation with government officials and business and political élites at national, regional and local level. Each year an Annual Action Programme has been drawn up which sets the parameters within which specific projects are evaluated and selected for funding. There has been close cooperation between the EU delegation based in Moscow and the TACIS Coordinating Unit responsible to the Russian government. The emphasis has been on working in partnership with the Russian authorities in order to identify priorities and needs and select those projects that can most effectively contribute to the achievement of the agreed objectives. TACIS Technical Offices have also been established in a number of major cities and regions in the belief that decentralization might increase the effectiveness of project management. Furthermore, the 1998 Action Programme specifically encouraged EU implementing bodies to work with and through Russian counterpart institutions and enterprises, and to use Russian consultants on projects whenever possible.[62] In this way it is hoped both to increase the effectiveness of the programme and overcome some of its earlier criticisms.

From the EU's perspective, the TACIS programme is very important because it involves the Commission, both in Brussels and more importantly also in the national and regional TACIS offices, in the management of a large number of very specific projects concerning the reform and restructuring of Russia's economy and infrastructure. In a limited way, this gives the EU some potential leverage over the way the Russian economy and society might evolve. However, from Russia's perspective, the EU is only one of many such actors proffering advice: the US and individual EU member states have their own programmes of technical assistance and international financial institutions such as the World Bank, the International Monetary Fund and European Bank for Reconstruction and Development are probably more influential than the EU.

TACIS Democracy Programme

The same note of caution needs to be sounded in assessing the significance of the EU's programme to support democratic reform in Russia.[63] EU teams have been sent to monitor parliamentary and presidential elections but here, of course, have found themselves operating alongside similar groups from the COE, the UN Committee for Europe and the OSCE. However, in the view of the European Parliament, measures to strengthen and consolidate the process of democratization should be one of the EU's key priorities and it has pressed for greater funds to be made available for the Democracy Programme. It regards Russia's democracy as 'still fragile' and in a recent resolution stressed the importance of fostering civil society and the emergence of a middle class to provide a firm basis for democracy, the rule of law and respect for human rights. It recommends that financial support is given to projects to foster the development of democratic political culture and a strong civil society particularly by encouraging and strengthening non-governmental organizations (NGOs).[64] An independent evaluation report on the TACIS Democracy Programme concluded that the most valuable part of its work was its contribution to the development of a 'lively NGO sector' for which external funding is vital given limited domestic resources.[65]

One example of the sort of project the EU has supported is the Specialist Information Centre: Prisoners' Rights, which was established under the aegis of the Moscow Centre for Prison Reform and has been very active in publicizing the appalling conditions prevalent in Russian prisons and campaigning for penal reform. The very fact that the EU is funding such organizations affords them a measure of protection as well as ensuring that they have the means to continue their work. In December 1998 the European Commission proposed that under the new TACIS regulation to cover the period 2000 to 2006, the promotion of democracy should be given a higher profile with particular emphasis on reinforcing the rule of law.[66] It also emphasized that the whole TACIS programme is strictly conditional on the continuation of the democratic reform process in Russia and it is clear that the EU hopes to be able to exercise significant influence over political developments in that country.

The EU's 'Common Strategy on Russia'

At the Cologne Council in June 1999 the EU adopted a 'Common Strategy on Russia' in order to build on the experience of the PCA and TACIS and to develop the Russia–EU relationship further. The introduction of the Common Strategy as a policy instrument was one of the key innovations of the new Treaty of Amsterdam which had come into force the previous month, so it was not surprising that the member states wanted to test out the new procedures in an area of obvious importance to them all. However, there were a number of additional reasons for deciding that a significant new initiative toward Russia was needed. Firstly, in the context of the EU's apparent preoccupation with ECE enlargement, it was important to send out a clear message of commitment to the development of much closer relations with Moscow and a determination that Russia should be fully integrated into a democratic and stable Europe. Secondly, there was a desire to respond to the criticism, for example in the European Parliament, that EU policy had been largely reactive and lacking any sense of long-term vision. Thirdly, it was hoped that a significant EU initiative would strengthen the position of the reformers in Russia in what was still an extremely uncertain domestic environment and send a positive signal in the run-up to the parliamentary and presidential elections scheduled for December 1999 and June 2000 respectively. Finally, the war in Kosovo and the subsequent commitment by the EU to develop a Stability Pact for the Balkans and to assume a lead role in a massive reconstruction programme gave rise to considerable Russian anxieties about a long-term shift in the balance of power in the region. It was, therefore, vital to seek new ways of strengthening cooperation with Russia in all aspects of European security, ranging from conflict resolution to combating international crime.

The Common Strategy was, therefore, an attempt to put a 'spin' on the work being undertaken within the framework of the PCA and TACIS, which remained the core of the relationship, and to identify specific initiatives for concrete action. It also suggested a number of potentially very significant new forms of cooperation in relation to foreign policy and security and placed a greater emphasis on joint efforts to deal with 'common scourges' such as organized crime, money-laundering, illegal immigration and trafficking in people and drugs. Above all, the Common Strategy attempted to give a clearer picture of long-term goals by spelling out a 'vision of the EU for its partnership with Russia'. This was seen in the following terms:

> A stable, democratic and prosperous Russia, firmly anchored in a united Europe free of new dividing lines, is essential to lasting peace on the continent. The issues which the whole continent faces can be resolved only through ever closer cooperation between Russia and the European Union. The European Union welcomes Russia's return to its rightful place in the European family in a spirit of friendship, cooperation, fair accommodation of interests and on the foundations of shared values enshrined in the common heritage of European civilisation.[67]

The reference to 'ever closer cooperation' clearly implied a progressive evolution of the relationship. One of the principal objectives of the Common Strategy was to enable Russia to integrate into a 'common economic and social area in Europe', particularly through the achievement of the free trade area and the accommodation of Russian legislation to EU norms. However, it is clear that the 'vision' extends beyond the creation of a form of European Economic Area extending from Reykjavik to Vladivostok. The partnership was now described as 'strategic', and the 'reinforced relationship' would include 'a permanent policy and security dialogue designed to bring interests closer together and to respond jointly to some of the challenges to security on the European continent'.[68] The newly appointed Secretary-General of the Council, the High Representative for the CFSP, was expected to play a key role in this security dialogue which was intended to become 'more operational and effective' than was the case under the PCA arrangements. It is not yet clear whether a new institution will be created, perhaps analogous to the Permanent Joint Council set up by NATO for dialogue with Russia, but the possibility is under consideration. The intention, however, was not just to institutionalize discussions on a wide range of issues, but to work toward joint foreign policy initiatives with regard to third countries, especially conflict prevention and crisis management in areas adjacent to Russia such as the Balkans and the Middle East. There was even a suggestion that Russia might in future participate in missions undertaken by the Western European Union at the request of the EU in relation to the 'Petersburg tasks' of peacekeeping, crisis management and humanitarian rescue operations.

The Common Strategy also contained numerous suggestions for specific actions to achieve the EU's strategic goals of promoting 'a stable, open and pluralistic democracy in Russia' and referred to 'intensified cooperation with Russia' in order to maintain European stability, promote global security and respond to the common challenges of the continent.[69] One of the significant aspects of the process of devising the Common Strategy was the extent of Russian involvement and indeed for the first time Moscow submitted a position paper outlining its views on the future development of relations with the EU.[70] Although there were some significant nuances in the language between the Russian and EU documents, the extent of agreement on the broad and ambitious objectives of the relationship was striking. Both parties referred to it as a 'strategic partnership' and it is clear that this reflected a significant shift in Russia's perception of the nature and role of the EU. Although economic objectives such as the free trade area remained important, it was also hoped that there would be joint development and implementation of the OSCE Charter on European Security. The overall goal, according to the Russian document, is of 'a mutually inter-connected and balanced strengthening of Russia's and the European Union's positions within the world community for the 21st century'.

The position paper stressed that Russian policy 'proceeds from the objective requirement of creating a multi-polar world and the responsibility of European states for the future of the continent, based on shared historical destinies as well as the complementarity of their economies'. It identified the principal objectives of Russia's strategy as being:

- to create a durable all-European collective security system (i.e. end the 'monopoly' of NATO and the US) in order to safeguard Russia's national interests and enhance its role and prestige in Europe and throughout the world;

- to help create a socially orientated market economy in Russia, based on principles of fair competition, by drawing on the EU's economic potential and administrative experience (i.e. different from the US free-market model);
- to establish an all-European economic and legal infrastructure or 'single European spaces';
- to further promote democracy and the rule of law;
- to ensure environmental protection and create decent living conditions in Europe;
- to work together to fight terrorism, drug trafficking and transnational organized crime;
- to strengthen partnership between Russia and the EU in European and world affairs.

The implicitly anti-American sentiments underlying some of Russia's objectives in relation to the EU are at odds with the policies of some, but by no means all, EU member states. However, a remarkable degree of consensus was apparent on both the objectives and specific content of the cooperation between Moscow and the EU.

Conclusion: Russia and the EU – conflict or cooperation?

The PCA, the 1996 Action Plan and the TACIS programme give a fairly clear idea of the EU's short- to medium-term objectives in relation to Russia. The Common Strategy even goes some way toward delineating the outline of the long-term shape of Russia–EU relations. Within the EU there is a recognition that the stability and security of Europe depend on the successful consolidation of economic and political reforms in Russia. This has meant, therefore, a strong sense of common interest with the westernizing/reforming groups in the Russian élite, something that has ensured continuing support for Yeltsin and his allies despite some of their less than democratic actions. It is assumed that Russia will not become a member of the EU, at least in the foreseeable future, but there has been a firm commitment to the development of a network of cooperative relationships covering trade, security, foreign policy, culture, the environment, research and development. The hope is that Russia will become so convinced of the benefits of cooperation and so integrated into all aspects of European life, that it will accept the role of equal partner with the EU in promoting the security and stability of the continent.

Although there are no comparable published documents enshrining Russia's policy toward the EU, the guidelines paper prepared in connection with the EU's Common Strategy provided a rare insight into the Yeltsin administration's thinking on the subject. It suggested a clear commitment to the development of a substantial partnership with the EU and broad agreement with it on the scope and direction of cooperation. However, Russian policy seems particularly susceptible to the political preferences of particular groups and individuals and it is not certain that a post-Yeltsin president would share the same objectives. There clearly are those within both Russian government and the business community who have a strong interest in gaining access to the EU's single market as a way of stimulating economic recovery, modernizing Russian industry and consolidating the capitalist economic system. However, there also seems to be evidence of a growing protectionist lobby that is resisting the opening up of the Russian market to competition from western goods and who argue that the Russian economy is big enough to be largely self-sufficient.[71] Similarly, while some groups welcome EU support for the consolidation of democratic institutions, others have seen it as an unacceptable interference in Russia's internal affairs and reject the assumption that there are shared universal values. Relations with the EU are inevitably caught up in the wider debate on Russia's identity and geopolitical vocation and, therefore, there are different perceptions of the importance of Russia's relations with the EU and of the particular form they should take. The EU is only one of several institutions seeking to influence the course of Russian reforms and to engage Moscow in cooperative actions. Ultimately, how much importance Russia attaches to the relationship with the EU, particularly its non-economic aspects, will depend on whether that relationship can deliver concrete results rather than just declarations of good intentions and whether a genuine sense of interdependence develops.

Notwithstanding the above caveat, there are two key factors that will inevitably make good relations with the EU increasingly salient to Russian policy-makers and which will, therefore, raise the potential costs of either confrontation or isolation. The first is the emergence of the EU as Russia's most important trading partner and the expectation that it is likely to remain so for the foreseeable future. The second is the prospect of EU enlargement over the next decade to the countries of ECE, including the Baltic states. This will not only further increase the EU's share of Russia's trade, but will also bring the EU closer to Russia's own borders. Both developments are likely to give rise to some tensions within the relationship and inevitably there will sometimes be conflicts of interest, but there will also be clear potential gains for both parties if cooperation can be strengthened and extended.

In the economic sphere, there is already evidence of growing interdependence and both parties would experience difficulties if trade were
to be interrupted or reduced.[72] In the case of Russia, the importance of
the EU market is obvious as long as a political leadership committed to
continuing economic reforms remains in power. Unless a future Russian
leadership decides to retreat into autarky, trade with the EU member
states is likely to continue to expand. Moreover, although statistically
EU trade appears to be much more important to Russia than vice versa,
Russia is a major supplier of energy and raw materials to the EU and also
a growing market for machinery, equipment, consumer goods and food.
From the EU's perspective, the 150 million Russian consumers are seen as
a very promising market, nearly one and a half times greater than the
combined market of all ten of the ECE applicant states. If the Russian
economy becomes more stable, then the development of a closer relationship with the EU may also contribute to a more favourable climate
for foreign direct investment, something which so far has been disap-
pointingly low. However, all these positive developments are dependent
on the success of political and economic transition and the development
of a stable, growing market economy in Russia. If all goes well, increased
business contacts, the development of trans-European communication
and supply networks, increased confidence and mutual trust will all make
Russia an integral part of the wider European economy. If a Russia–EU free
trade area becomes a reality, a genuinely pan-European marketplace will
be created and Russia could expect to share in the resulting economic
prosperity and stability. This growing economic interdependence which
gives Russia a stake in the new European order is the surest foundation
for the development of stable and peaceful political relations.

However, it would be unrealistic to expect that there will not be
some tension and occasional conflict in the economic relationship. In
the immediate future, trade disputes over such issues as dumping and
quotas are likely to continue to be a source of friction. The number of
cases and the amounts involved are actually quite small, but they
receive a disproportionate amount of negative coverage in the Russian
press and fuel suspicions that the EU is deliberately discriminating
against Russian exports. There have also been grievances on the West
European side over, for example, the high charges made to EU airlines
for over-flying Siberia, the stringent restrictions on imported beef and
other non-tariff barriers to trade arising from laws on standards and
technical specifications. In both Russia and the EU there are powerful
economic sectors and groups that expect to be protected against what
they regard as unfair foreign competition and there is inevitably a tension

between free trade and protectionism. What is important is that the institutions created under the PCA provide a framework for the resolution of such conflicts in a legal-bureaucratic environment so that they should not normally impact too seriously on the broader political relationship.

The other major factor that holds the potential for conflict in Russia–EU relations is that of EU enlargement. As has already been noted, reaction in Russia to the eventuality of enlargement has been generally relaxed and even quite positive. From Russia's perspective, the accession of its ECE neighbours to the EU could enhance regional stability and security by imposing a degree of external restraint over potentially excessive nationalism. Even the prospect of the three Baltic states becoming EU members seems to have been accepted. That said, there are two major potential flash-points in connection with the latter: the position of the large Russian-speaking minority in Estonia and Latvia and the region of Kaliningrad, formerly part of East Prussia and now a Russian enclave between Lithuania and Poland. The EU has been determined to ensure that as far as possible Russian grievances in relation to the treatment of Russian speakers in the Baltics are resolved as a precondition for EU membership of the Baltic states. It is clearly a nightmare scenario that a future nationalist-populist Russian president might launch a crusade to 'protect' fellow Russian-speakers in what might by then be an EU member state. There are also a number of issues arising from the fact that Kaliningrad will be physically located inside an enlarged EU. Issues such as transit rights across EU territory could potentially be difficult to resolve although so far all sides have been anxious to be accommodating. Current Russian policy is to emphasize the economic potential of Kaliningrad's location and exploit its status as a free economic zone to build a 'West–East trade bridge to Russia's Hong Kong'.[73] The fact that the enclave is also an important Russian naval and military base, however, increases the general level of sensitivity over its future position and could lead to tensions. The EU is very conscious of ensuring that Russia is fully integrated into the Baltic region and that relations between it and the Baltic states are normalized. Finland intends to mark its EU presidency in the second half of 1999 with a major package of measures to encourage greater cooperation with Russia as part of the EU's 'Northern Dimension', a project specifically intended to strengthen ties between Russia and the Baltic and Nordic states.[74]

Membership for the Balkan states could also be swallowed by Russia. Slovenia, at present the only probable candidate for accession, is already well integrated into regional networks involving Italy, Austria and Germany, and is marginal in any case to Russian interests in the region. While Slovenia's southern neighbours are unlikely candidates for EU membership, the proposed Stability Pact for the Balkans could involve states such as Bosnia, Albania and Macedonia being offered Europe Agreements and ultimately the prospect of full EU membership. If so, the impact on relations with Russia is difficult to predict, but it would not necessarily be negative if stability in the region is enhanced.

The one region where Russia would have real difficulties in accepting enlargement is among its Slavic neighbours. Although Belarus has not made a case for accession, Ukraine has been increasingly forceful in arguing that it should be regarded as a candidate for EU membership. Given that the Russian leadership (and, even more forcefully, the Russian Parliament) has regarded Ukraine as falling within Russia's legitimate sphere of influence, movement on Kiev's part toward western Europe could prove a major source of friction between Moscow and the EU.

Russia's most immediate concern, however, is to ensure that EU enlargement does not have a damaging impact on its own trade, especially in the light of the quite significant trade diversion experienced after Finland joined the EU in 1995. An 'exchange of letters on the consequences of enlargement' was appended to the PCA containing an undertaking by the EU to consult with Russia on the implications for its bilateral trade with the acceding countries prior to enlargement. This promise has already been invoked by the Russian delegations in the Cooperation Councils and Committees and is likely to be a significant item on the agenda for some years to come. The broader context is also important here. Russia's objective is to work toward the creation of 'a single economic space'[75] in Europe. Therefore, particular importance is attached to the evolutionary clause in the PCA, which could lead to the negotiation of a free trade area. Equally important would be the adoption by Russia of EU technical standards which otherwise could become the main barrier to trade with the rest of Europe, particularly as the ECE countries are already harmonizing their economic laws with those of the EU.

Potentially, the ECE states could prove an invaluable bridge between western Europe and Russia if their business and tourist links to the east are maintained and even increased after they join the EU. These states are concerned about the trade deficit they currently have with the EU and the large, and perhaps somewhat less sophisticated Russian market could be an attractive outlet for ECE manufactured goods. Many of them also rely heavily on Russian gas and oil. There is a growing tourist industry on both sides, which would be expected to expand with increased levels of prosperity. There is, therefore, no obvious reason why EU membership for the ECE states should not be combined with a high level of interaction with Russia.

Despite these potentialities, however, so far the signs have not been promising. The introduction by the ECE states of much tighter controls on their eastern borders to fulfil the pre-accession obligations imposed by the EU has aroused considerable bad feeling in Russia. In many respects it is becoming more difficult to move between Russia and Poland or the Czech Republic than it was during the Cold War, and, of course, border controls between Russia and the Baltic states are even more sensitive. One early casualty of these controls was the 'Russian bazaar' that took place in the sports stadium in Warsaw throughout the mid-1990s. Here, large numbers of small-scale traders from Belarus, Ukraine and Russia itself engaged in a primitive, but mutually advantageous, cross-border market. The imposition of border controls has virtually killed off this kind of informal cross-border trade, much to the dismay of many ordinary people, although the authorities on both sides were less concerned in view of the tax evasion it clearly encouraged. The introduction of visas for travel between Russia and some of its former allies is also bitterly resented as symbolic of new psychological as well as practical barriers. From the EU's perspective, strict controls of its external borders are an essential precondition of freedom of movement within the Union. The widespread belief that Russia is a base for organized crime, moreover, increases its anxieties about the permeability of the eastern frontier. However, in Russia there is a growing fear that measures associated with EU enlargement will resurrect the iron curtain, only this time further east.[76]

Although there are a number of potential sources of tension between Russia and the EU, there are also strong incentives for both parties to avoid open conflict and a mutual commitment to strengthen their relationship. The hope is that the PCA framework will provide channels through which conflicts of interest and straightforward differences of opinion can be discussed openly and dealt with in a constructive and peaceful manner between equals. Partnership does not mean always agreeing with one another: a mature relationship is one that recognizes that there will be differences, but at the same time accepts that a mutual interest exists, ensuring that these differences are settled in a manner that avoids inflicting permanent damage. However, there is no doubt that ultimately the critical factor that will determine the future relationship is whether Russia continues to be at least an aspiring democracy or whether the forces of reaction or extremism, or indeed anarchy, gain the ascendancy. The political conditionality of the PCA and TACIS is no empty threat and it is quite possible that if Russia was to relapse into authoritarianism, some or even all of the agreement could be suspended and aid frozen. Whether Russia is integrated or marginalized in Europe will ultimately depend on the success or failure of its own reforms and the EU can only hope that by holding out the prospect of a genuine partnership, the advantages of staying on the reform path will in some small way tip the balance in favour of democracy and stability.

Notes

1. Yeltsin's enthusiasm for 'trilateral meetings' between the Presidents of Russia and France and the German Chancellor are a reflection of this perception of a Europe dominated by 'great powers'.
2. A recent publication by the European Commission's Forward Studies Unit, *Shaping Actors, Shaping Factors in Russia's Future* (Kogan Page and the Official Publications of the EU, 1998) painted a pessimistic picture of the economic and political situation in Russia. Although not an official view, it has been influential in Brussels circles and seems to reflect the prevailing assumptions of many in the Commission.
3. EC Commission, 'Agenda 2000 – For a Stronger and Wider Union', *Bulletin of the European Union*, supplement 5/97 and supplements 6–15 for Commission opinions on the ten individual ECE applicants.
4. European Parliament Resolution on the Commission communication 'The Future of Relations between the EU and Russia', *Official Journal*, C138, 4 May 1998.
5. Y. Borko, 'The New Intra-European Relations and Russia', in M. Maresceau (ed.), *Enlarging the European Union: Relations between the EU and Central and Eastern Europe* (Harlow: Longman, 1997).
6. The Luxembourg European Council of December 1997 decided to launch the enlargement process in March 1998. The 'Agreement on Partnership and Cooperation between the European Communities and their Member States and the Russian Federation' (*Official Journal*, L327, 28 November 1997) came into force on 1 December 1997. It had first been proposed in 1992 and was signed by President Yeltsin and the EU Member States at the Corfu Council in June 1994.
7. The European Union only came into being in November 1993 when the (Maastricht) Treaty on European Union came into force.
8. V. Baranovsky, 'The European Community as Seen from Moscow: Rival, Partner, Model?', in N. Malcolm (ed.), *Russia and Europe: an End to Confrontation?* (London and New York: Pinter/London: Royal Institute of International Affairs, 1994).
9. J. Gower, 'EC Relations with Central and Eastern Europe', in J. Lodge (ed.), *The European Community and the Challenge of the Future*, 2nd edn. (London and New York: Pinter, 1993), p. 285.
10. 'Agreement between the EEC and Euratom and the USSR on Trade and Commercial and Economic Cooperation', *Official Journal*, L68, 15 March 1990.
11. Baranovsky, *op. cit.*, p. 66.

12. I. Leshoukov, 'Beyond Satisfaction: Russia's Perspectives of European Integration' (Discussion Paper C26 1998, Zentrum für Europäische Integrationsforschung, Bonn, 1998), p. 22.

13. V. Saveliev, 'USA-EU-Russia', *International Affairs* (Moscow), Vol. 43, No. 6, 1997.

14. Dmitrii Danilov (Head of Military-Political Studies at the Institute of Europe, Russian Academy of Sciences, Moscow), in 'A Piece of the Partnership', Institute for Journalism in Transition, <http: transitions/apieceof.html 1998>.

15. Leshoukov, *op. cit.*, p. 22.

16. Y. Borko, 'Russia and the EU in the 21st Century: Four Possible Scenarios of Relations', paper presented at Third European Community Studies Association World Conference and published in *The European Union in a Changing World* (Brussels: ECSA, 1996), p. 302.

17. *Ibid.*, p. 301.

18. Danilov, *op. cit.*

19. TACIS, *Russia and the EU Member States: Statistical Comparison 1990–96* (Luxembourg: OOPEC, 1998) p. 152.

20. Y. Borko, 'Economic Transformation in Russia and Political Partnership with Europe', in V. Baranovsky (ed.), *Russia and Europe: the Emerging Security Agenda* (Oxford: Oxford University Press/Frösunda, Sweden: Stockholm International Peace Research Institute, 1997).

21. For example see Tatyana Yakhlakova, 'Hard Talks between Russia and the EU', *Moscow News*, 31 July–6 August 1997.

22. A. Kondakov and P. Smirnov, 'Economic Diplomacy of Russia', *International Affairs* (Moscow), Vol. 43, No. 2, 1997, p. 13.

23. A. Kondakov, 'Russia's Economic Status: Transitory or Market Economy?', *International Affairs* (Moscow), Vol. 43, No. 6, 1997, pp. 53–8.

24. Differentiation in terms of the EU's aid programmes can be dated even earlier, with the decision in 1991 to establish TACIS rather than to extend the earlier PHARE programme to Russia. See Council Regulation No. 2157/91 concerning the provision of technical assistance to economic reform and recovery in the USSR, *Official Journal*, L201, 24 July 1991.

25. The European Council, 'Conclusions of the Presidency', *Bulletin of the European Communities*, 6.1993, point 1.4.

26. House of Commons, European Standing Committee B, *Relations with Russia*, 28 February 1995.

27. Two leading officials in the Commission report that 'to a large extent the countries with Europe Agreements chose themselves, by indicating their wish for full membership of the EU'. See G. Avery and F. Cameron, *The Enlargement of the European Union* (Sheffield: Sheffield Academic Press, 1998), p. 16.

28. 'Agreement on Partnership and Co-operation between the European Communities and their Member States and Russia', *Official Journal*, L327, 28 November 1997.

29. Y. Borko, 'The New Intra-European Relations and Russia', in M. Maresceau (ed.), *Enlarging the European Union: Relations between the EU and Central and Eastern Europe* (London and New York: Longman), p. 382.

30. *Ibid.*, p. 385.

31. See the Preamble and Article 2.

32. Article 10 requires the parties to accord most-favoured nation treatment to one another in the trade of goods according to WTO rules; Article 11 provides

for the elimination of non-tariff barriers; and Article 15 for the removal of quantitative restrictions. However, there is provision for exceptions to be made in respect of so-called 'sensitive' goods, as is discussed later.

33. See, for example, 'Europe Agreement between the European Communities and their Member States and the Republic of Poland', *Official Journal*, L348, 31 December 1993.

34. M. Maresceau and E. Montaguti suggest that Russia's objective was to secure an agreement as close and comparable to the Europe Agreements as possible whereas the EU favoured a much looser framework. See 'The Relations between the European Union and Central and Eastern Europe: a Legal Appraisal', *Common Market Law Review*, Vol. 32, No. 6, 1995, pp. 1327–67.

35. *Bulletin EC* 4–1993, point 1.3.18 and 11–1993, point 1.3.16. For a discussion of the negotiations, see D. Allen, 'EPC/CFSP, the Soviet Union, and the Former Soviet Republics: Do the Twelve Have a Coherent Policy?', in E. Regelsberger, P. de Schoutheete de Tervarent and W. Wessels (eds.), *Foreign Policy of the European Union: From EPC to CFSP and Beyond* (Boulder & London: Lynne Rienner, 1997).

36. First Meeting of the Cooperation Council between the European Union and the Russian Federation, Press Release (Council), DN: PRES/98/15, 3 February 1998.

37. External Affairs Commissioner Hans van den Broek pointed out to Russian MPs attending the third Parliamentary Cooperation Committee that tariffs on imports from the EU are on average over 20 per cent and make a substantial contribution to the Russian federal budget. EU Commission: SPEECH/98/170. Leshoukov, *op. cit.*, calculates that the creation of a free trade area would result in a 14 per cent reduction in federal budget receipts.

38. Article 17 permits safeguard measures and Article 18 covers anti-dumping or countervailing measures, in accordance with GATT rules.

39. For example, see T. Oganesyan, 'Iron Curtain Built Against Russian Steel', *Moscow News*, 27 August–3 September, 1997, p. 7, which reports that the EU has imposed such high anti-dumping duties on 14 categories of Russian goods that it is pointless to trade in them. See also *Izvestiya*, 22 July 1997, p. 2 as translated in *The Current Digest of the Post-Soviet Press*, Vol. 49, No. 29.

40. At the summit meeting in June 1997, Russian Prime Minister Viktor Chernomyrdin argued forcefully that 'there was no political or economic justification to maintain Russia's status as a non-market economy' and protested at the negative impact the EU's anti-dumping measures were having on Russia's export potential for finished and semi-finished goods. See 'Visit to the European Commission of the Prime Minister of the Russian Federation', Press Release (Commission), DN: IP/97/670, 18 July 1997. Similar complaints were made at the first Cooperation Council in January 1998, Press Release (Council), DN: PRES/98/15.

41. O. Ivanov and V. Pozdnyakov, 'Novi vozmozhnosti Rossii v Evropeiskom Soyuz', *Mezhdinarodnaya zhizn'*, No. 3, 1998.

42. *Sevodnya*, 28 January 1998 as translated in *The Current Digest of the Post-Soviet Press*, Vol. 50, No. 4.

43. Press Release (Commission), IP/98/373, Brussels, 27 April 1998.

44. These meetings have been held near enough according to schedule, the most recent being in Birmingham (May 1998), Vienna (October 1998) and Moscow (February 1999).

45. See 'Declaration by the Presidency on Behalf of the European Union on the Situation in Russia', Press Release: PESC/98/100 and J. M. Jil-Robles Jil-Delgado, 'European Union: Privileged Relations with Russia', *International Affairs* (Moscow), Vol. 44, No. 4, p. 41. For Russia's view see *Finansoviye izvestiya*, 2 December 1997, as translated in *The Current Digest of the Post-Soviet Press*, Vol. 49, No. 49, p. 24.
46. Press Release (Council) DN: PRES/98/15, 3 February 1998.
47. Hans van den Broek, at the Third Meeting of the EU–Russia Parliamentary Cooperation Committee, European Parliament, Strasbourg, 16 September 1998, Commission: SPEECH/98/170.
48. EU–Russia Summit, Vienna, 27 October 1998, Joint Press Release: PRES/98/360.
49. Second meeting of the Cooperation Council between the EU and Russia, Brussels, 17 May 1999, Press Release (Council), DN: PRES/99/152.
50. The report is generally known by the name of its rapporteur, Catherine Lalumière. It was published in February 1998. See European Parliament Report on 'The Future of Relations between the European Union and Russia', European Parliament Document, PE 223.304/fin.
51. European Parliament Resolution on the Commission communication 'The Future of Relations between the EU and Russia', *Official Journal*, C138, 4 May 1998.
52. *Bulletin EU*, 11-1995, point 2.2.1.
53. *Bulletin EU*, 5-1996, point 2.3.1.
54. 'Relations with Russia', report presented at the General Affairs Council Meeting, Brussels, 6 December 1996, Press Release, DN: PRES/96/366.
55. TACIS stands for 'technical assistance to the CIS' and was established in 1991 by Council Regulation 2157/91. It is similar to the PHARE programme established in 1989 for the countries of ECE.
56. European Commission, *The TACIS Programme Annual Report 1997*, COM (98), 416 final, 3 July 1998.
57. European Commission, *The TACIS Programme: an Interim Evaluation* (Office of Official Publications of the EC, 1997), pp. 22–3.
58. See Leshoukov, *op. cit.*, p. 15. The widespread criticism of the large number of western consultants employed on TACIS projects is shared by observers in the EU member states as well. See House of Lords Select Committee on the European Communities, 33rd Report, *Partnership and Trust: the TACIS Programme*, 1998, p. 55.
59. *The TACIS Programme: an Interim Evaluation, op. cit.*, p. 15.
60. For example, in November 1998 after Commission President Jacques Santer had visited Moscow, the Commission proposed that a food programme amounting to about EUR 470 million should be made available to Russia.
61. *The TACIS Programme: an Interim Evaluation, op. cit.*, p. 12.
62. European Commission, TACIS Action Programme 1998, <http://europa.eu.int/comm/dg1a/tacis/country close-up/Russia>.
63. In February 1997, the internal management of the TACIS Democracy Programme was integrated with the PHARE Democracy Programme to become the PTDP – the PHARE/TACIS Democracy Programme.
64. *Official Journal*, C138, 4 May 1998.
65. Mary Kaldor and Peter Wilke, 'Evaluation of the PHARE and TACIS Democracy Programme 1992–1997', <http://europa.eu.int/comm/dg1a/tacis/results>.

66. 'Democracy and Investment: New Focus of EU Assistance to Russia, Ukraine and other New Independent States', Press Release (Commission), IP/98/1159, Brussels, 22 December 1998.
67. 'Common Strategy of the European Union on Russia', Annex II, Council of the European Union, *Presidency Conclusions: Cologne European Council*, 3–4 June 1999, p. 1, Press Release Council, DN:PRES/99/1500, 9 June 1999.
68. *Ibid.*, p. 2.
69. *Ibid.*, p. 1.
70. 'Guidelines for the Strategy of Developing Relations of the Russian Federation with the European Union', circulated to EU Member States in 1999. Unpublished.
71. Tariffs have been increased on many imported goods in response to lobbying from domestic producers. Borko predicts that the Russian authorities will find it difficult to balance the demands for increased protection from domestic producers with the goal of integrating Russia in the world economy. See Y. Borko, 'The New Intra-European Relations and Russia', *op. cit.*
72. During the financial crisis 1998–99, EU farmers were badly hit by the collapse of the Russian market for imported meat, especially beef. Commission President Santer reported that 20 per cent of the EU's exports of agricultural goods goes to Russia. 'Intervention de M. Jacques Santer Président de la Commission Européenne Débat sur la Situation en Russie Session Plénière du Parlement Européen Strasbourg, le 16 Septembre', Press Release, SPEECH/98/169.
73. A. Sergounin, 'The Russia Dimension', in H. Mouritzen (ed.), *Bordering Russia* (Aldershot: Ashgate, 1998), p. 45.
74. 'Survey: the Baltic Sea Region', *Financial Times*, 11 June 1999; *The Economist*, 12 June 1999, p. 51.
75. I. Ivanov, 'Rasshirenie Evrosoyuza: stsenarii problemii, posledstviya', *Mirovaya ekonomika i mezhdunarodnye otnosheniya*, No. 9, 1998, p. 33.
76. *Pravda*, 20 February, 1998 as translated in *The Current Digest of the Post-Soviet Press*, Vol. 50, 1998.

5
Russia and the Organization for Security and Cooperation in Europe

Dov Lynch

Introduction

The authorities in Moscow have recognized the opportunities that exist for the integration of Russia into Europe as a 'normal' power. The Russian leadership has officially acknowledged that the main threats to Russian security arise to the south and south-west, and most importantly, from within Russia itself. Apart from the war-torn Balkans, Europe has been recognized as a relative zone of stability. However, despite these relatively positive circumstances, Russia's relations with Europe since 1992 have not been without difficulties.

Tensions have resulted, in part, from the manner in which Russia has confronted the challenges posed by this new 'window of opportunity' in Europe.[1] The Russian authorities face the question of determining what role their country will play in Europe. Will this role be that of a peripheral state or that of a key European power? How will relations between Russia and the rest of Europe be structured? In what ways will Russia be taken into account in decision-making on key issues of European security and cooperation?

The Organization for Security and Cooperation in Europe (now OSCE, until January 1995 the Conference on Security and Cooperation in Europe – the CSCE) has played an important part in Russian considerations of these questions. Interactions between Russia and the rest of Europe since the collapse of the Soviet Union have not occurred in an institutional vacuum. The collapse of the Cold War order occurred primarily along its Soviet and East European dimensions. In its search for an appropriate place, Moscow has, since 1992, aimed at increasing the role of the OSCE in regional peace and security. At various points since 1989, the Soviet and Russian leaderships have called for the

99

creation of a collective security system in Europe based around a reinforced OSCE, coordinating the activities of other security-related organizations. The Russian leadership has underlined the extensive
membership of the OSCE (by 1997, there were 54 members), the organization's comprehensive approach to security (including economic,
humanitarian as well as ecological dimensions), as well as its consensual
decision-making process. By this view, the OSCE stands in direct contrast to the North Atlantic Treaty Organization (NATO), a collective
defence organization from which Russia and many other European
states are excluded.

Moves toward an enlargement of NATO after 1994 resulted in an initial
deterioration of relations with the European powers. In the former Soviet
Union (FSU) these tensions were reflected in exclusive Russian policies
toward the OSCE in peacekeeping in post-Soviet conflicts. However,
during 1995–99, a normalization trend in Russian–European relations was
apparent as a special relationship was created with NATO, and the Russian
initiative to elaborate a 'Common and Comprehensive Security Model for
the 21st Century' within the OSCE kept the issue of pan-European
cooperation on the international agenda. Moreover, starting in 1994,
Russia sought the harmonization of its peacekeeping activities with
OSCE missions on the ground in post-Soviet conflicts. Even more fundamentally, the Russian authorities have allowed the deployment of an
OSCE mission inside Russia, which has performed a wide range of activities
in Chechnya since April 1995.

This discussion of Russian policy toward the OSCE is divided into
three parts. A brief first part will outline the Soviet perspective on the
CSCE in the late 1980s as an instrument to overcome the collapse of the
Warsaw Pact and the shifts occurring in the European security landscape. The second part will delineate the main objectives pursued by
the Russian leadership regarding the OSCE since late 1992. This discussion will make an important distinction between maximal and minimal
objectives in Russian policy. The final part will discuss the evolution of
Russian–CSCE/OSCE relations since late 1991, with a view to highlighting the emergence of more harmonious and routinized relations at the
strategic and tactical levels.

Gorbachev's 'common European home' and the CSCE

Before discussing Russian policy toward the OSCE, it is important to
examine briefly the evolution of Soviet policy toward the CSCE in the
late 1980s. This evolution highlights enduring elements that remain in

Russia's interaction with the OSCE. Until Mikhail Gorbachev's arrival in power in 1985, Soviet policy toward Europe had been largely linked to wider Soviet–American relations.[2] By 1985, elements in the Soviet leadership realized that this policy had not just decreased Soviet security in Europe but had resulted in the Soviet Union's isolation from an increasingly dynamic group of states.[3] With regard to the United States (US) meanwhile, the Soviet leadership faced an administration under Ronald Reagan bent on outpacing it in military and technological terms. Gorbachev's 'new political thinking' represented an attempt to redress this array of stalemates in order to create a favourable international environment for the internal revitalization of the Soviet Union. A critical part of this 'new political thinking' was the normalization of relations with western Europe and European organizations.

The concept of a 'common European home' became a central plank in Gorbachev's 'new political thinking.' This 'home' was defined as 'an integral political and legal, economic and cultural space, an alliance of states with common structures maintaining military and ecological security, and ensuring a high level of multifarious interaction'.[4] As such, the concept was not coterminous with the CSCE. Until 1989, it was associated with the broader objective of normalizing Soviet–European relations and, by extension, an improvement of relations with the US.[5]

The CSCE had played an important role in Soviet *détente* policies in the early 1970s. The Helsinki Final Act of 1975 was interpreted as an important success, standing as a *de facto* peace treaty in Europe enshrining the inviolability of post-war borders and the integrity of the Eastern bloc. In the initial years of Gorbachev's 'new political thinking', the CSCE had assumed some importance as a forum for discussion of confidence and security-building measures. Before the Council of Europe on 6 July 1989, Gorbachev called for greater dynamism to be imbued in the CSCE process through a second conference of the Helsinki type.[6] However, the emphasis in Soviet policy remained on the wider 'common European home', in which the CSCE was only one strand of a multifaceted set of both multilateral and bilateral relations.

The CSCE became a central pillar of Soviet European policy only in late 1989. The fast pace of events in east-central Europe (ECE) forced the Soviet leadership to propose a CSCE-based collective security system in order to offset the dangers arising from a fundamental transition in European affairs. The critical concern in this regard was the 'German problem' and the possibility that a reunified Germany might remain within NATO. Soviet policy sought to synchronize the reunification of Germany with the creation of a 'fundamentally new structure of European security which

[... would] replace the one based on blocs'.[7] The Soviet leadership placed great emphasis on the strengthening of the CSCE in order to eliminate the 'bipolar model' and to create a 'new European community based on confidence, mutual understanding and an effective system of collective security'.[8]

In advance of the scheduled CSCE summit in Paris in November 1990, Foreign Minister Eduard Shevardnadze called for the creation of new institutions within the CSCE to place the organization on a more permanent footing. These included a Council of Great Europe for regular meeting of Heads of State, a Foreign Ministers Committee to meet twice a year, a consultative mechanism of member-state Ambassadors, a permanent Secretariat, and a Centre for Military-Political Stability.[9] This Centre was to play an important role in a new bloc-free Europe as a mechanism for conflict prevention and mediation, as well as a forum for permanent military transparency.[10] Clearly in response to Soviet positions, the US government and NATO took up the theme of reinforcing the CSCE in advance of the Paris summit. At the US–Soviet summit in Washington in June, President George Bush offered a strengthening of the CSCE as a condition for Soviet acceptance of a reunified Germany within NATO.[11] However, while taking Soviet proposals into account, 'The Charter of Paris for a New Europe' reflected clearly the views put forth in July by NATO in its 'London Declaration on a Transformed North Atlantic Alliance'.[12]

The Soviet Union welcomed the institutional reform of the CSCE endorsed at Paris. However, the signing of the Conventional Forces in Europe Treaty, and the 'Joint Declaration of Twenty-Two States' (of NATO and the Warsaw Pact) were seen as more important.[13] The Paris Charter contained only one paragraph on the German issue, highlighting the shift in Soviet attention once this central question had been resolved outside the CSCE framework. Following US and NATO pledges to transform the role of the Alliance and the resolution of the status of Germany, Soviet proposals for the creation of a collective security system under the umbrella of the CSCE lost impetus. These proposals had played an important, if instrumental, role in framing Soviet security concerns with the radical shifts then occurring in the European order. The Soviet Foreign Ministry thereafter viewed the CSCE in a less ambitious manner, as a 'common roof' encompassing what one official called 'differently oriented vectors in European politics'.[14] Far less than a collective security system, these 'vectors' were to include cross-cutting cooperation between various organizations in Europe, and a network of bilateral security guarantees in eastern and western Europe.[15] This shift in Soviet policy favouring less ambitious policies toward the CSCE foreshadowed a similar change in Russian approaches in 1995.

Factors and objectives in Russian policy toward the OSCE

This section will examine the main trends in Russian policy toward the CSCE/OSCE as well as the balance between Russia's maximal and minimal objectives toward that organization. This discussion will establish signposts for a subsequent detailed examination of the evolution of Russian policy since 1992. The section begins, however, by highlighting three interacting factors that have influenced the Russian approach.

The interaction of these three factors has denoted the relative importance attributed to the OSCE in Russian policy, and the varying degree of 'functionality' the organization has assumed with regard to wider developments in European affairs. First, Russian policy toward the OSCE has been influenced by changes that have taken place in the structure of Russian security and foreign policy decision-making. Following the appointment of Yevgeny Primakov as Foreign Minister in January 1996, the Foreign Ministry managed to recapture ground that had been lost to the then Defence Minister Pavel Grachev. Its resurgence as a leading decision-maker in Russian policy also catalysed a conceptual shift in Russian approaches to the OSCE and European security away from the 'hard' geopolitical and conflictual approach adopted by Grachev.

The second factor has resided in military-security developments within Russia itself and a number of the Soviet successor states. The conflict in Chechnya and Russia's involvement in peacekeeping operations in the FSU have had a sobering effect on Russian ambitions to employ exclusive policies to advance its interests through the use of force.[16] By 1996, it had become painfully apparent to the Russian government that it no longer had the resources necessary for a strategy of forward positioning. The use of force in Russian policy had had unintended effects that often went counter to the pursuit of Russian interests. As a result, Russian and OSCE mediation has become increasingly harmonious and mutually supportive.

The third factor has been the wider development of events in Europe outside of the OSCE process. The enlargement of NATO and the development of Russian–NATO relations have constituted the strategic framework structuring much of Russian policy toward the OSCE. Russia's reaction to the initial discussions of NATO enlargement was reflected in its proposals for the creation of a pan-European collective security system under the coordinating framework of the OSCE. The creation of a formal special relationship between Russia and NATO in the Permanent Joint Council in 1997 (see Chapter 3) has led Russia to abandon its most ambitious plans regarding the OSCE. However, Russian–NATO ties remain significantly linked with Russian policy toward the OSCE and its desire to maintain an effective balance between 'mutually reinforcing institutions' in Europe.

In addition to these three factors, Russian (and earlier Soviet) policy toward the CSCE/OSCE has reflected two main trends – first, that of using the organization as an *agent to maintain the status quo* in Europe; and secondly, that of using the OSCE as an *agent to transform* European affairs. Between 1975 and 1989, the Soviet Union sought to use the CSCE as a means to reinforce the post-war *status quo* in Europe, by creating 'rules of the game' to normalize East–West relations. By contrast, between 1989 and 1995, the Soviet and then Russian leaderships sought to employ the OSCE as a mechanism to transform European security affairs, with the aim of eliminating the remnants of the bloc system in Europe. Since 1995, the Russian government has sought to use the OSCE once more as a *status quo* agent in Europe, in order to prevent the further enlargement of NATO and to establish 'rules of the game' for the interaction between Russia and the rest of Europe, and between various security-related organizations.

Related to these two wider trends, it is important to distinguish between maximal and minimal objectives in Russian approaches to the OSCE. Since 1992, Russia has put forth a series of optimal proposals for the reform of European security structures around the OSCE. Particularly in 1994, the Russian leadership called for the creation of a pyramid of security-related organizations, in which the OSCE would stand as the central coordinator.[17] In its minimal objectives, the Russian authorities have been intent on codifying Russia's voice as a great power in European affairs. At the very least, Moscow has sought to prevent the isolation of a Russia which now finds itself geographically distant from the heart of Europe. It has also sought to obtain the legitimation and support of the OSCE for Russian peacekeeping operations. However, the means by which these minimal objectives have been pursued have changed in Russian policy.

After failing to oppose the enlargement of NATO, Moscow has sought to prevent NATO becoming the main axis of security in Europe. In search of multipolarity in international affairs, Russia has been intent on the elaboration of 'modalities of cooperation' between different security-related organizations in order to create a network of mutually reinforcing institutions.[18] It has de-emphasized the notion of a hierarchy of institutions under the OSCE and has rather claimed to place this organization at the heart of discussions of both 'hard' and 'soft' security as a mechanism for systematic consultation. Combined with the formation of formal ties between Russia and NATO, the OSCE would formalize 'rules of the game' for the cooperative pursuit of European security, in which Russia would have a 'special' as well as an 'equal' voice.[19]

At the heart of Russia's minimal objectives stands an attempt to answer the question posed by Kozyrev in 1995 on 'how to form the optimal ratio of global, regional and sub-regional approaches to the solution of European problems'.[20] The Russian proposal of July 1997 for a European Security Charter explicitly aimed 'to develop a concept of the indivisibility of security'.[21] As defined by Primakov, indivisible security requires avoiding the introduction of 'new elements in the system, which would ensure the security of certain participants at the expense of others'.[22] These Russian proposals represented a retreat from calls for a collective security system under the OSCE. In the words of Andrei Kokoshin, former Secretary of the Defence Council and State Military Inspectorate, codes of interaction between mutually reinforcing institutions would offset the dangers of seeking pure geopolitical objectives while mitigating the inefficiency of international organizations.[23] In this, Moscow has sought to prevent the further division of Europe along geographical lines, as well as any division of labour in the activities of European security organizations between 'hard' (i.e. NATO-led) and 'soft' security responsibilities.

The evolution of Russian policy toward the OSCE

Russian policy toward the OSCE has evolved in three periods since late 1991. The first period, which lasted until July 1992, corresponded with Russia's embrace of the West and with the objective of rejoining Europe and its institutions as a 'normal' state. The second period, from July 1992 until the OSCE's Budapest summit of December 1994, was characterized by maximalist Russian proposals for the reform of the then CSCE. The most recent period, starting in 1995, has featured an increasing normalization of Russian relations with the OSCE as well as the harmonization of Russian and OSCE mediation efforts in post-Soviet conflicts. This evolution highlights the increasing importance of the OSCE for Russian policy as a cooperative mechanism to address Russian security concerns on a pan-European and sub-regional level. It also underlines the shift in Russian policy toward a greater understanding of the utility of the OSCE for relations with Europe.

Each period will be examined in terms of two levels of interaction between Russia and the OSCE: first, Russian policy toward the OSCE as a pan-European security organization; and, secondly, Russian policy toward OSCE conflict mediation in the FSU region. This discussion will also address elements of soft cooperation between Russia and the OSCE, particularly regarding the OSCE Human Dimension and the role of the High Commissioner for National Minorities (HCNM).

Late 1991–July 1992: 'romantic westernism'

Russian approaches to the OSCE during this short period reflected a pursuit of integration into international, and mainly western, economic and political organizations. The focus in Russian policy was on the creation of 'all-azimuth partnership', with the West and international organizations.[24] This policy followed on the shift that had occurred in Soviet approaches to European security organizations in mid-1990, in which the OSCE was downgraded in importance. The OSCE subsequently became only one forum addressed by Russia and not the central one. Oleg Bykov, Deputy Director of the Institute of World Economy and International Relations (IMEMO), explained Russian policy during this period as a reorientation away from a 'predominant fixation on the CSCE towards a wide range of dynamics in European politics'.[25] The Yeltsin leadership sought to develop closer ties with the NATO states, as a stabilizing factor in the nascent European order.

The Russian policy of 'all-azimuth partnership' was also reflected in its approach to security threats emerging in the FSU. In early 1992, it had become painfully evident that the presence of some 25 million ethnic Russians outside Russia represented a critical security issue. Kozyrev undertook to protect the rights of these 'national minorities' by engaging the OSCE in the region. As early as September 1991, Kozyrev proposed to a meeting of the CSCE on the Human Dimension that cases of alleged human rights violations in the FSU could be a matter for CSCE inspection.[26] Following the tensions that arose in June 1992 after the passage of restrictive Estonian laws on voting rights, the Russian Foreign Ministry made a concerted effort to make use of the CSCE to place pressure on the Estonian government. In Deputy Foreign Minister Fedor Shelov-Kovedyaev's words, this would 'solve the problem without bloodletting'.[27] Kozyrev welcomed the creation of the new HCNM during the 1992 CSCE Helsinki review conference as a 'mechanism that could be used to protect the Russian-speaking population'.[28]

The Russian Foreign Ministry also sought to engage the CSCE in mediation in conflicts in the region of the FSU. By March 1992, all of the

Soviet successor states had joined the CSCE. A representative of the CSCE Chairman-in-Office was sent to the Moldovan capital of Chisinau in mid-April to follow developments in the quadripartite mechanism set up by Kozyrev to promote conflict resolution in the Transdniestrian region.[29] The CSCE also became deeply involved in mediation of the conflict in Nagorno-Karabakh (Azerbaijan): the CSCE's Senior Council created the so-called Minsk Group in March to direct mediation activities toward the eventual convening of a peace conference.[30]

Russian peacekeeping policy in early 1992 was explicitly inclusive. The Russian Foreign Ministry sought to prevent any burdensome entanglement in the FSU in order to focus on internal reform. The decisions adopted at the CSCE summit in Helsinki in July reflected the nature of Russian policy at this point. As well as supporting the creation of the HCNM, Russia also welcomed a decision to discuss procedures for CSCE peacekeeping.[31] Yeltsin, moreover, was also able to place nascent Russian threat perceptions on the CSCE agenda with a statement on the dangers of nationalism as 'a plague of the 20th century'. However, the CSCE was not fundamentally reformed. The summit placed emphasis on the CSCE as only one 'forum for dialogue, negotiation and cooperation' in Europe.[32]

July 1992–December 1994: unilateralism and grand designs

During this period, Russian relations with the CSCE deteriorated quite dramatically. In conflict mediation in the FSU, Russia pursued exclusive policies. At a wider level, the Russian leadership proposed a significant strengthening of the CSCE. In this, the CSCE was to emerge as the central coordinator of a pan-European collective security system to which other security-related structures would be subordinated. This shift in policy reflected the 'push' and 'pull' interaction of four factors.

First, President Yeltsin and Andrei Kozyrev came under intense political pressure from critics inside the government and in the Parliament. State Counsellor Sergei Stankevich called for rectifying the 'obvious distortions caused by the creators of the concept of the common European home'.[33] The nationalist opposition criticized Kozyrev's reliance on international organizations to defend Russian interests and the Russian-speaking population in the Soviet successor states. These critics argued that Kozyrev's 'priority of civilized methods' was useless.[34] In this view, the Russian leadership had to recognize that the main threats to its interests emerged from the FSU. As a result, it was considered vitally important for Russia to become the 'political and military guarantor of stability' in this region.[35] This pressure placed intense stress on Kozyrev's approach to conflict mediation in post-Soviet conflicts.

Second, and perhaps most fundamentally for the Foreign Ministry's position, in May 1992, President Yeltsin created a Ministry of Defence under Grachev. One reason behind this decision was the perceived need to respond to local conflicts in more assertive ways. On 1 July 1992 Grachev stated that 'in conditions of civil chaos, clashes and reprisals, only the army can save thousands of lives, preserve morsels of good and defend what is sacred'.[36] The influence of the new Ministry was immediately felt in conflicts in the FSU. In June–July 1992, Colonel-General Aleksandr Lebed intervened in the conflict in Moldova, lending former Soviet 14th Army support to Transdniestrian forces (in addition, 1200 Russian peacekeepers drawn from the 14th Army were deployed in July). Elsewhere, the Russian 201st motorized rifle division in Tajikistan was given a 'peacekeeping' role in November 1992 in order to strengthen the position of the former communist government in this country crippled by civil war. The Russian Defence Ministry also deployed peacekeeping forces in the South Ossetian region of Georgia in mid-July 1992, and throughout 1993 Russian forces deployed in the Abkhaz region provided armed support to local forces in their struggle with Georgian troops (the Defence Ministry subsequently deployed peacekeeping forces in Abkhazia in June 1994).

The activities of the Defence Ministry signalled the end of Kozyrev's initial policy of 'benign neglect' toward the FSU. The Foreign Ministry had sought to avoid becoming entangled in the 'chaos' of the Soviet collapse in order to focus on Russia's internal revitalization and integration into the international community. Yet, by mid-1993, Russia had become deeply involved militarily throughout the FSU. These circumstances highlighted the predominance of the Defence Ministry in critical areas of Russian foreign policy-making. With privileged access to President Yeltsin, it rapidly seized the initiative and excluded the Foreign Ministry from policy-making.

Third, these shifts also led to a change in the conceptual basis of Russian policy. A consensus emerged in the Russian leadership on the need to actively defend Russian interests abroad: arms and drugs smuggling, the spill over of conflicts, refugee flows and Russian out-migration posed a threat to Russian reform.[37] Under the influence of the Defence Ministry, geopolitical perceptions increasingly framed Russian foreign policy. Military officials focused on the geopolitical loss suffered by Russia and the need to regain the initiative in the threatening post-Soviet space through an assertive, even interventionist, policy.[38]

A final factor influencing Russian policy toward the CSCE during this period resided in the debates that emerged over NATO enlargement and of Russia joining the Partnership for Peace programme. As early as May 1992, the Russian press had raised with anxiety the possibility that NATO might intervene in conflicts in the FSU.[39] At the wider European level, Moscow evinced increasing anxiety about the possibility of NATO becoming the principal axis of security and thus of Russia being marginalized from the heart of European developments. More fundamentally, enlargement was interpreted as an affront to Russia's status as a great power.

The interaction of these internal and external factors produced distinct shifts in Russian policy toward the CSCE. In conflict mediation, Russian policy became increasingly exclusive regarding CSCE activities. Yeltsin's appeal to the international community to recognize Russia's 'special responsibility' in the FSU in February 1993[40] initiated a campaign to secure international support for Russian peacekeeping operations. Russian peacekeeping activities became officially integrated into a policy which sought to defend and promote Russian interests. Kozyrev stressed that: '[u]nless we find the political will and real resources [...] for peacekeeping in the former Soviet zones, this vacuum will be filled by others, above all by the forces of political extremism, which threaten Russia itself'.[41] In November 1993, Kozyrev affirmed that Russia would 'not abandon the FSU to international organizations'.[42]

Between mid-1993 and the CSCE's Budapest summit of December 1994, Moscow actively sought CSCE support for Russian peacekeeping. The CSCE Helsinki Declaration of July 1992 stated that the organization might seek the support of 'other institutions and mechanisms, including the peacekeeping mechanism of the CIS [Commonwealth of Independent States]' for CSCE operations. Following this, in 1993 Moscow initiated a discussion of the possibility of CSCE support for 'third party' peacekeeping activities. The CSCE's Rome Council meeting in December 1993 endorsed the possibility that the CSCE might support such activities if accompanied by CSCE cooperative arrangements 'to ensure that the role and functions of a third party force in a conflict area are consistent with CSCE principles and objectives'.[43]

In the run-up to the Budapest summit in December 1994, Russia sought a loose framework for CSCE support for third-party peacekeeping. In February 1994, the Head of the Russian delegation to the CSCE, Vladimir Shustov, presented Russian objectives in this area. Shustov called for CSCE sponsorship of the peacekeeping activities of a 'single state or a group of states belonging to a regional organization' (i.e. Russia and the other CIS member states). In Shustov's view, CSCE support would consist ideally of a 'blessing', in which actual monitoring would be 'qualified, limited and distant'. The third parties themselves would pursue 'voluntary monitoring' to ensure compliance with CSCE principles. The Russian official maintained that Russian/CIS peacekeeping operations did not require CSCE legitimation, as these were already in full accordance with UN and CSCE norms.[44]

Shustov's proposals underlined Russia's desire to limit the actual involvement of the CSCE in the FSU, while still obtaining its financial support and mandating legitimacy. In its 'Programme to Increase the Efficiency of the CSCE' distributed at the preparatory talks before the 1994 Budapest summit, the Russian Foreign Ministry called for the creation of a 'compensation regime' within the CSCE to support Russian/CIS operations.[45] Moscow justified its search for a loose CSCE monitoring framework on the basis that Russian peacekeeping had already proved its efficiency. A Foreign Ministry official, Yury Ushakov, stated at the preparatory talks for the Budapest summit: '[t]he CSCE is just beginning in peacekeeping. It has no experience in military matters or peacekeeping and is not suitable to supervise them. We don't want the CSCE to be giving us orders'.[46]

During this period, the CSCE deployed long-term missions in Georgia in November 1992, Moldova in April 1993 and Tajikistan in February 1994. The CSCE also continued mediating via the Minsk Group in Nagorno-Karabakh. These efforts were not well met by Moscow as its search for international support for CIS peacekeeping translated, at this point, into exclusive policies toward the CSCE on the ground. In Moldova, Russian mediation obstructed Moldovan government attempts to widen the negotiation framework to include Ukraine, Romania and the CSCE. The Russian leadership also repeatedly ignored CSCE calls for the rapid withdrawal of the Russian 14th Army from the Transdniestrian region, and rejected any CSCE presence in negotiations on this issue. With regard to CSCE mediation in the Nagorno-Karabakh conflict, the appointment of Vladimir Kazimirov as Russian presidential envoy to this conflict in July 1993 marked the start of a campaign to exclude the CSCE. Defence Minister Grachev secured a ceasefire in Moscow on 16 May 1994, which was thereafter to provide for the deployment of a CIS peacekeeping operation. This ceasefire regime held throughout 1994. However, Azerbaijan rejected any Russian-dominated CIS operation, calling for a multinational operation under the aegis of the CSCE. The possible deployment of a CSCE operation, however, became entangled in the wider Russia–CSCE discussions about the modalities for 'third party peacekeeping', in which Russia rejected any deployment of 'foreign' troops in the post-Soviet space.[47] Moscow sought to prevent the Minsk Group from becoming the main mediator in this conflict. In November

1994, the Foreign Ministry stated that CSCE activities 'in fact undermine the very core of the peace process, no matter what statements about the importance of other international efforts are used to conceal this'.[48] Moscow viewed the activities of the Minsk Group in geopolitical terms, as an attempt to limit Russian influence in the Transcaucasus.

Despite confounding CSCE initiatives regarding conflict management, Russia was a little more generous toward the organization's efforts in the fields of conflict prevention and the human dimension, particularly in the Baltic states where this was geared toward the rights of Russian minorities. Russian relations with Estonia and Latvia were strained over Russian protests at the treatment of Russophone minorities in these states. At times, this controversial issue became a central theme in Russia's internal foreign policy debate. The populist and hostile rhetoric adopted by the Russian leadership reflected these circumstances. In general, however, it welcomed the use of the OSCE intermediary. Indeed, the HCNM, Max van der Stoel, played an important role in promoting changes in Estonian residency and citizenship legislation.[49] Further, a local OSCE Mission developed good ties with Russophone organizations in Estonia, and it is notable also that Russia agreed to OSCE monitoring of Skrunda radar station in Latvia in the period before its dismantling. Despite apparently tense relations, therefore, Russian policy in the Baltic states demonstrated an early willingness to draw upon the OSCE as neutral intermediary to mediate issues of soft as well as hard security.

At the wider strategic level, the Russian leadership elaborated ambitious proposals for a reform of the CSCE. The Russian 'Programme to Increase the Efficiency of the CSCE' in September 1994, called for attributing to the CSCE a 'coordinating function' with regard to other security-related organizations, such as the CIS, NATO's North Atlantic Cooperation Council (NACC), NATO itself, and the Western European Union (WEU). As a pan-European body with consensus decision-making and a comprehensive approach to security, Moscow argued that the CSCE was the most appropriate organization to address the new array of 'soft' security threats facing Europe. In particular, the CSCE would become the mandating authority for peacekeeping operations undertaken by regional arrangements such as the CIS and would be placed on a legal-treaty footing in order to enhance compliance with its decisions. Russian proposals, finally, called for the creation of an OSCE Executive Committee to provide streamlined direction to CSCE activities through great power cooperation.[50]

In the run-up to the Budapest summit, the Russian government presented these proposals as an alternative to the prospect of NATO enlargement. Kozyrev, moreover, had earlier called for expanding the role of the NACC as a 'peacekeeping laboratory,' with its own small secretariat.[51] This mechanism would complement a network of overlapping guarantees for ECE by Russia and the West under the aegis of the CSCE. Yet in defining the future role of the CSCE in a collective security system, Moscow left its proposals quite vague, something which allowed for a certain distinction to emerge between the views of the Russian Foreign and Defence Ministries. The former remained equivocal about the nature of institutional coordination.[52] The latter called for the creation of a strictly hierarchical system, with the CSCE as a 'leading' organization in a bloc-free Europe.[53]

Despite the clear elevation of the CSCE in these various proposals, the Russian position, moreover, contained other ambiguities. As evidenced in peacekeeping, the Russian leadership did not seek to provide the CSCE with a 'leading' role in the FSU. Its major thrust was, in fact, to prevent the emergence of NATO as the main axis for European security and thus the marginalizing of Russia as a European power. Yet this itself conflicted, in part, with another strand of Russian policy. The Russian proposal for a CSCE Executive Committee drew upon the model of great power interaction in the UN Security Council (UNSC) in which Russia maintained a veto. The latter was, in fact, more important to Russia because of its wider influence in international affairs. It was not, therefore, to be undermined. For this reason, the Russian delegation to the CSCE rejected a German–Dutch proposal to the Budapest summit for 'CSCE-first response' to security issues in Europe, fearful that it would undercut UNSC responsibility.

Whatever the subtleties of Russian suggestions, they eventually came to little. At the Budapest summit Russian proposals on third-party peacekeeping were rejected by a number of CSCE member states as were Moscow's more ambitious plans for the wholesale reform of the organization. Realizing, in fact, that its plans would be frustrated Russian foreign policy had already started in November 1994 to search for alternative models for Russian involvement in Europe. In Paris on 18 November, Kozyrev stressed the 'historical Russian-French alliance'.[54] In early December, Kozyrev spoke of the WEU in exactly the same terms as he had previously of the NACC.[55] These various proposals were, however, to become over-shadowed by events within Russia for later in December Russian armed forces became engaged in a brutal struggle to suppress Chechen independence.[56]

January 1995–April 1999: security models and peacekeeping cooperation

Following this low point, Russian policy toward the OSCE has become more conciliatory. This shift has laid the basis for a more mutually supportive relationship between Russia and the OSCE, both in the FSU and on issues of wider European security. Three developments have stimulated these changes in Russian policy.

First, Russia's experience of fighting in Chechnya during 1994–96 dramatically highlighted the dangers of the use of force. The lessons learnt from this conflict have reverberated throughout wider Russian peacekeeping policy. Its operations in the FSU have left Russia entangled in a series costly engagements at a time when its armed forces are collapsing and subject to a decreasing resource base. Between 1992 and 1995, the Russian leadership had used peacekeeping as an instrument to advance exclusive Russian interests abroad. Since at least late 1995 it has sought to deinstrumentalize these operations and thus lessen Russia's involvement in what are now seen as intractable internal conflicts.[57] In this new policy framework, Moscow has been increasingly willing to allow for international peacekeeping efforts in order to share the political and material burdens of conflict management.

Secondly, the appointment of Yevgeny Primakov as Foreign Minister in January 1996 altered the balance of power in Russian policy-making. The military High Command, still reeling from the Chechen experience, had been in disarray since the dismissal of Grachev as Defence Minister in mid-1996. This, coupled with the Defence Ministry's new focus on military reform (after a decade of ineffectual discussion), allowed Primakov to restore the balance between political and military tools in Russian policy. The Defence Ministry subsequently took on an increasingly passive role in Russian peacekeeping, taking a strong line only in objecting to further deployments. The appointment of Primakov also produced a shift in policy-making toward the OSCE and other European security organizations. Since 1996, Yeltsin has reinforced the Foreign Ministry's formal position in security decision-making. Notably, in late 1997 Yeltsin decreed the creation of an inter-departmental agency in the government to direct Russian policy toward NATO under the leadership of Primakov.[58] Perhaps more importantly, Primakov moved rapidly in 1996 to prevent the involvement of other departmental actors in Russian policy toward European security organizations. As a result, the Foreign Ministry has played a leading role in policy-making toward the OSCE and NATO since late 1996.[59]

These shifts in policy-making were also accompanied by significant changes in the conceptual basis of Russian foreign policy. The National Security Concept, adopted in December 1997, stressed that the main threats to Russian security arose from within Russia in a wide spectrum of 'domestic, political, economic, social, environmental and information' challenges.[60] The instability in Chechnya and increasing tension in Dagestan have dramatically underlined the nature of these threats. Combined with the pressures of ongoing economic dislocation, the Russian leadership has shifted its foreign policy in order to secure a predictable international environment conducive to Russia's internal revitalization.

A final development that has affected Russian policy toward the OSCE has been the ongoing ascendancy of NATO in European security matters. Particularly after Russia joined PfP in May 1995, Russian analyses of European security structures have stressed the weakness of the OSCE as a framework for ensuring a Russian voice in European security affairs and have underlined the need to form a special partnership with NATO. As Dmitry Trenin stated in 1995 'the OSCE can hardly transform itself into a security alliance or a regional military body within a hierarchical structure [dominated by NATO]'.[61] A dialogue with NATO is thus necessary if Russia is to have any hope of retaining a role in the creation of what Secretary of the Defence Council Yuri Baturin referred to in November 1996 as 'a common European security arena'.[62] In line with this view, Deputy Foreign Minister Nikolai Afanasyevsky stated that the Founding Act between Russian and NATO signified that 'Russia is recognized as an equal pole in world and European politics'.[63]

Despite the formal downgrading of the position of the OSCE in Russian policy, the organization has remained an important pillar in Russian foreign policy. In the FSU, and indeed in Russia itself, Moscow's interactions with the OSCE have changed dramatically, as the Russian leadership has realized the utility of the OSCE in the mediation of intractable conflicts. Most fundamentally, the Russian authorities allowed the deployment of an OSCE Assistance Group in Chechnya in April 1995. The acceptance of an OSCE mission inside Russian frontiers is striking. The Assistance Group has played a limited but important role in mediation in the Chechen conflict. The Personal Representative of the OSCE Chairman-in-Office, Istvan Gyarmati, detailed the difficulties the OSCE faced in 1995 in dealing with the Russian authorities, and the Defence Ministry in particular.[64] Moreover, the Assistance Group suffered at different times very dangerous circumstances on the ground in the conflict zone.[65] However, the Assistance Group helped to oversee negotiations between the parties after the hostage taking crisis in Budyennovsk in June–July 1995, and in the run-up to the Khasavyurt Agreement reached in August 1996. Since then, the OSCE has been deeply involved in monitoring the human rights situation, overseeing the presidential elections in January 1997 and maintaining a forum for dialogue between the parties.

In early 1995, the Russian government had established quite strict conditions for the deployment of the OSCE Group.[66] As Ushakov stated, 'it was not an easy decision'.[67] Yet, it is surprising how rapidly the Russian authorities then took an OSCE presence on Russian territory for granted. The Russian experience in working with the OSCE in conflicts outside Russia was an important reason for this. As part of its campaign to secure OSCE support for Russian peacekeeping, Moscow had developed mechanisms of interaction on the ground with the OSCE in the run-up to the Budapest summit. In March 1994, it agreed to allow the OSCE a much larger role in monitoring developments in and around the conflict zone in South Ossetia (Georgia). It also granted the OSCE the right to participate as an observer in a Joint Control Commission comprised of representatives from the peacekeeping contingents of Russia, Georgia and the Russian republic of North Ossetia. Since then, the OSCE Mission has assumed an important role not only in negotiations between the parties to this conflict, but also on the ground.[68] In a more limited manner, the OSCE Mission to Moldova reached an agreement with Russia and the parties to the conflict on the 'Principles of Cooperation Between the OSCE Mission and the Joint Control Commission in the Security Zone' on 20 July 1994 (updated on 16 January 1996). While not providing for OSCE 'monitoring', these principles have allowed it to patrol the Security Zone and to participate in the Joint Control Commission (made up of Moldovan, Transdniestrian, Russian and Ukrainian representatives).[69]

More generally, the Russian position in conflict mediation has shifted distinctly toward OSCE positions. The war in Chechnya dramatically highlighted the dangers of separatism throughout Russia and the FSU. In line with OSCE proposals, the Russian Foreign Ministry has proposed peace plans in these conflicts, which maintain the territorial integrity of the states concerned. This shift has been most evident in Russian mediation in the Nagorno-Karabakh conflict. At the 1994 Budapest summit, the OSCE named Russia as co-chair of the Minsk Group and called for a 'single coordinated effort' in mediation.[70] Within the Minsk Group framework, western and Russian proposals have agreed on the need to ensure Azeri territorial integrity while providing for extensive autonomy to Nagorno-Karabakh.[71] Vladimir Kazimirov stated that the decision to appoint Russia as co-chair 'allowed the consolidation of the mediating efforts'. In his words, the Minsk Group had become a 'creative laboratory of the peace process and an instrument of collective influence'.[72] These coordinated international efforts had produced significant progress by late 1997. However, prospects for conflict resolution and the deployment of international peacekeeping forces were then put off as a result of the changes in the Armenian leadership in early 1998.[73]

In parallel, the Russian leadership has pursued further cooperation with the OSCE in non-intrusive areas of soft security. OSCE monitoring of elections in Russia are notable examples of Moscow's intent to demonstrate its good will and democratic credentials. On the controversial issues of the Russian minorities in the Baltic states, Moscow has developed a routine reliance on the OSCE as the central intermediary of Russian protest. This has not excluded unilateral Russian measures, nor toned down Russian rhetoric. However, as then Russian Security Council Secretary Ivan Rybkin stated in January 1998, Russia welcomed the positive role of the HCNM in resolving these disputes.[74] It is notable that the Russian Duma appealed first to the OSCE and the HCNM following the small-scale march of neo-Nazis in Riga in March 1998.[75]

As for broader security matters, the 1994 Budapest summit endorsed a Russian proposal to launch a discussion on a 'Common and Comprehensive Security Model for the 21st century' (CCSM). In 1995 this discussion was seen as compensation to Russia for NATO enlargement. The discussion since has been taken very seriously by most OSCE member states. In December 1995, a 'Security Model Committee' was created under the OSCE's Permanent Council, supported by three informal working groups. A series of discussion seminars have been held since 1995 with the active participation of member states and other security-related organizations. At first, Russian proposals for the CCSM remained quite vague, with remnants of its previous ambitious plans. A Russian proposal presented by Kozyrev to a meeting of OSCE Foreign Ministers in December 1995 called for the formulation of a Charter to place the organization on a legal footing, the creation of a European security council and coordinated activities between the OSCE, the CIS and NATO.[76]

Since late 1996, Russian policy has shifted toward more moderate positions although the OSCE still remains potentially very important. The Russian 'Outline of the Charter on European Security' distributed to the OSCE on 17 July 1997 focused on the 'central role of the OSCE in fostering better cooperation between complementary and mutually reinforcing institutions in Europe'.[77] The Outline Charter underlined Russian objectives to create rules of conduct in European security affairs. These principles included provisions to prevent one state from strengthening its security at the expense of another. In this, member states must develop national security policies 'bearing in mind the legitimate security concerns of other participating states'. This document includes a section detailing a 'Platform for Cooperative Security' (originally a UK–EU initiative). This Platform formulated six principles of interaction between security-related organizations, including transparency, information exchanges and function sharing. Importantly, the Platform would ensure the 'consistency of the projects and programmes with the concept of comprehensive and indivisible security [...] in a comprehensive security space where all the participating states will enjoy equal rights and obligations'.[78] By this view, the OSCE would become the main forum for cooperation and coordination among security-related organizations in Europe.

Russia aims via the CCSM to create a 'code of conduct' for the interaction between security-related organizations in Europe under the loose framework of the OSCE.[79] Having established a special mechanism for Russia–NATO relations, the Russian leadership still seeks to ensure that NATO does not become the central axis for European security. The Russian focus is no longer on hierarchy but on equality. In this view, an 'equality' of security-related agencies will accord Russia a special place as a key hub for their coordination. After the OSCE Ministerial Council meeting in Copenhagen in December 1997, at which guidelines on an OSCE 'Document-Charter on European Security' were adopted, Primakov stated 'we were able to lessen the possibility that European security will be established on the basis of NATO-centrism'.[80] Igor Ivanov, Primakov's successor as Foreign Minister, was to subsequently argue in early 1999 that the Charter could be the 'linchpin' of a 'new, stable and balanced structure of European security' that stands in juxtaposition to a model based on NATO.[81]

In the Russian view, the formulation of 'modalities of interaction' between security-related organizations would create a normative framework preventing any further waves of NATO enlargement, and enshrining the role of the OSCE as a non-hierarchical coordinator in European security. These proposals reflected what Russia regarded as a model of interaction between various organizations in the peacekeeping and peacebuilding missions in Bosnia. Hence, Extraordinary Ambassador Vladimir Shustov called for the CCSM to build upon the Bosnian 'model' with the OSCE as a 'roof' coordinating other organizations.[82] Ivanov, meanwhile, has called upon the new Euro-Atlantic Partnership Council created at the NATO Madrid summit in July 1997 to coordinate future peacekeeping activities undertaken by the OSCE. In this respect, it is notable that the Russian Charter proposal called for the creation of reserve peacekeeping forces under the OSCE, as well as the formation of a staff structure under the OSCE's Permanent Council. Such forces would increase the role of the OSCE beyond 'soft' security activities.

The Russian objective has been to prevent firm divisions of labour between 'hard' and 'soft' security tasks among security organizations, which might allow a NATO monopoly on the use of force.

Conclusions

Russian policy toward the OSCE has shifted from the exclusive pursuit of maximalist aims towards the search for more moderate objectives. In this shift, Russian–OSCE relations have become more harmonious. Interestingly, the significance of the organization for Moscow has not diminished even though Russian objectives regarding the OSCE have shifted. The OSCE has always been important for Soviet and Russian policy in relation to wider developments in Europe. After 1994–96, Russian ambitions regarding the OSCE were directly linked to the issue of NATO enlargement. However, the Russian authorities have also increasingly perceived the importance of the organization in its own right as a means to institutionalize Russian involvement in wider European security discussions, and, perhaps more fundamentally, as a mechanism to address some of the security predicaments faced by Russia in Europe and the FSU.

This position has been clearly apparent in relation to discussions on the guidelines on a 'Document-Charter on European Security' issued in December 1997. Although the Document fell far short of some of the more ambitious clauses in the Russian Charter proposal, it did stress the need to 'strengthen non-hierarchical cooperation' and to 'devise optimal cooperative solutions to specific problems' on the basis of 'common, comprehensive and indivisible security'.[83] The Ministerial Council meeting in Oslo in December 1998 affirmed these provisions and agreed that work on a final document would be completed in time for the OSCE's Istanbul summit in November 1999. The Russian leadership has, therefore, successfully placed on the agenda the need to devise 'rules of the game' for the interaction of states and security organizations which would prevent a NATO monopoly on 'hard' security decision-making and hopefully ensure a Russian voice at the heart of these interactions. The Russian objective has not simply been to prevent any further geographical divisions in Europe. Moscow is also intent on avoiding any division of labour in Europe between 'hard' and 'soft' security activities. In Russian policy, 'indivisible security' must reside at both of these levels.

Russia's interaction with the OSCE has been a learning process since 1992. Clearly, Moscow has come to consider the OSCE as an important mechanism for embedding Russia into a multilateral framework for the resolution of European security issues and the pursuit of Russian security aims. Furthermore, Russia's relatively more positive and routinized experience with the OSCE on the ground in Chechnya and other post-Soviet conflicts has had some wider effects on Russian policy toward the role of the OSCE in European security as well as toward international organizations in general. The routinization of Russian–OSCE interaction has been reinforced by shifts in the Russian decision-making process which have seen a movement of influence away from the Ministry of Defence toward the Foreign Ministry. These developments reflect the fact that at a time of pressing internal problems, Russia has shifted from a policy of 'stand-off' in Europe to one of 'neutralization' of negative developments. In a manner reminiscent of Gorbachev, the Russian government seeks to create a favourable 'breathing space' for domestic reform.[84]

These developments, however, should not obscure the ongoing process of evolution in Russian policy. The relative importance that Russia attaches to the OSCE as an instrument to reflect Russia's great power status in Europe and as an inherently valuable organization in itself, remains subject to the unfolding of events in Europe. The pragmatic adjustment of policy toward the OSCE after 1994 may well have reached its limits with the 1998–99 Kosovo crisis. The sidelining of the OSCE (as well as the UN) by NATO gave the lie to the notion that the predominance of the Alliance in European security affairs does not rule out a role for other international organizations (and thus, by extension, Moscow). All the rhetoric over establishing 'modalities of interaction' between security organizations in response to such crises was shown to be ineffective, as the Russian President accused NATO of failing to consult with Russia and of monopolizing the use of force.[85] In the Russian view, NATO actions had contravened the OSCE Document-Charter's principle of indivisible security, in which 'optimal' (that is inclusive) solutions are devised for specific crises. The normalization of Russian–European relations thus remains a process rather than a state of affairs. This process will remain vulnerable to regional crises, reflecting the friction involved in Russia's search for the establishment of a new European security order – one in which Russia insists on an equal voice in all organizations and regarding all security issues.

Notes

1. *Russia and the Maintenance of International Stability* (Moscow: IMEMO, 1995), p. 57.
2. R. W. Clawson, 'Changes in Soviet National Security Policy towards Europe under Gorbachev', in G. E. Hudson (ed.), *Soviet National Security Policy under Gorbachev* (Boston: Unwin Hyman, 1989), pp. 197–220.

3. S. Karaganov, 'The Soviet Union and the New European Architecture', in A. Cleese and L. Ruhl (eds.), *Beyond East–West Confrontation. Searching for a New Security Structure in Europe* (Baden Baden: Nomos Verlagsgesellschaft, 1990), pp. 429–35.

4. See N. Malcolm, 'The Soviet Concept of a Common European Home', in J. Livonen (ed.), *The Changing Soviet Union in the New Europe* (Hants: Edward Elgar, 1991), pp. 45–82. Brezhnev had first used the concept in a visit to Bonn in 1981. It had been taken up by Soviet Foreign Minister Andrei Gromyko in another visit to Bonn in 1983. Gorbachev himself placed his first use of the concept to his speech before the British House of Commons in December 1994; see M. S. Gorbachev, 'Plaidoyer Une Maison Commune', *Politique Internationale*, No. 68, 1985, pp. 105–12.

5. H. Adomeit, 'The Impact of Perestroika on Soviet European Policy', in T. Hasegawa and A. Pravda (eds.), *Perestroika: Soviet Domestic and Foreign Policies* (London: Royal Institute of International Affairs and Sage Publications, 1990), pp. 242–66.

6. See 'M. S. Gorbachev Address to the Council of Europe', 6 July 1989, reproduced in *Soviet News*, 12 July 1989.

7. See interview with Gorbachev in *Pravda*, 21 February 1990, reproduced in *Soviet News*, 28 February 1990.

8. See the detailed proposal of Vladimir Shustov, Deputy Head of the Soviet Mission to the United Nations, 'From Interbloc Confrontation towards a New Peaceful Order in Europe', in Cleese and Ruhl, *op. cit.*, pp. 436–45.

9. See Eduard Shevardnadze, *Izvestiya*, 30 May 1990, cited in A. D. Rotfeld, 'New Security Structures in Europe: Concepts, Proposals and Decisions', in *SIPRI Yearbook, 1991: World Armaments and Disarmament* (Stockholm: SIPRI, 1991), p. 595. These proposals were raised again by Shevardnadze at the Conference on the Human Dimension of the CSCE in Copenhagen in early June.

10. See the proposal of M. V. Shikolov, Soviet delegate to the CSCE, 'Soviet Perspectives on the Future Role of the OSCE', in K. Holder, R. E. Hunter and P. Lipponen (eds.), *CSCE: the Next Phase* (Washington D.C.: CSIS Significant Issues Series, No. 7, Vol. 13, 1991), pp. 44–9.

11. An important reason for this Soviet acceptance may have resided in the Soviet leadership's realization that maintaining Germany within NATO would, in fact, be a stabilizing factor in the turbulent transition that Europe was then undergoing.

12. See, for example, the comparison drawn by Rotfeld, *op. cit.*, p. 595. The Paris Charter endorsed the creation of a Council of Foreign Ministers, a Committee of Senior Officials, a permanent Secretariat, a Centre for the Prevention of Conflict based in Vienna as well as an Office of Free Elections.

13. Heather Hurlburt has advanced the view that the predominance of arms control experts in the Soviet delegation to the preparatory talks and the summit itself goes far in explaining this position. See her 'Russia, the OSCE and the European Security Architecture', *Helsinki Monitor*, Vol. 6, No. 2, 1995, p. 7.

14. Shustov, *op. cit.*, pp. 444–5.

15. A. Kokoshin, 'The Security Interests of the USSR and the New European Structures', in Cleese and Ruhl, *op. cit.*, pp. 424–8.

16. For a detailed examination of Russian peacekeeping policy, see D. Lynch, *Russian Peacekeeping Strategies towards the CIS, 1992–1997* (London: Royal Institute of International Affairs/Houndmills: Macmillan Press, 1998).
17. 'Programme to Increase the Effectiveness of the CSCE', distributed to CSCE member states in preparation for the Budapest summit, *Diplomaticheskii vestnik*, Nos. 17–18, 1994, pp. 13–16.
18. 'Speech by Y. M. Primakov to Meeting of Council of Ministers in Copenhagen, 18 December, 1997', *Diplomaticheskii vestnik*, No. 1, 1998, p. 25.
19. Deputy Foreign Minister Nikolai Afanasyevsky, 'The Founding Act Between Russia and NATO', *Mezhdunarodnaya zhizn'*, No. 6, 1997, pp. 8–12.
20. A. Kozyrev, 'For a New Model of Security', *Moscow News*, 30 June–6 July 1995, p. 5. This question had been raised earlier by Yevgenny Primakov, *Izvestiya*, 26 November 1993.
21. Preamble to 'An Outline of the Charter on European Security', Russian proposal to the Security Model Committee under the Permanent Council, 17 July 1997 reproduced in B. George (rapportuer), 'Complementary Pillars of European Security: the OSCE Security Model and the Euro-Atlantic Partnership Council' (Draft Interim Report, North Atlantic Assembly, International Secretariat sub-Committee on Transatlantic and European Relations, 26 August 1997), p. 15.
22. Y. Primakov, 'The World on the Eve of the 21st Century', *International Affairs* (Moscow), Vol. 42, Nos. 5–6, 1996, pp. 2–14.
23. A. Kokoshin, *The New Russia: Inheritance and Perspectives* (Frankfurt: PRIF Reports, No. 43, August 1996), p. 38.
24. A. Kozyrev, *Izvestiya*, 2 January 1992.
25. O. Bykov, 'The Role of the CIS in the New European Security System', in I. M. Cuthbertson (ed.), *Redefining the CSCE, Challenges and Opportunities in the New Europe* (Helsinki: Institute of East–West Studies and the Finnish Institute of International Affairs: 1992), pp. 147–8.
26. *Komsomolskaya pravda*, 5 September 1991, cited A. Rotfeld, 'European Security Structures in Transition', *SIPRI Yearbook, 1992: Armaments, Disarmament and International Security* (Oxford: Oxford University Press/Frösunda, Sweden: Stockholm International Peace Research Institute, 1992), p. 572.
27. Interview in *Izvestiya*, 26 June 1992. See also the Foreign Ministry statement that Russia 'reserves the right to use appropriate international mechanisms to draw the attention of the world community to the human rights situation in the Estonian Republic', cited in *Izvestiya*, 2 July 1992.
28. Cited in *Izvestiya*, 10 July 1992.
29. This mechanism included the Foreign Ministers of Moldova, Russia, Ukraine and Romania.
30. The Minsk Group then contained representatives from Armenia, Nagorno-Karabakh, Azerbaijan, Belgium, the Czech and Slovak Republics, France, Germany, Italy, Sweden, Russia, Turkey and the US. See the discussion in O. Paye and E. Remacle, 'UN and CSCE Policies in Transcaucasia', in B. Coppeters (ed.), *Contested Borders in the Caucasus* (Brussels: Vubpress, 1996), pp. 103–36.
31. *Izvestiya*, 10 July 1992.
32. 'Helsinki Summit Declaration on the Promises and Problems of Change', 10 July 1992, paragraphs 10 and 22, <http://www.osce.org/indexe-da.htm>.
33. *Nezavisimaya gazeta*, 28 March 1992.

34. *Izvestiya*, 7 July 1992.
35. See Member of Presidential Council, A. Migranyan, *Rossiskaya gazeta*, 4 August 1992; and K. Eggert, *Izvestiya*, 7 August 1992.
36. Itar-Tass, Moscow, 1 July 1992, BBC, Summary of World Broadcasts (henceforth *SWB*) SU/1421, i.
37. See the Foreign Policy Concept, summarized by Vladimir Chernov, Deputy Secretary of the Security Council, *Nezavisimaya gazeta*, 29 April 1993.
38. Colonel C. Pechorov, *Krasnaya zvezda*, 20 March 1992.
39. *Pravda*, 26 May 1992; *Izvestiya*, 5 June 1992.
40. Yeltsin's speech to the Civic Union, 28 February 1993, cited in SWB, SU/1626, B/1–3.
41. *Nezavisimaya gazeta*, 22 September 1993.
42. *Nezavisimaya gazeta*, 24 November 1993.
43. *CSCE and the New Europe, Our Security is Indivisible* (Decision of the Rome Council Meeting, December 1993), <http://www.osce.org/indexe-da.htm>.
44. S. Crow, 'Russia Promotes the CIS as an International Organization', *Radio Free Europe/Radio Liberty Research Report*, Vol. 3, No. 11, 1994, pp. 133–8.
45. 'Programme to Increase the Effectiveness . . .', *Diplomaticheskii vestnik*, Nos. 17–18, September 1994, pp. 13–16.
46. Yu. Ushakov, cited in M. Mikhalka, 'Restructuring European Security', *Transition*, Vol. 1, No. 11, 1995, p. 6.
47. At most, the Russian government was willing to accept CSCE observers; see interview with Kozyrev, *Nezavisimaya gazeta*, 24 November 1994.
48. Cited in *Segodnya*, 18 November 1994.
49. See Ambassador Klaus Tornudd, 'The Role of the CSCE Mission in Preventive Diplomacy: the Case of Estonia', in *The Challenge of Preventive Diplomacy* (Stockolm: Swedish Ministry of Foreign Affairs, 1994), pp. 73–86.
50. *Diplomaticheskii vestnik*, Nos. 17–18, 1994, pp. 13–16.
51. *Nezavisimaya gazeta*, 3 March 1994.
52. Kozyrev in *Segodnya*, 25 February 1994.
53. Grachev in *Segodnya*, 27 May 1994.
54. *Segodnya*, 18 November 1994.
55. *Segodnya*, 2 December 1994.
56. The Russian offensive in Chechnya in late December 1994 violated a number of international agreements on the use of force and military transparency, most notably the OSCE Code of Conduct which Russia had signed two weeks earlier at the OSCE's Budapest summit. See M. Lucas, 'The War in Chechnya and the OSCE Code of Conduct', *Helsinki Monitor*, Vol. 6, No. 2, 1995, pp. 32–42.
57. On these shifts in Russian peacekeeping policy, see Lynch, *op. cit.*, passim, and D. Lynch, *The Conflict in Abkhazia* (London: Royal Institute of International Affairs (Chatham House Discussion Paper)), February 1998.
58. Itar-Tass, Moscow, 17 December 1997, *SWB*, SU/3106, B/10.
59. Although the development of military-to-military ties between Russia and NATO in 1997–98 did increase the role of the Ministry of Defence, sometimes to the frustration of the Foreign Ministry.
60. *Diplomaticheskii vestnik*, No. 2, 1998, pp. 7–9.
61. D. Trenin, 'How to Avoid Confrontation: NATO', *International Affairs* (Moscow), Vol. 41, No. 7, 1995, pp. 20–6.

62. Cited in A. D. Rotfeld, 'Europe: In Search of Cooperative Security', *SIPRI Yearbook, 1997: Armaments, Disarmament and International Security* (Oxford: Oxford University Press/Frösunda, Sweden: SIPRI, 1997), p. 138.
63. Afanasyevsky, *op. cit.*, pp. 8–12.
64. C. Pursianen, 'The Impact of International Institutions on Russia's Behaviour: the Case of the OSCE and Chechnya' (unpublished paper, spring 1997).
65. The mission was surrounded in Grozny in late September 1995 by armed local forces and the Head of the Group, Tim Guldiman, had to leave the region on several occasions because of threats. Relations between the OSCE and the Chechen authorities have remained tense because of the OSCE's bias toward the principle of Russian territorial integrity.
66. In early 1995, the government insisted on the recognition of Russian territorial integrity, placed limits on the territorial scope of any mission, and rejected the right of the OSCE to investigate the human rights situation.
67. *Segodnya*, 21 April 1995.
68. This point was stressed in interviews with members of the Mission by the author in June 1997. The Mission played an important role in securing a Memorandum of Understanding signed in May 1996 by the Georgian government and South Ossetian representatives.
69. The OSCE has been limited in these activities by the Transdniestrian authorities not necessarily by the Russian Foreign Ministry; interviews conducted by the author with military members of the Mission to Moldova, May 1998.
70. *Budapest Decisions* (Section II, 'Regional Issues', para. 1), <http://www.oscep-rag.cz/indexe-da.htm>.
71. M. Mikhalka, 'A Marriage of Convenience: the OSCE and Russia in Nagorno-Karabakh and Chechnya', *Helsinki Monitor*, Vol. 7, No. 2, 1996. These conditions were reaffirmed in the 1996 OSCE Lisbon summit statement despite Armenia's objection. See *Lisbon Document* (Annex I), <http://www.oscep-rag.cz/indexe-da.htm>.
72. V. Kazimirov, 'The OSCE and Nagorno-Karabakh', *European Review* (Special Issue), Vol. 8, 1995, pp. 81–7.
73. The nature of a possible operation is outlined in an unpublished paper by H. Vilen, M. Karie and R. Biesel, 'Preparations for a Peacekeeping Mission for the Nagorno-Karabakh Conflict by the OSCE High Level Planning Group' (May 1996).
74. Interfax, 26 January 1998, *SWB*, SU/337, B/11.
75. Interfax, 20 March 1998, *SWB*, SU/3181, B/7.
76. *Diplomaticheskii vestnik*, No. 1, 1996, pp. 11–13.
77. 'An Outline of the Charter on European Security', in George, *op. cit*, p. 15.
78. *Ibid.*, pp. 16–17.
79. Primakov, 'The World on the Eve of the 21st Century', *op. cit.*, pp. 2–14.
80. *Nezavisimaya gazeta*, 24 December 1997.
81. I. Ivanov, 'Europe on the Threshold of the 21st Century', *International Affairs* (Moscow), Vol. 45, No. 1, 1999, electronic edition <http://home.mosinfo.ru/news/int-aff/1999/data/01990In.htm>.
82. V. Shustov, 'The European Security Charter', *International Affairs* (Moscow), No. 9, 1997, pp. 7–13.
83. OSCE Ministerial Council, 19 December 1997 (OSCE document MC(6).DEC/5).

84. V. N. Tsygichko, 'Geostrategic Aspects of Russia's National Security Policy', *Voennaya mysl'*, Nos. 5–6, 1996, pp. 39–45.

85. *Russia Today*, 25 March 1999, <http://www.russiatoday.com/rtoday/special/yeltsnato.html>.

6
Russia and the Council of Europe
Mark Webber

Introduction

If we are to believe the 'democratic peace' hypothesis, stability in Europe relies, in large part, on the extension of democratic, pluralistic political systems to the east of the continent, Russia included. The spread of democratic institutions, it is argued, provides domestic obstacles to belligerent acts by governments, while the diffusion of democratic norms promotes compromise and cooperative practices among states. The process of democratic transition, however, is far from trouble free. As noted in Chapter 1, the interactions of consolidated democracies may be peaceful, but the foreign policies of those in the early stages of demo-cratization are more likely to be unpredictable and bellicose. Thus, stability relies not just on democratic development, but on the parallel assimilation of democratizing states into international institutions that may act to blunt the external consequences of domestic political trans-formations.

In this regard, the Council of Europe (COE) is particularly important. Unlike say the North Atlantic Treaty Organization (NATO) and the European Union (EU), the organization has expanded at a rapid rate. Its core rationale has also essentially remained unaltered: the promotion of cooperation among the states of Europe based on a shared adherence to human rights standards, democratic norms and the rule of law. What has changed, however, is the scope of this mission. In the 40 years fol-lowing its formation in 1949, the work of the COE had been under-taken almost solely among established democracies, and even though the roots of democracy were fragile in some cases (as in Spain, Greece, Portugal and Turkey), the coherence and solidity of the organization as a whole was facilitated by its location firmly on one side of the Cold

War divide. During this period its only dealings with the communist states to the east was to condemn their authoritarian forms of rule and to assert in the process the moral supremacy of Western forms of political life.[1] All of this changed in 1989, when the COE was faced with the prospect of establishing relations with, and ultimately extending its membership to, states which were both large in number and wanting in their democratic credentials.

Given this context, the COE is of significance for Russia on at least three grounds. First, because political cooperation is the principal purpose of the organization;[2] the COE is, therefore, a potential prop for Russia along the trouble-strewn route toward democratic consolidation. Second, because this form of cooperation among states is generally recognized to be the most problematic; if success can be registered here it bodes well for cooperative efforts more generally. Third, and related, because it involves a supranational element in the form of the judgements of the European Court of Human Rights; Russian involvement within the COE, therefore, amounts to a potential crossing of the Rubicon toward acceptance of external interference in its internal affairs.

This chapter, then, describes and evaluates Russia's relations with the COE. It examines the manner of Russia's accession to the organization, and highlights how this process of admission was well-served by bargaining and compromise; Russia entered the COE with a less than sound record on human rights and democracy but was only permitted to do so on the basis of implementing an exhaustive set of political commitments. The character of relations after this point is also detailed, focusing on Russia's fulfilment of COE obligations, programmes of assistance involving Russia, and member-state disputes involving Russia. In conclusion, the chapter will consider the impact of COE membership upon Russia's domestic political development and its relationship with Europe.

Russia – the road to membership

The debate within the Council of Europe

Russia's relationship with the COE has its roots in the late Soviet period. In recognition of the democratic transformation in the former Communist bloc, the Parliamentary Assembly of the COE (PACE) introduced in 1989 a pre-membership 'special guest status' for delegations from national parliaments willing to adhere to human rights provisions laid down in agreements and conventions of the United Nations and the then Conference on Security and Cooperation in Europe (CSCE) (including the 1975 Helsinki Final Act).[3] Such status was extended to the Soviet

Congress of People's Deputies in June 1989 and, perhaps fittingly, one month later, Mikhail Gorbachev chose a session of the PACE at Strasbourg to outline his vision of a 'common European home'.[4] At a special meeting in March of the following year, the COE's Committee of Ministers welcomed the 'important reforms' underway in the Soviet Union and decided to initiate closer contacts with the country.[5] In keeping with these approaches, the Soviet Union acceded to a total of seven COE conventions (mainly in the cultural sphere) and began to participate in a small number of COE expert committees. Unlike former communist countries in east-central Europe (ECE), however, the Soviet Union was not a prominent recipient of COE cooperation and assistance programmes[6] – a state of affairs that reflected a caution in the COE at the Soviet Union's uncertain democratic credentials and, on Gorbachev's part, a lingering belief in the autonomous nature of his political reforms.

With the dissolution of the Soviet Union in 1991, special guest status was extended to the Russian Parliament and the Russian government submitted a formal application for full state membership in May 1992. Admission was, however, delayed until February 1996 following an arduous and at times controversial accession process. In examining this, an important distinction needs to be made between the inter-governmental element of the COE located in the Committee of Ministers and the PACE. The former is representative of official opinion among member states, while the latter is composed of individual parliamentary delegations. Although the Committee is responsible for inviting new members, it does so, decisively, only after a recommendation from the PACE. During the debates on Russian membership the Committee of Ministers, reflecting the opinion of home governments (and particularly the caucus of EU states), was generally sympathetic to Moscow;[7] opinion in the PACE, meanwhile, although eventually in favour, struck an at times ambiguous and even hostile posture.

Russian admission also needs to be placed in the context of the rapid enlargement of membership that the COE has experienced since 1989 (involving an increase in the number of member states from 23 to 40 as of 1999), something that distinguishes the organization from the far more limited processes of enlargement begun within NATO and the EU. In explaining this difference attention should be drawn to the perceived role of the organization in post-Cold War Europe. From its rather exclusivist function as the guardian of western democratic norms among the established European democracies, the organization has moved to take on the related, but nonetheless innovative role of champion of these principles in the uncertain environment of post-communism. By definition, this is a mission the COE cannot undertake unless it is prepared to embrace formerly excluded states.

This view of the COE as an inclusive organization has been most obviously apparent among some of its permanent officials.[8] Speaking in 1990, COE General Secretary Catherine Lalumière suggested that the COE was 'the organization around which [. . . a] future European confederation [. . . could] be constructed'.[9] While this level of euphoria did not last long after 1989, Lalumière nonetheless continued to argue that the COE had a valuable role to play, particularly in ECE. By promoting its core concerns – pluralistic democracy, human rights and the rule of law – and by encouraging tolerance among different ethnic and religious groups, the COE could make a unique contribution to stability in the region, engineering a 'democratic security' that would complement the potential military and economic benefits of partnership with other international organizations.[10] Lalumière's successor, Daniel Tarschys, has argued in a similar vein. Writing in 1995, he contended that 'democracy and democratic security must be extended eastwards'. While this should not entail any lowering of the COE's ambitions 'for the defence of democracy and human rights', Taraschys suggested that it was right to accept new members on the basis of their *commitment* to meeting COE standards. A less than perfect record was to be expected in fledgling post-communist democracies, and once an 'acceptable level of democratic development' had been attained, membership should follow, for '[i]nclusion [. . . was] far preferable to exclusion' if democratic construction was to be encouraged.[11]

In practice, the requirements of accession have been rather exacting for the post-communist states.[12] Yet this should not detract attention from an obvious predisposition in favour of enlargement within the COE. And this is a position that has been held not just by its Secretaries-General. The 'Vienna Declaration' issued by the first ever summit meeting of COE heads of state and government in October 1993 referred, in glowing terms, to the Council as 'the pre-eminent European political organization capable of welcoming [. . .] the democracies of Europe freed from communist oppression'. Accession of these countries was consequently viewed as 'a central factor in the process of European construction'.[13] The COE's second summit in October 1997 voiced a similar sentiment, the summit document on this occasion referring to the COE's role in preparing countries in transition for 'their full integration into the wider European family'.[14]

Such statements may well mask somewhat instrumental calculations on the part of the COE's more established members. A preference for extending membership represented, in part, a need to offer a sop to those states blocked from the concrete benefits of EU and/or NATO membership. Yet whatever the reasons for the COE's enlargement, that it occurred in such an expansive manner in the first half of the 1990s is important. It meant that Russia's continued exclusion appeared incongruous and, from the perspective of Moscow, increasingly unacceptable.

In light of these preliminary considerations, how then did Russia obtain entry into the COE? Following Russia's initial application, the Committee of Ministers, meeting in June 1992, agreed unanimously that membership was desirable once Moscow had demonstrated sufficient progress in the fields of pluralist democracy, human rights and the rule of law. On the basis of an exchange of views with Russian Foreign Minister Andrei Kozyrev the previous month, moreover, the Committee accepted the Russian position that the scale of post-communist transformation required 'time [in order] to translate theoretical freedoms into actual practice' and that this, in turn, necessitated an intensification of cooperation and assistance. Even so, the Committee looked forward to Russian membership 'as soon as possible'.[15]

These auspicious moves were, however, subsequently interrupted by domestic developments within Russia. In view of the COE's strong parliamentary dimension, the deterioration of relations between the executive and legislative branches of Russian government during 1993 led to a waning of interest in the COE on the part of the Russian leadership. Indeed, the Russian Foreign Ministry, then responsible for dialogue with the COE, was even charged by Ivan Rybkin (the coordinator of the Communists of Russia parliamentary faction) of deliberately conspiring to hamper Russian admission as a means of undermining parliamentary influence.[16] These events were not, however, sufficient to dispel the basic goodwill shown toward Russia. The violent *dénouement* of the crisis between Boris Yeltsin and the parliamentary opposition was, for instance, met with some indulgence on the part of the COE's member states. The Vienna summit in October 1993 issued a 'Declaration on Russia' which placed the blame for events in the country firmly upon the shoulders of the 'opponents of reform' and which made clear its 'solidarity' with Yeltsin's democratic leadership.[17] Events in Chechnya, similarly had little impact at the governmental level. The Committee of Ministers meeting in January 1995 (one month after the launch of the Russian military campaign) issued a communiqué which not only made no mention of these events, but which congratulated Russia on 'the progress achieved in building a democratic society' and welcomed its admission into the COE 'at the earliest possible date'.[18]

Somewhat less amenable, however, was opinion within the PACE. A 'Report on the Conformity of the Legal Order of the Russian Federation with Council of Europe Standards' written under the aegis of the PACE concluded in September 1994 that, despite some notable achievements in the post-Soviet period (for instance, the adoption of the 1993 constitution and the parliamentary elections of the same year), the political and legal order in Russia still failed to meet COE standards as enshrined in its Statute and the European Convention on Human Rights (ECHR).[19] Seemingly confirming some of the doubts levelled against Russia, the launch of the offensive in Chechnya provided cause for a suspension of consideration of Russia's membership application. Russia's actions were considered to be in violation of COE and other international humanitarian standards to which Russia was party.[20] In February 1995, the PACE decided by a large majority (just one abstention and one vote against) to defer consideration of Russia's application citing the indiscriminate use of force in Chechnya and the imbalance of political power in Russia in favour of the executive.[21]

Despite its deep reservations, examination of Russia's application was resumed by the PACE in September. The decision to do so was ostensibly taken on the back of what was seen as a renewed Russian willingness to find a political solution to the Chechen imbroglio. Yet as the relevant PACE resolution made clear, longer-term considerations were also important. Russia had by this point displayed a clear wish for integration in European structures (evident from its acceptance of mediation by the Organization for Security and Cooperation in Europe (OSCE) in Chechnya and the signing of an interim trade agreement with the EU). In this light, exclusion from the COE was anomalous. Furthermore, Chechnya notwithstanding, the transition toward democracy was seen as ongoing, even if its conclusion required decades to complete. While this was not evidence sufficient to approve Russian membership, it was enough to reactivate the accession process.[22]

The subsequent six months witnessed a charged debate on Russian entry. Indicative of the controversies thrown up by the issue, the PACE, in January 1996, published two authoritative reports which reached differing views on the merits of the Russian case. The first, a report of the PACE Political Affairs Committee (the formal body charged with issuing a recommendation to the Assembly on new applications) came out in favour of extending an invitation to Russia, not so much on the grounds of Russia's conformity with COE standards in the spheres of democracy, the rule of law and human rights, but rather on the basis of assurances given by the Russian leadership that the limited progress in these regards would continue via legislative initiative and other reforms. Furthermore, conceding the peculiar difficulties of the Russian transition (specifically, the absence of a prior democratic tradition), the report suggested that inclusion rather than exclusion from the COE was a better means of promoting favourable change.[23] Somewhat more conditional was a report issued by the PACE Committee on Legal Affairs and Human Rights. This concluded that 'for the time being, considerable deficits remain in the application of laws and regulations and the observance of human rights'. Russia, consequently, could not be regarded as a state based on the rule of law and thus its membership of the COE ought to be ruled inadmissible. The report did suggest, however, that if a pragmatic political judgement was to be made, this opinion be revised; that is, entry would be permitted as a means of encouraging the development of the rule of law through Russia's accession to the mandatory judgements of the COE's European Court of Human Rights.[24]

These two reports formed the basis of a debate within the PACE that same month. The minority view, held most strongly by delegations from the Baltic states, argued against Russian entry. Amidst an escalation of the Chechen war, the Chair of the Latvian delegation argued that admission was tantamount to condoning Russian aggression and casting a veil over continuing human rights abuses in the conflict zone. Moreover, to allow Russia into the organization would grant it the right to judge – from a somewhat corrupted position – the democratic credentials and human rights practices of other candidates for membership.[25] By contrast, the majority opinion, voiced loudly by parliamentary delegations from the EU states[26] and certain ECE states (Bulgaria, Romania, Poland and Ukraine) was in favour of Russian admission on several counts; these reflected a largely pragmatic set of calculations, rather than an exacting application of COE standards. It was recognized, for instance, that Russia had introduced legal and political reforms since 1992 in a deliberate effort to meet COE principles.[27] Russia had also made certain strides toward democracy (specifically two sets of parliamentary elections), and, as one delegate pointedly suggested, was closer to COE standards than some existing member states.[28] The positive signal sent by membership, it was argued, would help counteract undemocratic forces inside the country and avail Russia more extensively of COE assistance. As for the COE, it would be able to apply even more intrusive monitoring procedures.[29] More symbolically, acceptance of Russia's application would pre-empt any division of Europe while simultaneously confirming Russia's European (as opposed to its Asian) orientation. This, ultimately, would staunch isolationist and anti-western currents in the country.[30]

The majority view was to win out. In opinion 193 adopted on 25 January 1996 the PACE recommended that the Committee of Ministers formally invite Russia to join the COE.[31] This invitation was extended the following month, and on 28 February Yevgenni Primakov in his then capacity as Foreign Minister travelled to Strasbourg for the formal ceremony of admission.

Russian views of the Council of Europe

While the COE has not figured large in official Russian opinion of European institutions, neither has it been overlooked. Membership of the organization has held a certain attraction for Moscow, based in part on principle and in part on more instrumental concerns.

During the first year of Russian statehood – a year characterized by a near unabashed courting of the West in foreign policy and a domestic programme committed at least rhetorically to democratic consolidation and economic liberalization – statements on the COE emanating from the Yeltsin leadership tended to view membership as part and parcel of Russia's desire, in Kozyrev's words, to embrace universal democratic values and thereby to 're-join the mainstream of Western civilization'.[32] Speaking in Strasbourg in May 1992, the Foreign Minister, while admitting that Russia was far from a mature democracy, committed his government to the development of pluralistic democracy, something that would embed the country in 'the (COE's) standards and rules of conduct'. Although a sensitivity to Russia's purported great power status led Kozyrev to argue that membership would enable it to join Europe as an equal of its western partners, there was at least an implicit note of deference in the Russian application. '[Y]oung Russian democracy' he suggested 'will not be able to flourish without Europe with its huge democratic experience'.[33] Yeltsin's message to the COE's Vienna summit the following year made a similar case. Russia's participation would, he suggested, help the country's democratic consolidation, would confirm its position as 'an inalienable part of European civilization' and would see it welcomed as a member of 'the family of law-governed [*pravovykh*], democratic states'.[34]

Such idealism was stressed less often after 1993. This did not mean that Russian attitudes toward the COE became entirely negative, but simply that Moscow came to view the organization in a more utilitarian light. This, in turn, reflected the general stiffening of attitudes in foreign policy as a whole during 1993–94 (see Chapter 2) and the related assumption that Russian interests ought be pursued more emphatically in international fora (a position not unique to Russia and certainly not absent from the positions of the COE's longer-standing member states). It is also worth remembering the changing context of Russia's relations with Europe after 1993. The mooted enlargements of the EU and NATO to the exclusion of Russia increased the relevance to Moscow of more obviously pan-European bodies in which it could play a part. In this connection the OSCE stood out more so than the COE, given the fact that Russia was already a member and because that organization had begun to instrumentalize a variety of non-traditional security functions. Yet the COE too had its attractions; in general terms, because it would allow Moscow an entrée into continental affairs and, more specifically, because it would provide a platform for the projection of Russian concerns (the plight of Russian minorities in the Baltic states, the defence of the principle of territorial integrity etc.).[35]

The lengthy process of admission, however, rendered these calculations moot – something which in its own right became an object of concern to Moscow. As was noted above, one of the main reasons for the delay was the use of force in Chechnya. This was an important test case for Russia's relations with the COE, not only because the military operation violated COE standards, but also because breaches of human rights in the conflict were precisely the sort of situation the organization would want to monitor and, if possible, correct upon Russian accession. In this sense, statements from the Russian Foreign Ministry that the conduct of the campaign was a purely internal matter[36] were contrary to the *modus operandi* of the COE's human rights' regime. Moreover, in making a case for exclusive domestic jurisdiction, Russia was in contradiction of international texts to which it had already acceded and which shared the spirit of key COE conventions.[37] Eventually, Moscow was to concede that human rights within the conflict zone were a matter of international concern, and accordingly, along with missions from the OSCE and the UN Commissioner for Human Rights, the Russian authorities facilitated entry of a PACE delegation to Chechnya in 1995.[38]

While these concessions suggested a movement toward international opinion, Russia was far less forthcoming in accepting the Chechen conflict as a pretext for deferring consideration of its application. The suspension was criticized as counter-productive to the COE's mission of strengthening the rule of law and human rights and as freezing its 'transformation into an organization for all Europe'.[39]

What made the suspension even more irksome for Russia was the seeming readiness of the COE to accept into its number post-communist states with what Moscow regarded as dubious human rights practices.

As early as 1993, Foreign Ministry officials had bemoaned the delay over Russian accession and contrasted this with the goodwill shown toward Romania and Estonia, both of whom had entered the organization with little controversy.[40] Similarly, in view of its alleged discrimination against ethnic Russians, Latvia's admission to the COE in January 1995 (at the height of the debate over Chechnya) was met with accusations of 'double standards' in Moscow.[41]

The Yeltsin leadership was also of the opinion that, Chechnya notwithstanding, Russia had exhibited otherwise commendable progress toward COE principles. Indeed, some frustration had been voiced when, following the holding of parliamentary elections and the adoption of a new Constitution in December 1993, membership continued to be withheld. This sense of injury was compounded further by the exhaustive set of commitments the Russian leadership had given toward honouring COE obligations. A 'High Level Message' of January 1995, for instance, signed by President Yeltsin, Prime Minister Viktor Chernomyrdin and the Chairs of the two chambers of the Russian Parliament suggested that Russian membership would 'not result in any lowering of the high standards' of the organization.[42] To back this case, a 29-page Appendix charted recent legal, constitutional and political changes, international treaty obligations, as well as intended reforms that would bring Russia into line with COE practices.[43]

Given these arguments, Russia clearly welcomed both the re-activation of its application by the PACE and its subsequent entry into the COE. Speaking at the ceremony of admission, then Foreign Minister Primakov hailed the decision as confirmation of Russia's democratic transformation and 'a major step towards the genuine unification of Europe'. Despite all the delay, moreover, Russia, it was argued, should not be regarded as a second-class member. Its 'huge cultural, historic, scientific and intellectual potential [would] enrich the activities of [the] organization'.[44]

Yet membership, as the debate of the previous three years had suggested, would not be trouble-free. In order to boost its case, upon admission Russia undertook to meet an extensive list of commitments. This will be examined in some detail in the following section. However, at this point it is worth making three points that would come to have some bearing on the matter. First, and to reiterate, Russian entry was permitted largely on political rather than legal grounds. Whatever the wisdom of that position (that reform in Russia would be better pursued if the country was within rather than outside the organization), a strong counter-case had been made that Russia did not meet standard

COE criteria on human rights practices, the rule of law and good democratic practice. Indeed, the war in Chechnya, the major cause of the delay in accession, remained unresolved at the point of admission. The importance of the legal case would, however, increase once Russia had entered the organization and the statutory bodies and instruments of the COE extended their remit into the country. The political leniency shown toward Russia at the inter-governmental level would, consequently, count for less. Second, the Russian leadership made much during the admission process of Russia's European orientation. Yet, at times, reference was also made to the exceptionalism of the country: the colossal problems of democratic consolidation that stemmed from its multinational and 'post-totalitarian' character.[45] By the same logic, the obligations of membership could also be downplayed. Thus, amidst the hand-clapping at the time of Russian entry, less noticed statements emanating from the President and the Interior Ministry suggested that conditions in the country rendered premature the speedy implementation of its COE undertakings.[46] Third, the cause of Russian entry, unusual in Russian foreign policy, generated a near consensus in domestic opinion. While the position of the Yeltsin leadership has been mapped out above, it is also worth noting that political factions (with the notable exception of Vladimir Zhirinovsky's Liberal Democrats)[47] were united in favour of Russian entry, in part, for similar reasons to those outlined by the leadership, but also because membership would permit them a fuller role in the PACE. Yet, the Russian delegation to the PACE would, of course, be drawn from the Russian Parliament, a body which, following elections to its lower chamber, the State Duma, in 1995 remained ill-disposed toward the Yeltsin leadership.

Russia's involvement with the Council of Europe

Many of the issues surrounding the process of accession to the COE have remained at the forefront of Russia's relations with the organization in the period since 1996. In this section three aspects of Russia's interaction with the COE will be considered.

Russia and the obligations of Council of Europe membership

Russia assumed that certain benefits would follow from accession to the COE. Membership is significant, however, in that it also entails some fairly weighty responsibilities. In the case of new members these take two broad forms: first, specific commitments entered into as part of the accession process, and second, the standard obligations which follow from the operation of mechanisms such as the European Court of Human Rights linked to the provisions of the ECHR. If fully operative, these can have a transformative effect on domestic political and legal development. They are benchmarks against which a state's seriousness in accepting international obligations and assimilation into multilateral structures can be judged. In Russia's case, although the period of COE membership has been short, sufficient movement has occurred for an interim judgement in these regards.

Taking specific pledges first, as noted above, upon its accession in 1996 Russia took upon itself an exhaustive list of commitments; these formed the basis of PACE Opinion 193 and the Committee of Ministers' Resolution 96(2) inviting Russia to join the COE. Opinion 193 contains no less than 34 itemized pledges on the part of Russia. Several of these are vague in meaning and almost impossible to quantify – for instance, a commitment to settle both internal and international disputes by peaceful means and a clause disavowing the 'near abroad' as 'a zone of special influence'. Others, however, are far more precise. Table 6.1 groups together a large selection of these pledges and where appropriate notes the level of compliance on Russia's part.

Table 6.1 suggests a mixed picture. On the one hand, there has been a clear lack of progress in terms of prison conditions, freedom of movement and religion, and the reform of the security services. Arbitrary arrest, lengthy pre-trial detention, the torture of detainees and conscripts, and infringements on citizens' rights to privacy have also attracted criticism within the COE.[48] The fact that COE requirements have not been fully conveyed into Russia is, of course, to be expected given the early and still uncertain stage of its democratic consolidation. As figures within the Russian leadership have continued to point out, the sheer scale of the political, legal and cultural alterations required to give effect to these commitments suggests a necessarily prolonged period of reform.[49]

In view of these qualifications it should come as no surprise that progress has been most evident in a declaratory sense (see the large number of conventions signed by Russia noted in Table 6.1) rather than in the field of substantive implementation where fundamental changes to domestic law and practice are required, as well as negotiation and compromise among domestic institutional actors. That important qualification aside, a picture of tentative change is nonetheless apparent when one considers three other developments. First, some of the procedural attributes of democracy such as elections have been clearly evident. And while in this regard there was not a specific pledge on Russia's part at the time of accession, the ongoing march of democracy is a *sine qua non* of its participation in the COE.[50] Second, Russia's commitments, in some respects, go beyond normal standards set by the COE and international law more generally – this is true, for instance, regarding the status and powers of national security services – and are suggestive, at least, of good intent. Third, action on the part of the executive has expedited accommodation with COE standards even in the face of considerable domestic opposition. Take, for instance, Russia's commitments on the matter of capital punishment. Developments here have at times placed Russia in open conflict with the COE.[51] The rate of executions actually increased in the first few months following Russian admission.[52] The death penalty was also retained in the new Russian Criminal Code, which went into force in January 1997[53] and Russian judges have continued to hand down the sentence such that an estimated 700 persons were on death row as of January 1998.[54] The State Duma refused in March 1997 to support a draft law imposing a legal moratorium by a wide margin of 177 to 75 and at the time of writing has yet to ratify Russia's signature of Protocol 6 of the ECHR which prohibits the use of capital punishment in peacetime. Officials at the Justice Ministry, the Supreme Court and the office of the General Prosecutor are also reportedly in favour of retaining capital punishment.[55] In December 1998 Prime Minister Primakov alluded to his personal support for the 'physical elimination of those who raise their hands against society, the public and children'.[56] Public opinion, meanwhile, has registered consistently large majorities in favour of the death penalty.[57]

Where movement has occurred on the issue it has been due largely to presidential intervention; this, moreover, has been a consequence of pressure mounted directly upon Russia within the PACE and the Committee of Ministers and, indirectly, through a 'shaming' campaign led by domestic non-governmental organizations (NGOs) enjoying COE support.[58] A presidential moratorium on the death sentence was introduced in August 1996, and in January 1998 Yeltsin signed a law on amendments to the 1996 Penitentiary Code which allowed the President to review all death sentences, in effect institutionalizing the practice of presidential pardons for those on death row.[59] By June 1999 this meant that all prisoners awaiting execution had had their sentences commuted to terms of life imprisonment or 25 years. When coupled with a Constitutional Court decision of February 1999 that prohibited courts from issuing death sentences until the introduction of jury trials throughout Russia, these interventions meant that capital punishment was *de facto* no longer in use in Russia by mid-1999.[60] The process of abolition is, admittedly, incomplete in the absence of a durable legislative or constitutional

Table 6.1   Russian commitments upon entering the Council of Europe and compliance as of February 1999

Type of commitment	Comments
Signatures and ratifications	
Sign the ECHR at the moment of accession.	Done.
Ratify the ECHR within 1 year.	Instruments of ratification deposited in May 1998 with two reservations.
Ratify ECHR protocols 1, 2, 4, 7 and 11 within one year.	Instruments of ratification deposited in May 1998.
Recognise articles 25 and 46 of the ECHR concerning the right of individual petition and the compulsory jurisdiction of the European Court of Human Rights.	Done, May 1998. (Article 25 superseded in November 1998 by Article 34 of the ECHR as amended by Protocol No. 11. Russia has ratified the latter – see above item.)
Sign within one year of accession protocol 6 of the ECHR abolishing capital punishment in peacetime.	Done, April 1997.
Ratify ECHR protocol 6 within three years of accession.	Unratified.
Put in place a moratorium on capital punishment from the day of accession.	Done *de facto* by presidential intervention from August 1996.
Sign and ratify within one year from accession: (i) the European Convention for the Prevention of Torture; (ii) the Framework Convention for the Protection of National Minorities; (iii) the European Charter of Local Self-Government; (iv) the European Charter for Regional or Minority Languages.	(i) and (iii) signed February 1996, ratified May 1998; (ii) signed February 1996, ratified August 1998; (iv) unsigned and unratified.
Ratify the European Social Charter.	Unsigned; unratified.
Sign and ratify conventions on (i) extradition; (ii) mutual assistance in criminal matters; (iii) on the transfer of sentenced persons; and (iv) laundering of criminal proceeds.	(i) and (ii) signed November 1996; (iii) and (iv) unsigned and unratified.
Domestic reform	
Revise the law on the federal security services within one year of accession.	Law of April 1995 unamended.
Adopt a law on alternative military service and reduce incidents of ill-treatment in the armed forces.	Law rejected by the state Duma at its second reading in 1995 and no subsequent law passed as of February 1999; conditions of conscripts unimproved according to PACE Document 8127 (2 June 1998).

Pursue legal reform and in particular revise Presidential Decree1226 (allowing detention without trial for up to 30 days).	Decree 1226 repealed June 1997 but replaced by a decree permitting detention without charge for up to 10 days for those suspected of ties to organized crime.
Adopt the following: (i) Criminal Code; (ii) Code of Criminal Procedure; (iii) Civil Code; (iv) Code of Civil Procedure.	(i) Entered into force January 1997; (ii) 1960 Soviet Code still in force; (iii) Entered into force March 1996; (iv) Not yet considered by state Duma.
Adopt laws protecting: (i) freedom of assembly; (ii) freedom of religion; (iii) rights of national minorities.	(i) Law on Public Associations passed May 1995; (ii) Law on Religion entered into force October 1997 but its restrictive clauses criticized in PACE Document 8127 (2 June 1998).
Bring to justice those responsible for human rights violations in Chechnya.	23 persons convicted for crimes against the civilian population as of June 1998.
Improve conditions of detention.	No improvement according to PACE Document 8127 (2 June 1998).
Transfer the administration of prisons from the Ministry of the Interior to the Ministry of Justice.	Formal transfer occurred September 1998.
Guarantee freedom of movement and choice of place of residence.	Stipulated in Article 27 of the Russian Constitution but restricted by the internal passport system and unofficial use of resident registration rules (especially in Moscow).
Foreign Policy Ratify within six months of accession the October 1994 agreement on a withdrawal of Russian troops from Moldova; withdraw troops by 21 October 1997.	Agreement unratified; troop withdrawal in train but incomplete.
Fulfil obligations under the Conventional Forces in Europe Treaty.	Partially fulfilled (see Chapter 7).

Sources: PACE Opinion 193 (1996) reprinted in *Human Rights Law Journal*, Vol. 17, Nos. 3–6, 1996, pp. 185–7; PACE, Document 8127, 2 June 1998, 'Honouring of Obligations and Commitments by the Russian Federation'; 'Treaties of the Council of Europe Ratified by Russia, <http://www.coe.fr/eng/legaltxt/ratstates/eratrus.htm>; 'Treaties of the Council of Europe Signed but Not Ratified by Russia', <http://www.coe.fr/emg/legaltxtsignstates/esignrus.htm>; COE Directorate of Human Rights, *Human Rights Information Bulletin*, No. 45, November 1998–February 1999, pp. 8, 33, 35, 41; United States, Department of State, 'Russia Country Report on Human Rights Practices for 1998', <http://www.state.gov/www/global/human_rights/1998_hrp_report/russia.html>.

framework. However, while not sufficient to fully meet Russia's accession commitments regarding capital punishment, the developments noted above have gone a substantial way to altering actual practice within the country.

Turning to Russia's compliance with standard COE working practices, a number of significant steps have been taken. In May 1998 Russia completed the ratification process relating to the ECHR and, in addition, recognized with immediate effect Articles 25 and 46 of the Convention. The first of these was, in fact, superseded in November 1998 by Article 34 to the ECHR as amended by Protocol No. 11 (which Russia too has recognized). This permits individuals and private groups to directly petition the European Court of Human Rights in cases of alleged breaches of the ECHR by their government. Article 46, meanwhile, grants the Court compulsory jurisdiction thereby requiring national governments to implement changes in light of adverse findings. Interestingly, Article 15(4) of the 1993 Russian Constitution also establishes the supremacy of international law over domestic legislation.[61] As of November 1998 over 1500 letters of complaint from Russian citizens were awaiting processing. It is the norm for the majority of complaints under the ECHR to be declared inadmissible (admissibility criteria include that an alleged violation of the ECHR has occurred after a state's formal accession to the ECHR and that the appellant has exhausted all approaches to domestic courts). Some 70 cases brought by Russian citizens had been declared admissible by November 1998,[62] something that raises the possibility of adverse judgements being made against the Russian authorities. At this point, two scenarios are possible: either the COE displays some form of leniency toward Russia in terms of compliance with adverse judgements (based on similar political considerations to those that facilitated Russian entry into the COE in the first place) or it retains rigour in the application of Court findings.[63] Should the latter occur, Russia's credibility within the COE will be measured by its willingness to admit domestic human rights abuses and, more significantly, by its ability to remedy these infractions either by legislative revision or the payment of reparations. The indications of possible Russian compliance with the Court have thus far been mixed. Merely signing up to Articles 25 and 46 shows a seeming intent to submit to external jurisdiction. However, COE membership has also been accompanied by high-level statements (from Yeltsin amongst others) that the organization should not be an instrument for unwarranted interference in Russia's internal affairs,[64] a position that could be used to deflect unwelcome judgements of the Court.

Whatever opinion one is to hold of Russia in terms of its COE obligations, it has to be placed in context. Russia has clearly made some progress and although it has been laggardly in some areas it is no different in this respect from certain other new entrants. While Russia has not progressed as swiftly as, say, Poland, Hungary and the Czech Republic toward COE standards, it compares favourably with Albania and Croatia, for example. Russia can also be seen in a positive light when compared to other former Soviet republics: Latvia and Ukraine (COE members since 1995) have been berated just as roundly as Russia for their failings on the issue of capital punishment[65] whereas Belarus has effectively experienced a suspension of its membership application (it applied in March 1993) owing to the quasi-authoritarian rule of its President, Aleksandr Lukashenko.[66] Furthermore, the prospects of Russia's adherence to COE norms should also be set against the record of the organization's longer-established members. Their democratic credentials may be stronger than Russia's (although Turkey, a member since 1950 has long been criticized for democratic and human rights abuses and was actually suspended from the PACE between 1981 and 1984), but their attitude toward the COE's human rights regime has not always been exemplary. Whereas Russia took a few years to recognize Articles 25 and 46, some western democracies, the United Kingdom, France and Italy included, did so after a delay of 20–30 years. Similarly, while these states have generally been willing to accept the judgements of the European Court of Human Rights, they have delayed and at times resisted acting upon adverse opinions.[67]

Russia and Council of Europe assistance

COE activity occurs in many fields. These include science, social policy, sport, education, crime prevention and environmental protection. Through the COE's numerous conventions, member states cooperate in joint activities, codification and standardization, and the dissemination of good practice. The assimilation of new members into these activities has progressed within the COE and Russia too has partaken in them to a certain degree via activities related to the 'Octopus' programme (on organized crime), the Pompidou Group (drug abuse) and the New Initiative of the Secretary General (education, culture and civil society).

More pertinent to its core missions and of specific relevance to the post-communist states, the COE has also sought to foster the political incorporation of new members. Of particular note here are programmes which fall under the broad rubric of 'democratic assistance' designed to enable applicant countries to fulfil admission requirements and, subsequently, to undertake political, judicial and administrative reforms to match COE standards. Such assistance is also intended to increase public and élite familiarity with the organization and, more imperceptibly, to promote democratic norms in new member states.[68]

In Russia's case, initial contacts in this context were formalized during 1992 through small-scale seminars and consultations with representatives from the judiciary, local and regional government and NGOs, and through the establishment of contact groups drawn from the COE Secretariat General and the Russian Foreign Ministry. More substantively, a Joint Programme of Activities was launched in 1993. Again the focus was on expert meetings: the programme of activities for 1995, for instance, involved a total of 37 meetings on the themes of federalism, human rights, the media, local government (through the COE's 'Lode' programme), legal cooperation (the 'Demo-droit' and 'Themis' programmes) and civil society.[69] In 1992 Russia also joined, as an associate member, the COE's European Commission for Democracy through Law, a body which provides advice on constitutional and legal reform. Since Russia's accession, LODE and Themis have continued to run. Russia has also become involved with 'Demosthenes' (a specially tailored assistance programme for new members) and has become the beneficiary of a Joint Programme involving the COE alongside the Commission of the European Communities. This latter initiative has pursued activities under two broad themes: constitutional arrangements and institution building (federal structures, local government and human rights protection mechanisms), and legal reform (legal education and training, the development of legislation compatible with the ECHR, and prison reform).[70] These have involved the establishment of working relations with the presidential administration, the Justice Ministry, the Procuracy, the federal subjects of the Russian Federation and with the Russian Parliament. The COE has also worked increasingly with the media and NGOs working in the human rights field in Moscow and other large Russian cities.[71]

These contacts have resulted in numerous exchanges, conferences, seminars, working groups and so on.[72] Their impact, however, is difficult to judge. Legislation in Russia does reflect COE language and norms (the human rights provisions of the Constitution itself are seemingly modelled on COE conventions)[73] and the COE has claimed credit for directly shaping specific legislative acts and presidential decrees.[74] It has also claimed to have had a beneficial impact on official opinion in areas such as penal reform and, more generally, a discrete influence upon government and Parliament, which has in turn facilitated Russia's honouring of COE commitments.[75] Yet by its own admission, COE assistance is still considered transitional and success in obtaining its objective – the '[b]uilding up of a democratic infrastructure' – is something that can be 'perceived only in the long-term'.[76] Caution is also in order when one considers the scale of the challenge – overcoming a heritage of hierarchical, closed and undemocratic practices within state structures and transforming bureaucratic attitudes ill-disposed to, or at least unfamiliar with, the COE's human rights and legal regime. All of this, moreover, has been attempted by the COE through programmes with limited funding[77] in a country of enormous geography and experiencing profound economic and social dislocation.

Member states' disputes within the Council of Europe

The opportunities for foreign policy activism within the COE are far fewer than within other international organizations (the EU, the OSCE and NATO) considered in this volume. This reflects the absence of any meaningful security or economic functions enjoyed by the Committee of Ministers and the derogation of important tasks to the PACE, and the European Court of Human Rights. That said, accession issues and controversies over human rights commitments do often touch upon the foreign policy concerns of member states. Since obtaining membership, Russia has been the target of criticism by other member states, but has itself also utilized the COE to highlight certain foreign policy issues.

Taking the former first, Russia has been censured by the Moldovan government for a failure to withdraw troops from its national territory. The fact that such a withdrawal was a commitment entered into by Russia upon accession to the COE (see Table 6.1) has added strength to the Moldovan case.[78] As for Russia's own favoured causes, it has continued to emphasize the COE's pan-European credentials (contrasting this with the closed and divisive nature of NATO) and has pressed for an enhancement of the organization's profile in non-traditional security matters (arguing in favour of a strengthening of its links with the OSCE and welcoming the COE's involvement in post-conflict Bosnia).[79] Russia has also argued in favour of a continuing enlargement of the COE and, consequently, has been critical of the PACE's suspension of Belarus.[80] Such emphases reflect Moscow's continuing anxieties at the effects of NATO and EU enlargement. With regard to matters closer to the COE's traditional missions, Russia has been a persistent critic of alleged human rights infringements of Russian speakers in Latvia and Estonia. This matter is of note, moreover, because the COE has played a direct role in dealing with the issue. Of the two cases, Latvia has been the subject of greater concern within the COE.[81] Although an applicant since September 1991 this state had, in effect, been barred from admission owing to its overly restrictive citizenship requirements. Accession, when it came in February 1995, followed amendments to a 1994 citizenship law (in part inspired by criticisms within the COE) and undertakings on Latvia's part that it would avoid any discrimination between citizens and 'non-citizens' (i.e. Russian speakers).[82] Some three years later a PACE fact-finding visit to Riga, however, concluded that Latvia had 'not yet achieved a successful integration of its non-citizens' and had not put in place fair and efficient naturalization procedures.[83] This seemingly confirmed criticisms of Latvia made on several occasions by Russia within the PACE, the Committee of Ministers and at the 1997 COE summit.[84] In response to the chorus of complaints,[85] further amendments to citizenship legislation were adopted in June 1998 and in October of that year Latvians voted in a referendum to grant virtually automatic citizenship to stateless (i.e. resident Russian) children born after the re-establishment of independence in 1991. Russia has, however, given these initiatives only a cautious welcome.[86]

Conclusion

In the context of its broader relations with Europe, Russia's relationship with the COE is potentially important in at least two senses. The first of these concerns the promotion in Russia of democratic consolidation with its associated features of respect for human rights and the rule of law. As noted already, consolidation of this type is by no means a pre-ordained outcome given the obstacles to transition in the country. The possibility of a relapse into authoritarianism or the persistence of an oligarchic, quasi-democratic polity remains a real possibility. In this environment, the COE, and indeed international actors more generally, can at best play only a marginal role. What does such a role amount to? To begin with, the COE can have some effect through its established human rights machinery. Russia's acceptance of the right of individual petition under Article 25 (and subsequently Article 34) of the ECHR will inevitably lead to adverse opinions against the Russian authorities and while the COE lacks any real powers of enforcement to ensure sub-sequent compliance, its judgements will at least provide a yardstick against which the good faith and the democratic credentials of the Russian state can be measured. Of course, applying this yardstick as a means of pressurizing Russia does depend on the strength of the domestic human-rights lobby and the boldness of the COE's more influential member states. Both these constituencies have their limitations (of influence and size in the case of the former and those stemming from pragmatism and *realpolitik* in the case of the latter); however, there are some signs already that COE membership has forced the hand of the Russian leadership. The case of the death penalty is particularly instructive here, Russian policy being directly determined by its membership of the COE and indirectly influenced by domestic NGOs enjoying COE assistance. Yet ultimately, the effectiveness of the organization will depend upon the authority it enjoys among Russia's political élites.[87] In this regard, it is far too early to judge the COE's impact. The organization has to overcome a political and legal culture in Russia not well-inclined to the encroachments of external jurisdiction. While the role of the COE as an institution for the diffusion of norms should not be ruled out, such a role may take several generations to effect and even then depends upon a range of proximate uncertainties regarding political, economic and cultural change. In this light, it has been argued that the COE is far more suited to improving established democracies than it is to assisting the consolidation of fragile ones.[88]

If acculturation into COE standards is only a long-term prospect in Russia, then the organization's influence may well be derived from more pragmatic considerations. This follows from the second important aspect of the Russian–COE relationship, that involving the consolidation of Russia's European orientation and its integration into European institutions. The desire of the Russian leadership for membership of the COE arguably reflects perceptions of state interest (the need to avoid isolation, to compensate for the effects of EU and NATO enlargement and to soothe its great power sensibilities which demand a say in European affairs) as much as any accommodation with the 'European' principles of democracy, human rights and the rule of law. However, once inside the organization Russia will, of course, want to stay there and will want to be seen to play by its rules. To do otherwise, opens it up to censure and ultimately the risk of expulsion. Admittedly, the latter is rare within the COE; however, the former is commonplace and, at times, highly effective owing to the organization's intrusive monitoring procedures. The need to avoid pariah status will mean that Russia has a pragmatic interest in complying, at least to a degree, with COE standards and, as we have seen above, in committing itself to obligations against which it can subsequently be judged.

Notes

1. J. E. Manas, 'The Council of Europe's Democracy Ideal and the Challenge of Ethno-National Strife', in A. Chayes and A. H. Chayes (eds.), *Preventing Conflict in the Post-Communist World* (Washington D.C.: The Brookings Institution, 1996), pp. 102–4.
2. By contrast, in NATO, the OSCE and to some extent the EU, political cooperation is a by-product of other more pressing missions relating to respectively security, inter-state dialogue and confidence building, and economic integration.
3. B. Kovrig, 'Creating Coherence: Collective Contributions to the Political Integration of Central and Eastern Europe', in J. R. Lampe and D. N. Nelson (eds.), *East European Security Reconsidered* (Washington D.C.: Woodrow Wilson Centre Press, 1993), pp. 171–2.
4. R. L. Garthoff, *The Great Transition. American–Soviet Relations and the End of the Cold War* (Washington D.C.: The Brookings Institution, 1994), p. 587.
5. Parliamentary Assembly of the Council of Europe (PACE), Document 6203, 4 April 1990, p. 3.
6. *'Demosthenes' and other Cooperation and Assistance Programmes for Countries of Central and Eastern Europe* (Strasburg: Council of Europe, 1991).
7. Personal correspondence with the German and Austrian permanent missions to the COE dated 16 July 1998 and 3 November 1998 respectively. (The EU member states had decided at their European Council meeting in Madrid in December 1995 to support Russian entry into the COE.)
8. Although not all of them. The deputy Secretary-General Peter Leuprecht resigned in July 1997 in protest at what he saw as a watering down of the COE's values owing to its overly fast expansion. At the time, Leuprecht referred to the admission of Croatia, Romania and Russia as being mistaken. See J. Blocker, 'Council of Europe's "Soft" Standards for East European Members', Radio Free Europe/Radio Liberty (RFE/RL), *Newsline*, End Note (newsline@list.rferl.org), 8 July 1997.
9. Cited in PACE, Document 6216, 26 April 1990, p. 12.
10. From a lecture given at St Anthony's College, Oxford, cited in A. Hyde-Price, *The International Politics of East Central Europe* (Manchester and New York: Manchester University Press, 1996), p. 194.
11. D. Tarschys, 'The Council of Europe: the Challenge of Enlargement', *The World Today*, Vol. 51, No. 4, 1995, pp. 62–4.
12. H. Storey, 'Human Rights and the New Europe: Experience and Experiment', *Political Studies*, Vol. 43 (special issue), 1995, pp. 142–3.
13. 'Vienna Declaration of the Heads of State and Government of the Member States of the Council of Europe on the Reform of the Council Mechanism of the ECHR, on National Minorities, and on a Plan of Action against Racism', reprinted in *Human Rights Law Journal*, Vol. 14, Nos. 9–10, 1993, pp. 373–6.
14. 'Final Declaration and Action Plan of the 2nd Summit of the Council of Europe', reprinted in *Objective 1998. The Council of Europe's Intergovernmental Programme of Activities* (Strasburg: Council of Europe, 1998), p. 55.
15. Committee of Ministers Resolution (92) 27, 25 June 1992.
16. A. Zagorsky, 'Russia and European Institutions', in V. Baranovsky (ed.), *Russia and Europe. The Emerging Security Agenda* (Oxford: Oxford University Press/

Frösunda, Sweden: Stockholm International Peace Research Institute, 1997), p. 537.

17. PACE, Document 7000, 24 January 1994, p. A5.
18. PACE, Document 7224, 27 January 1995, p. A3.
19. The report is reprinted in full in *Human Rights Law Journal*, Vol. 15, No. 7, 1994, pp. 249–300. See especially, the Conclusions on p. 287.
20. PACE, Document 7231, 2 February 1995, pp. 3–4 cites Russia's abrogation of the 1949 Geneva Conventions for the Protection of Victims of War, the OSCE's 'Code of Conduct' signed by Russia in December 1994 and a variety of resolutions adopted by the UN General Assembly dealing with the protection of civilian populations in time of war.
21. PACE, Resolution 1055 (1995), reprinted in PACE, Document 7443, 2 January 1996, Annex 4, p. 29.
22. PACE, Resolution 1065 (1995), reprinted in *Human Rights Law Journal*, Vol. 17, Nos. 3–6, 1996, p. 196.
23. PACE, Document 7443, 2 January 1996.
24. PACE, Document 7463, 18 January 1996.
25. Speech of Mr Sinka (Latvia) transcribed in PACE, Official Report, AS (1996) CR 6, p. 26.
26. EU governments also indulged in discrete lobbying of the PACE in the run-up to the debate on Russian membership. For statements of support by the Danish, German and French Foreign Ministers see respectively, Foreign Broadcast Information Service (FBIS)-WEU-96-013, 8 January 1996; The Jamestown Foundation, *Monitor* (webmaster@jamestown.org), 22 January 1996 and FBIS-SOV-96-017, 25 January 1996, p. 10.
27. Speech of Mr Laakso (Finland) on behalf of the Group of the Unified European Left, in PACE, Official Report, AS(1996) CR 6, *op. cit.*, p. 11.
28. Speech of Mr Atkinson (UK), Rapportuer of the Committee on Relations with European Non-Member Countries in *ibid.*, p. 6.
29. Speech by Mr Iwinski (Poland), in *ibid.*, p. 15.
30. Speech of Mr Baumel (France), in *ibid.*, p. 14.
31. The motion was passed by a large majority (164 votes in favour), although 15 delegates abstained and 35 voted against. Most of the dissenters were drawn from delegations from the Baltic states and the Czech Republic. See J. Blocker, 'Vote on Russia Marks Council's Most Historic Day' (RFE/RL, 26 January 1996).
32. As cited in 'A Transformed Russia in a New World', *International Affairs* (Moscow), April–May 1992, p. 86.
33. FBIS-SOV-92-090, 8 May 1992, pp. 15, 17.
34. *Diplomaticheskii vestnik*, Nos. 21–2, 1993, p. 1.
35. Speech of First Deputy Foreign Minister, A. L. Adamishin, to the COE's Vienna summit as transcribed in *Diplomaticheskii vestnik*, Nos. 21–2, 1993, p. 11; meeting of First Deputy Foreign Minister I. S. Ivanov with COE officials as reported in *ibid.*, No. 10, 1995, p. 22.
36. Open Media Research Institute (OMRI), *Daily Digest* (OMRI-L@UBVM.cc. buffalo.edu), 19 January 1995.
37. The 1991 Moscow document of the then CSCE states that CSCE participating states 'declare that the commitments undertaken in the field of the human dimension of the CSCE are matters of direct and legitimate concern to all

participating States and do not belong exclusively to the internal affairs of the State concerned'. In 1992 Russia inherited the Soviet Union's membership of the CSCE and thus commitments entered into with that organization.

38. A delegation from the PACE Sub-Committee on Human Rights visited the region in June and August 1995. See PACE, Document 7384, 15 September 1995, Appendix. For the OSCE and UN missions see T. Gazzini, 'Considerations on the Conflict in Chechnya', *Human Rights Law Journal*, Vol. 17, Nos. 3–6, 1996, pp. 101–5.

39. Deputy Foreign Minister Nikolai Afanasyevsky cited in FBIS-SOV-95-008, 12 January 1995, p. 10; Deputy Prime Minister Sergei Shakrai cited in OMRI, *Daily Digest* (OMRI-L@UBVM.cc.buffalo.edu), 1 February 1995.

40. *Diplomaticheskii vestnik*, Nos. 21–2, 1993, p. 61.

41. Aleksandr Udalstsov (Deputy Director of the Russian Foreign Ministry's Second European Department) cited in FBIS-SOV-95-022, 2 February 1995, p. 5.

42. PACE, Document 7443, 2 January 1996, Annex 3.

43. *Ibid.*, Addendum B, pp. 5–34.

44. <http://stars.coe.fr/act/compress/russia_p.htm>.

45. Meeting of First Deputy Foreign Minister I. S. Ivanov with COE officials, as reported in *Diplomaticheskii vestnik*, No. 10, 1995, p. 22.

46. FBIS-SOV-96-019, 29 January 1996, p. 15; FBIS-SOV-96-049, 12 March 1996.

47. For quite different reasons, the former Presidential Commissioner for Human Rights Sergei Kovalev also opposed entry. See *Nezavisimaya gazeta*, 25 January 1996.

48. PACE, Document 8127, 'Honouring of Obligations and Commitments by the Russian Federation', 2 June 1998, pp. 9, 13–16, 19–20. See also Human Rights Watch, 'World Report 1999: the Russian Federation', <http://www/hrw.org/hrw/worldreport99/europe/russian.html>.

49. Justice Minister Sergei Stepashin cited in RFE/RL, *Newsline* (newsline@list.rferl.org), 3 July 1997; Yevgenni Primakov (then Russian Foreign Minister) cited in FBIS-SOV-98-125, 5 May 1998.

50. The judgement of the PACE in this regard is that '[p]olitical developments in Russia reflect a progressive shift from a totalitarian political system to a liberal democracy based on democratic elections'. See PACE, Document 8127, 2 June 1998, p. 25.

51. In January 1997, the PACE passed a resolution threatening to bar the Russian delegation owing to Russian tardiness in abolishing capital punishment.

52. *The Guardian*, 2 May 1996.

53. The number of offences carrying the death sentence was reduced from 28 to five. However, as a PACE report noted, none of the prisoners condemned to death in recent years was sentenced on the basis of the 23 offenses for which punishment had been revised. See PACE, Document 7746, 28 January 1997, p. 5.

54. The Jamestown Foundation, *Monitor* (webmaster@jamestown.org), 15 January 1998.

55. *Moscow News*, 16–22 October 1997, p. 5; comments of Justice Minister Pavel Krashennikov cited in FBIS-SOV-98-149, 29 May 1998.

56. RFE/RL, *Newsline* (newsline@list.rferl.org), 1 December 1998.

57. A poll taken in March 1997 found that only 14 per cent of the 1630 adult Russians questioned were in favour of abolition. See FBIS-SOV-97-073, 14 March 1997. *Izvestiya* reported on 13 January 1999 that 50 per cent of Russians

were in favour of maintaining the death penalty in its current form and 22 per cent wanted to broaden its application.

58. J. Checkel, 'Empowerment, Ricochets and End-Runs: Russia's Integration with Western Human Rights Institutions and Practices' (Programme on New Approaches to Russian Security, Harvard University), Memo No. 14, October 1997, <http://www.fas.harvard.edu/~ponars/POLICYMEMOS/Checkelmemo.html>.

59. The moratorium has held since August 1996 with the exception of Chechnya where, following the cessation of hostilities, the local authorities have continued to use the death penalty. Four executions were recorded by the COE in the region in 1997. See PACE, Press Release, 17 November 1997 and PACE, Document 8127, 2 June 1998, pp. 10–11.

60. 'Russia and the Death Penalty: a Fact Sheet' (Human Rights Watch, Moscow, June 1999) as carried by *Johnson's Russia List* (davidjohnson@erols.com), 3 June 1999.

61. On the significance of this provision see V. S. Vereshchetin, 'New Constitutions and the Old Problem of the Relationship between International Law and National Law', *European Journal of International Law*, Vol. 7, No. 1, 1996, pp. 29–41.

62. *Noviye izvestiya*, 5 November 1998 translated in *The Current Digest of the Post-Soviet Press*, Vol. 50, No. 45, 1998, p. 18.

63. M. Janis, 'Russia and the "Legality" of Strasbourg Law', *European Journal of International Law*, Vol. 8, No. 1, 1997, p. 41. The leniency scenario would follow from the fact that the inter-governmental element of the COE, the Committee of Ministers, supervises the execution of judgements of the Court in cases where the ECHR has been deemed to be violated.

64. Yeltsin cited in FBIS-SOV-96-049, 12 March 1996.

65. PACE, Document 7589, 25 June 1996, pp. 9–11; PACE, Press Release 660a(97), 17 November 1997; and PACE, Document 8136 Addendum I, 9 June 1998.

66. In January 1997 the Political Bureau of the PACE decided to suspend the Belarus Parliament's special guest status. This followed charges of irregularities in the conduct of a referendum the previous November on a new Constitution and criticism of the Constitution itself for not respecting 'minimum democratic standards'. See PACE, Press Release 11(97), 13 January 1997.

67. See the cases drawn from Belgium, Ireland, Italy, Switzerland and the UK detailed in C. Tomuschat, 'Quo Vadis, Argentorium? The Success Story of the European Convention on Human Rights – and a Few Dark Stains', *Human Rights Law Journal*, Vol. 13, Nos. 11–12, 1992, pp. 401–6.

68. D. Pinto, *From Assistance to Democracy to Democratic Security* (Strasburg: Council of Europe, n.d.), p. 7.

69. PACE, Document 6750, 1 February 1993, Addendum II, pp. 20–1; PACE, Document 7443, 2 January 1996, Addendum C, pp. 36–41.

70. 'Activities for the Development and Consolidation of Democratic Stability. Joint Programmes between the European Commission (PHARE and TACIS) and the Council of Europe' (Council of Europe, Information Document ADACS/JP[98] 1, 18 March 1998), p. 7.

71. J. T. Checkel, 'International Norms and Domestic Politics: Bridging the Rationalist–Constructivist Divide', *European Journal of International Relations*, Vol. 3, No. 4, 1997, pp. 484–5; Pinto, *op. cit.*, pp. 10–15.

72. Division for Pan-European Cooperation Programmes, Directorate of Political Affairs, 'Assistance with the Development and Consolidation of Democratic Security. Cooperation and Assistance Programmes with Countries of Central and Eastern Europe. Annual Report 1996' (Council of Europe, Document SG/INF[7]1), pp. 55–61; Division for Pan-European Cooperation Programmes, Directorate of Political Affairs, 'Activities for the Development and Consolidation of Democratic Stability (ADACS). Synopses of Activities – 1997. Russian Federation' (Council of Europe, Document SG/INF[98] 1 add/ Russia, 14 April 1998); Division for Pan-European Cooperation Programmes, Directorate of Political Affairs, 'Activities for the Development and Consolidation of Democratic Stability (ADACS). Programme 1998' (Council of Europe, Document SG/INF[98]2), pp. 85–113.

73. The COE's European Commission for Democracy through Law offered advice during the drafting stage of this document.

74. 'Final Report. Joint Programme between the European Commission and the Council of Europe for Strengthening of the Federal Structure, Introduction of Human Rights Protection Mechanisms and Legal System Reform in the Russian Federation' (Council of Europe, Document JP/RUSSIA[98]1, 30 April 1998), p. 2. The laws mentioned here are the Presidential Decree on Plenipotentiary Representatives in the Subjects of the Federation, the Law on Competencies of the Russian Federation and the Subjects of the Russian Federation and the Local Authorities (Financial Basis) Act.

75. *Ibid.*, pp. 3, 8.

76. *Ibid.*, pp. 8–9.

77. For example, the joint European Commission/COE initiative was allocated funds of just ECU 3.75 million for 1996–98. See 'Activities for the Development . . .' (footnote 70 above), p. 7.

78. Speech of President Petru Lucinschi to the Second COE summit, October 1997, <http://www.coe.fr/summit/discours/mold.htm>.

79. Primakov cited in FBIS-SOV-96-088, 3 May 1996; speech of Primakov to the COE Committee of Ministers transcribed in *Diplomaticheskii vestnik*, No. 6, 1997, pp. 15–16; speech of Boris Yeltsin to the COE summit, *Diplomaticheskii vestnik*, No. 11, 1997, p. 9; V. Shustov (Russian Ambassador at Large), '"Wise Persons" and the Council of Europe', *International Affairs* (Moscow), Vol. 45, No. 2, 1999, electronic edition <http://home.mosinfo.ru/news/int-aff/1999/data/002hust.htm>.

80. Speech by Primakov on the occasion of a visit to Moscow by COE Secretary General Daniel Tarschys transcribed in *Diplomaticheskii vestnik*, No. 4, 1997, p. 15; Foreign Ministry spokesman V. Andreev cited in OMRI, *Daily Digest* (OMRI-L@UBVM.cc.buffalo.edu), 17 January 1997.

81. Moscow has raised the Estonian case in the COE. However, here it has found little sympathy. The Committee of Ministers in October 1996 commended Estonian legislation on citizenship, minority issues and the rights of resident aliens. See PACE, Document 7689, 29 October 1996, p. 3. The PACE report on 'Honouring of Obligations and Commitments by the Russian Federation' cited in footnote 48 above, states in paragraph 93 that allegations of the Russian PACE delegation regarding Estonia were 'unsubstantiated'.

82. Janis, *op. cit.*, pp. 70–1; PACE, Opinion 183 (1995).

83. PACE, Document 8136, 9 June 1998, Addendum I.

84. Primakov cited in FBIS-SOV-98-124, 4 May 1998; draft resolution submitted by Segei Glotov – PACE, Document 7879, 9 July 1997; *Diplomaticheskii vestnik*, No. 11, 1997, p. 9.

85. As well as Russian demands within the COE, the NATO Secretary General and the OSCE's High Commissioner for National Minorities have also been instrumental in recommnding changes. Perhaps even more significantly, the European Commission in its 'Opinion on Latvia's Application for Membership of the European Union' concluded that 'steps need to be taken to enable the Russian-speaking minority to become better integrated into society'. See <http://europa.eu.int/search97cgi/s . . . te=EC_HTML-view. hts&hlnavigate=ALL>.

86. Primakov cited in FBIS-SOV-98-174, 23 June 1998; Foreign Minister I. Ivanov cited in RFE/RL, *Newsline* (newsline@list.rferl.org), 2 December 1998. It might also be noted that a PACE Report of May 1999 concurred with the Russian view, suggesting that 'Latvia has not yet honoured one major commitment [to the COE]: to integrate its non-citizen population.' See PACE, Document 8426, 24 May 1999, p. 15.

87. For the general proposition that élite attitudes are pivotal to the impact of organized human rights provisions see J. Donnelly, 'International Human Rights: A Regime Analysis', *International Organization*, Vol. 40, No. 3, 1986, pp. 614–19.

88. See A. Moravscik, 'Explaining International Human Rights Regimes: Liberal Theory and Western Europe', *European Journal of International Relations*, Vol. 1, No. 2, 1997, p. 159.

7
Russia and Issues of Demilitarization
Derek Averre

Introduction

The fundamental political changes of the last decade have unquestionably led to the emergence of a new Europe, a continent if not yet free of military tensions then at least one in which the major powers have negotiated their way toward relative stability. The seeds of this change were sown in the years preceding the collapse of Soviet-dominated communism in east-central Europe (ECE). Mikhail Gorbachev's leadership inspired new Soviet approaches to international security issues and offered concessions in arms control to further these approaches. The most visible result of these policies was the Intermediate Nuclear Forces (INF) Treaty signed in 1987, a historic agreement which effectively eliminated an entire category of weapons from Europe. The late 1980s also saw the beginning of negotiations leading to agreements which were to have a substantial impact upon the size, structure and operational aims of military forces in Europe and which established a considerable degree of openness and transparency in military relations between the North Atlantic Treaty Organization (NATO) and its former adversaries in the Warsaw Pact. The 1990 Treaty on Conventional Armed Forces in Europe (CFE), the Concluding Act of the Negotiation on Personnel Strength of Conventional Armed Forces in Europe (the 1992 CFE-1A agreement), the 1992 Vienna Document on Confidence and Security Building Measures (CSBMs) and the 1992 Treaty on Open Skies together represented a package of measures designed 'to replace military confrontation with a new pattern of security relations' in Europe, thereby helping to overcome the division of the continent.[1]

The process of structural change in the international system has also had a far-reaching effect on demilitarization in Europe. As Barry Buzan points out, '[i]t makes a big difference to the whole calculation of deterrence whether the relationship involved is bipolar or multipolar [. . .]. In arms racing and arms control, the dynamics of interaction and the availability of parity are both deeply affected by the variable of polarity.'[2] This has raised a number of problems with which those trying to reconceptualize European security and elucidate the dynamics in Russian–western relations are having to grapple.

Agreements on disarmament, arms control and reduction, and CSBMs are, of course, vital components of the security-building process. The term chosen for the title of this chapter is 'demilitarization'. This implies an added dimension, to wit, reducing the weight of the military factor in, and essentially rethinking, security relations. This is particularly crucial to Russian political, economic and societal development in the current period and, in turn, determines the way agreements are interpreted and whether they are adhered to.

This chapter briefly outlines the agreements listed above and considers their significance in terms of the international political events, which marked the end of the Cold War. It then goes on to analyse the implementation of arms control agreements and related initiatives within the wider context of Russia's place in the contemporary European security framework. The problems posed to Russia by demilitarization and military reform are then discussed and an attempt made to examine how these problems are affecting Russia's defence capability. Finally, the debate on military security in the new Europe is considered and prospects for future cooperation in the sphere of demilitarization assessed.

Arms control agreements and CSBMs in post-Cold War Europe

The lack of any real progress in East–West conventional arms control prior to 1986 stemmed largely from the participants' reluctance to compromise over what were then considered to be vital strategic interests. The core of the problem was twofold and stemmed, first, from the ideological conflict which had dominated post-war relations and second, from the absence of a 'solid conceptual framework of conventional arms control',[3] itself the legacy of an era dominated by nuclear arms control theory. Proposals by the Warsaw Pact and NATO regarding limited cuts in weaponry and troop levels in the central European area were perceived by both sides to be aimed at securing strategic advantage by altering the existing balance of forces. NATO's argument, which formed the rationale for the Allies' nuclear deterrent, that the Soviet Union enjoyed critical superiority in conventional forces, was rejected by the pre-Gorbachev Soviet leadership.

The deadlock was, however, broken following a change of leadership in the Soviet Union. In April 1986 Gorbachev proposed to reduce substantially, across the entire Atlantic to the Urals (ATTU) region, troop units and weaponry held by all European states and those deployed by the US and Canada in Europe. These measures were to be backed up with means of verification as well as ideas for CSBMs. The Warsaw Pact summit in Budapest in June 1986, moreover, implicitly recognized traditional western fears over attack by 'excessively large military forces structured and trained according to an offensive military doctrine'.[4] Meetings between the sixteen NATO and seven Warsaw Pact states, in what was essentially an alliance-to-alliance framework, to formulate a new conventional arms control mandate began in February 1987. Sufficient progress, including an agreement on verification and data exchange, was made over the next two years – again, largely as a result of substantial Soviet concessions[5] – to have the mandate included as an annex to the Concluding Document of the Vienna follow-up meeting of the Conference on Security and Cooperation in Europe (CSCE) signed on 17 January 1989. It was agreed, notwithstanding a proposal on Gorbachev's part to leave tactical nuclear weapons (TNWs) for separate talks and to exclude naval forces from the agenda. The negotiations, which culminated with the signing in November 1990 of the CFE Treaty (an agreement of unlimited duration), thus covered the land-based conventional armed forces, including conventional and dual-use arms and equipment, of the 23 countries of NATO and the Warsaw Pact within the ATTU territory. The legally binding obligations of the treaty – providing detailed information on national armed forces within the ATTU zone, adhering to numerical ceilings on military equipment, reducing set amounts of excess treaty-limited equipment (TLE) and accepting inspections to verify the fulfilment of these obligations – were aimed at greatly enhancing transparency and thus allowing defence planners to formulate policy based on a clearer appreciation of other states' military capabilities.

Few would dispute that the remarkable progress between April 1986 and November 1990 would not have been possible without the radical rethinking of foreign and security policy which emerged under Gorbachev and which forced the West to recognize the conceptual link between conventional arms control and the future of European security, and indeed, to re-examine the assumptions upon which its whole military strategy rested. This shift in Soviet policy was motivated by the need to restructure the heavily militarized Soviet economy in pursuit of economic regeneration and to end the Soviet Union's isolation from the developed western community of nations. This meant, in turn, that it was imperative to resolve the security dilemma whereby Soviet defence policies had prompted the perception of a high-level threat and consequent response from NATO. The strategic concepts articulated to deal with these challenges were those of 'reasonable sufficiency' and 'non-offensive defence'. At the root of both was an assumption that, henceforth, conflict could be averted through political rather than military means. The change in approach, however, had fundamental domestic repercussions. It affected deep-seated institutional interests in the Soviet defence establishment and military-industrial complex, required attempts on Gorbachev's part to gain greater control over military spending, and was accompanied by the involvement in military decision-making of new civilian experts, the ideas of which often conflicted with the interests of defence officials.[6]

The political upheavals in ECE in 1989 presaged a substantial revision of the security map of Europe. The Soviet Union was deprived of the basis for forward operations built up after the Yalta agreement in 1945 – the 'buffer zone' separating Soviet territory from the formerly hostile West. The CFE talks were interpreted by conservative forces, including the military, as widening the Soviet Union's window of vulnerability and the Gorbachev leadership came under increasing political pressure. Indeed, with the tumultuous events of 1989, it became clear that the main perceived threat which guided NATO's approach to conventional arms control – large-scale Soviet forces poised in forward positions facing the Alliance – would disappear before the CFE Treaty could be ready for signing. This evident weakening of the Soviet Union's geostrategic situation in fact made little impact on the progress of the negotiations other than the need to confirm force ceiling allocations; the Gorbachev leadership remained committed to the Treaty, while arguing for an increase in the single-country limit on force sizes and calling for the simultaneous transformation of NATO and the Warsaw Pact into military-political organizations with diminished military features.[7]

The signing of the CFE Treaty and the establishment of meaningful verification provisions laid the foundations for separate follow-on negotiations on troop levels. A major Soviet concern was the size of German forces. However, a German commitment to reduced personnel levels in the reunified state made speedy progress possible. Although complicated by the break-up of the Soviet Union the politically binding CFE-1A agreement was signed in July 1992 by NATO member states, former

Warsaw Pact countries and eight Soviet successor states with territory in the ATTU region (excluding the Baltic states of Estonia, Latvia and Lithuania). It covered personnel located in ground, air and air-defence forces and land-based naval formations, but excluded internal security forces.

The evolution of CSBMs within the CSCE framework, from the 1975 Helsinki Final Act through the 1986 Stockholm Document to the period of CFE Treaty talks, provided an important complement to arms control. Aimed at reducing the risk of military confrontation by monitoring and regulating the activities of conventional forces, CSBMs culminated in the Vienna Document of 1992, which encompassed all the measures agreed since Helsinki and 'for the first time, addressed the real limitations on military activities at the same time as it included new measures to enhance transparency'.[8]

Closely linked, in turn, with arms control and CSBMs was the Open Skies Treaty, signed in March 1992 (originally by Russia, Ukraine and Belarus and subsequently by Georgia, as well as by five former Warsaw Pact countries and NATO's then 16 member states). This allows reconnaissance flights for observation purposes over the territory stretching 'from Vancouver to Vladivostok'. Open Skies (not yet ratified by Russia at the time of writing, despite repeated promptings from western partners) provides a complementary confidence-building and verification function aimed at greater openness and transparency in military activities.

Turning to nuclear weapons' issues, the threat of a nuclear conflict in Europe (which appeared only too real as the US under President Ronald Reagan considered a substantial rearmament programme including improved TNWs) abated with Gorbachev's initiative to remove INF from Europe. Although the INF Treaty came in for some criticism – notably from the west European allies who wanted to stabilize nuclear deterrence and avoid a total denuclearization of Europe which would have left them vulnerable to the Soviet conventional threat – the fact that it involved large and verifiable reductions represented a significant milestone in overcoming Cold War tensions. Little progress was made on short-range TNW until after the conclusion of the CFE Treaty. However, initiatives on the part of both Washington and Moscow (particularly those of Gorbachev in October 1991 and of Boris Yeltsin in January 1992 on unilateral and reciprocal reductions in both strategic and TNW)[9] eventually led to the withdrawal and elimination of substantial numbers of short- and medium-range land-based missiles formerly deployed by the US and the Soviet Union in Europe. With parallel initiatives on nuclear testing and production of fissile material, the shift in defence postures to minimal nuclear deterrence was clearly underway by the early 1990s.

As the above account suggests, both the Soviet government under Gorbachev and subsequently the newly established Russian state played full parts in the demilitarization process which followed the end of the Cold War and in building up mutual trust between former adversaries. Despite the extraordinary complications in the security situation brought about by the collapse of the Warsaw Pact[10] and the disintegration of the Soviet Union, the transition was made from implacable military confrontation to a much higher level of stability based on negotiated agreements.

Russia and demilitarization in Europe: conventional arms

Latent divisions between the more conciliatory foreign policy élite and the defence establishment in Moscow lay behind a number of disputes surrounding the CFE Treaty process in the late Soviet period. Western policy-makers feared that the 'window of opportunity' provided by Gorbachev's initiatives was about to close as the problems stemming from *perestroika* began to mount, and thus 'the dominant military objective of the talks [for the West] became the placement of binding limits on the size of the Soviet military' rather than Europe-wide stability based on reduced force levels.[11] Disagreements arose over data declared by both sides, and NATO voiced concern about the removal of large quantities of Soviet TLE beyond the Urals (out of the ATTU region) and the transfer of three Soviet motorized rifle divisions into force units not covered by the CFE Treaty. Although compromises were reached, the impression remained that by trying to circumvent certain technical provisions of the Treaty, the Soviet military was not acting in the spirit of the political relationship built up in the previous three to four years. Instead, it was pursuing what it perceived as immediate and important security interests which had been jeopardized by Gorbachev's diplomacy.

While the dissolution of the Warsaw Pact complicated but ultimately did not derail the arms control process and the broader trend toward demilitarization, the emergence of independent sovereign states in place of the Soviet Union necessitated a radical reassessment by defence planners in Moscow of the balance of forces and its implications for national security. Loss of territory and strategic installations and reductions in troop levels have been compounded by a failure to establish any kind of far-reaching military cooperation within the Commonwealth of Independent States (CIS). Russia, moreover, in meeting its defence requirements has also had to cope with profound economic difficulties which have hit both the armed forces and the military-industrial complex. All this has thrown up a number of challenges involving Russia to arms control implementation and verification.

The reluctance of the Russian military leadership to accept the creation of independent armies in the Soviet successor states and to relinquish control over forces there led to concerns during 1992 that ratification of the CFE Treaty would be delayed. Pressure was, however, placed on Moscow to accept a division of entitlements within the former Soviet zone of application. Despite its initial opposition, a desire to stabilize force levels in the former Soviet Union finally prompted Russia to give way. At a summit of the CIS in May 1992 the 'Tashkent Document' was signed. This divided Soviet entitlements into new national ceilings to be held by the successor states within the ATTU region. These provisions included Russia, Ukraine, Belarus, Moldova and the three Transcaucasian states of Armenia, Azerbaijan and Georgia, but did not impinge upon the Baltic states who had previously declared that they would not be associated with CFE obligations first entered into by the Soviet Union.[12] This re-allocation, in turn, paved the way for Russia's ratification of the CFE Treaty itself in October 1992.

Geographical considerations have, however, meant that implementing the Treaty has become a contentious issue. The north Caucasus military district (MD) in the south of Russia (relatively unimportant in the Soviet period) has become a vital front-line district in an unsettled region. Russia's Leningrad MD, meanwhile, borders on the now independent Baltic states which desire to join NATO. The Russian military thus believes it has a sound case for disputing the special 'flank' ceilings agreed in the CFE Treaty and proposals to modify them were made by Russia as early as 1993. Four major reasons for amending the flank provisions were forwarded. First, the Treaty was agreed when the Soviet Union possessed unified and powerful armed forces in a stable region, a situation which had changed radically. Second, conflicts in the Transcaucasus and the threat of separatism in Russia's own north Caucasus region required a substantial Russian military presence, with possibly more armaments than permitted under CFE limits, to ensure the country's security and integrity. Third, preservation of existing flank limits hampered redistribution of Russian forces from an east–west to a north–south orientation better suited to Russia's new security environment. Fourth, amendments were seen as necessary in order to accommodate TLE re-allocated to Russia as part of the former Soviet army's withdrawal from ECE. Russian proposals on these grounds, however, met with resistance from most states party to the Treaty, who feared that they would encourage larger revisions, which could, in turn, threaten the Treaty as a whole. Those with most to fear from flank limit increases, Turkey and Norway, mounted stiff opposition to the initiative.[13]

As noted, Russia's Caucasus region presents a major problem to the implementation and proper verification of the CFE Treaty. Even prior to the conflict in Chechnya, Russia had demonstrated its resolve to build up its forces in the area.[14] As the conflict progressed after 1994 it became clear that Russia would be unable to comply with CFE Treaty provisions by the compliance deadline of November 1995. Moreover, alleged movements of military hardware into and within the wider Transcaucasus region (partly resulting from illegal transfers from military bases, some in Russia) has made reliable counting of items difficult. Tension between Azerbaijan and Armenia, both signatories to the CFE Treaty but both failing to comply with its provisions, has spilled over into mutual accusations of exceeding TLE levels.[15] While this does not amount to a direct large-scale threat to the stability of the ATTU region, the potential effect of relatively small changes of force structures and capabilities on regional balances of power is a security issue which Russia – and indeed the larger European security community – must address.

By the November 1995 deadline, Russia had met aggregate limits on its forces but not the CFE flank ceilings.[16] The 'Flank Document', which NATO and Russia had agreed to negotiate at the first CFE Treaty Review Conference in May 1996 entered into force in May 1997. This brought into effect new higher ceilings on Russian tanks, armoured combat vehicles (ACVs) and heavy artillery deployed or stored in now revised flank zones. The document reduced the size of the flank zones by moving the Volgograd, Astrakhan and part of the Rostov region in the North Caucasus MD and the Pskov region in the Leningrad MD to the CFE rear zone without changing the limits on pieces of ground equipment fixed for the redefined flank zones. This revision has allowed Russia to deploy a greater concentration of weapons and has had the effect of raising the ceilings in the area covered by the original flank zones (although individual limits were placed on ACVs in the four regions mentioned and Russia agreed, in return, to provide more information about its flank holdings and accept additional site inspections in the excluded regions). Russia was given until 31 May 1999 to comply with the new flank limits.[17]

Nevertheless, concerns remain among neighbouring countries, notably Azerbaijan, Georgia, Moldova, Ukraine (the 'GUAM' group) and the three Baltic states, that the flank agreement favours Russia to the detriment of their own national security. In particular, the GUAM states have sought to ensure that Russia is not in a position to pressurize them to accept the stationing of troops or the redeployment of Russian TLE on their territory unless specifically requested. The Baltic states have also protested against the increased Russian military presence on the region's borders resulting from the new flank provisions.

The political context of the CFE Treaty negotiations also needs to be examined. At a time of turmoil and disunity in Russian foreign policy-making much of the western-oriented foreign policy pursued by Andrei Kozyrev came under increasing criticism as harmful to Russian national interests. Following his replacement by the pragmatic Yevgeni Primakov in January 1996 and subsequently by Igor Ivanov, a more independent and assertive policy has been pursued and, in spite of continuing bitter domestic political debates, more of a consensus has built up among foreign policy and defence officials and the Russian political establishment as a whole against further erosion of Russian military-political influence abroad. Even if this has not always been translated into cohesive policy, the more forthright assertion of Russian national interests has, since 1996, been a factor to be reckoned with.

Against this background, the link between NATO enlargement and the CFE Treaty has prompted heated discussion. The 1995 NATO 'Study on Enlargement' noted that 'NATO as such is not a signatory of the CFE Treaty [. . .]. Therefore, from a legal point of view, NATO's enlargement per se has no impact on the Treaty [. . .] possible implications of NATO's enlargement for the CFE Treaty can only be assessed when the actual enlargement is taking place'.[18] Moscow has, however, argued that the Treaty should be reconsidered in the light of the invitations extended to the Czech Republic, Poland and Hungary to join NATO in 1999. It has also attempted to limit the effect of NATO enlargement through a series of proposals for treaty adaptation.

Russian proposals have insisted that the new NATO countries' entitlements be absorbed into present NATO's aggregate allotments and that substantial combat forces should not be deployed near Russia's borders.[19] Russia has also sought some kind of compromise arrangement that corresponds to NATO's pledge in the 1997 NATO–Russia Founding Act to carry out collective defence operations by means that avoid the 'additional permanent stationing of substantial combat forces' in ECE other than in the event of a threat of aggression, for peacekeeping or for other purposes consistent with the CFE treaty. The Act (section IV) committed Russia and NATO to negotiate a CFE adaptation agreement and to work towards establishing lower TLE levels.[20] The imprecise definition of 'substantial combat forces', however, and the restrictions on NATO's flexibility in combat operations which Russian proposals would have involved constituted a delicate military-political matter for further negotiations. Russia's security concerns were also reflected in its calls for the strengthening of CSBMs in the sphere of naval and coalition military activities.

With a view to reassuring Russia that enlargement would not entail a destabilizing eastward shift in its military capabilities, NATO tabled a number of proposals in February 1997. These included, first, replacing the group (bloc) and zonal structure of the Treaty with a system of national (what a state party may hold) and territorial (what may be stationed on the territory of a state party) equipment limits and guaranteeing that aggregate ground TLE levels of its then 16 members would be lower than existing group ceilings. Second, introducing a new zone of stability in ECE (covering Poland, Hungary, the Czech Republic, Belarus, Slovakia, the Russian region of Kaliningrad and Ukrainian territory outside the flank zone) in which territorial ceilings would be no higher than current national entitlements, with temporary exceptions in certain cases. And third, altering the Treaty provision by which an increase in one state party's entitlement is to be offset by a corresponding reduction by other parties in the same group in favour of a situation whereby redistribution of TLE allocations is to be agreed between the parties involved.[21]

The Russian Foreign Ministry welcomed the initiative while stating that it did not fully meet Russian concerns about the impact of enlargement. It responded by agreeing to the abolition of the former group (bloc) and zone structure but proposed to retain aggregate ceilings for 'a particular military alliance' (i.e. NATO), to prohibit the stationing of foreign TLE not stationed at the CFE compliance deadline of November 1995 (something that would preclude NATO stationing military equipment in new member states), and to revise the existing mechanism of regional limitations to provide a better solution to the flank problem.[22] A senior Russian defence official has argued that the Flank Document of May 1996 'cannot be mechanically projected into the Treaty's new territorial structure [. . .] the inclusion of revised flank arrangements in an adapted Treaty is the issue which will test the worth of political assurances of genuinely partner relations between parties to the Treaty. We regard attempts to leave the previous arrangements intact as the old view of Russia as a threat.'[23]

Despite these differences, agreement was reached in July 1997 on an interim document entitled 'Certain Basic Elements for Treaty Adaptation' after talks involving all 30 CFE states' parties. The document established several general principles: levels of armaments deployable in the ATTU region as a whole would be lower than in the original CFE treaty provisions; group (bloc) entitlements would be abolished in favour of national and territorial ceilings (Moscow's caveat on an aggregate limit for NATO was rejected); and states would be permitted to station foreign TLE subject to territorial ceilings. The new national ceilings, which would not exceed the levels permitted by the original Treaty, would be codified as binding limits and reviewed every five years at periodic review conferences. The Flank regime would be maintained but reconciled with any adapted Treaty. To guard against destabilizing accumulations of forces, territorial ceilings would be established covering both national and stationed TLE within individual states parties and temporary deployments in excess of these territorial ceilings would be provided for only in specific instances.[24]

Substantial points of contention remained, however, including compliance issues between Russia and its neighbours, flank adaptation, the relationship between national and territorial ceilings, difficulties surrounding restrictions in the zone of stability, the stationing of NATO forces on new members' territories and technical issues of information exchange and verification. Subsequent negotiations in Vienna on a final agreement to amend the Treaty proceeded with some difficulty. However, a further preliminary agreement was reached in March 1999. This reiterated important aspects of the 1997 'Basic Elements' document (the use of national and territorial ceilings rather than bloc limits) and, as a concession to Russia, the Czech Republic, Hungary and Poland agreed to equipment entitlements lower than those under the 1990 Treaty. Compromises were also reached on the flank issue, the stationing of foreign TLE in the new NATO states and the stationing of Russian TLE in Kaliningrad and Pskov district (bordering Poland and Lithuania, and Estonia respectively).[25] A final adaptation agreement incorporating these provisions was due to be signed at a summit meeting of the Organization for Security and Cooperation in Europe (OSCE) in Europe in Istanbul in November 1999, although this was rendered that much more difficult by the Kosovo crisis earlier that year.[26]

Russia and demilitarization: nuclear weapons

Since the late 1980s considerable progress has been made on nuclear arms control. A reduction of 80 per cent of NATO's TNW arsenal has been effected, while all former Soviet TNWs deployed in ECE and the Soviet successor states were transferred to Russia by mid-1992. The denuclearization of Ukraine, Belarus and Kazakhstan, involving the removal of strategic nuclear warheads, was completed by the end of 1996. These and other developments – reductions in strategic nuclear missiles effected or envisaged by the two START treaties,[27] measures to 'dealert' US and Russian nuclear strike forces and commensurate responses by the European nuclear powers of France and the United Kingdom (UK), and assistance provided to Russia for the dismantling and storage of nuclear warheads and for non-proliferation purposes – have contributed to a significant reduction in nuclear tension in Europe.

Yet many issues remain to be resolved. Russia's non-strategic nuclear capability remains substantial. Authoritative sources estimate that as of early 1998, apart from its strategic holdings (6240 warheads in strategic forces), around 4000 TNW remained operational together with approximately 12 000 nuclear warheads overall in reserve or awaiting dismantling.[28] Moscow, for its part, has been concerned – despite the assurances written into the NATO–Russia Founding Act – about the future possibility of NATO siting nuclear infrastructure on the territory of new member states, as well as over US capability in nuclear-armed sea-launched cruise missiles.[29]

These concerns stem, in part, from changes in Russia's geopolitical situation and from its altered strategic requirements. The main focus of Moscow's immediate security concerns has during the 1990s switched away from large-scale conflict to internal or local threats. Consequently, the need for a massive nuclear capability along Soviet lines has been rendered redundant. However, the role played by nuclear weapons in Russian defence policy more broadly is still seen as crucially important. The requirement remains, both for military and political reasons, to balance the US strategic nuclear capability as well as (in the absence of multilateral nuclear disarmament talks) the more modest inventories of the UK, France and China. There is also concern – graphically demonstrated by the nuclear tests on the Indian sub-continent in summer 1998 – over the potential emergence of new nuclear powers in regions close to Russia's borders. Finally, there is a possible future need for nuclear weapons in deterring a large-scale conventional attack, in view of the loss of buffer zones formerly provided by Soviet republics and Warsaw Pact allies and the deterioration in Russia's conventional capabilities, particularly compared with those enjoyed by NATO.[30]

The implications for demilitarization in Europe are important, particularly in view of the removal of the Soviet commitment of 'no first use' of nuclear weapons in the 1993 Russian military doctrine.[31] A situation has arisen whereby there is a plausible argument that the defence of

Russia, pending far-reaching reform of the armed forces to provide flexible and well-equipped conventional forces, depends primarily upon nuclear deterrence. With the reductions in NATO's nuclear stockpile since 1991, Russia has come to possess overwhelming superiority in TNW above and beyond its still formidable strategic nuclear forces. The rationale for Russia's retention of these weapons is clear. One authoritative commentator has argued that:

> as NATO expands eastward, the imbalance of [conventional] forces will grow [to Russia's disadvantage] up to a ratio of approximately 4:1. In this respect Russia now faces the very important question of how to devaluate this imbalance. Given the geopolitical and economic status of Russia, as long as an effective system of collective security is lacking, Moscow will be bound to ensure its security, sovereignty, and territorial integrity by having nuclear weapons, particularly TNW. Highly cost-effective, TNW can serve as an equalizer of forces, stripping NATO of its military superiority. Under current circumstances, Russia can borrow NATO's recent theory of the necessity to compensate for Soviet predominance in conventional weapons by means of the US TNW arsenal in Europe. Here, history repeats itself, but in reverse [...] there is ample evidence that TNW have been given a role not only as deterrence weapons but also as a means to fend off aggression if deterrence fails.[32]

Other reports indicate that the Russian military has endorsed a decision to reverse stated obligations to reduce TNW in case Russia has to adopt military counter-measures against NATO enlargement.[33] In this connection, in April 1999 Yeltsin endorsed a document entitled 'Main Provisions of Russia's Nuclear Defence Policy'. This specifically highlighted the importance of TNWs and provided for their use in situations involving conventional weapons' attacks upon Russia. It was seemingly not a coincidence that the document was considered shortly after the entry of the three ECE states into NATO and the adoption by the Alliance of its new 'Strategic Concept' (see Chapter 3).[34]

Since the geopolitical and economic status of Russia is unlikely to change much in the foreseeable future, the question must be asked whether the retention of a robust tactical nuclear deterrent will remain part of Russian defence strategy in the long term and what effect this will have on European security. While there is no evidence to suggest the deployment of new Russian TNW at present – economic realities mean that Russia is likely to concentrate on its existing TNW and strategic forces – there have been recent reports of the completion of a new tactical missile system due to be commissioned in 1999.[35] Pressure is still being placed on Russia to reduce further its TNW stockpile and the issue has been placed on the agenda of the NATO–Russia Permanent Joint Council (PJC).[36] Progress, however, has been minimal here.

Debate over the finer points of nuclear doctrine is likely to continue for some time, even if the tension engendered by NATO enlargement abates and despite the question-mark placed by several prominent analysts over the utility of nuclear arms to combat a conventional attack. Certainly, mainstream opinion in Russia is that total nuclear disarmament is at present undesirable and unfeasible and thus the immediate task is to ensure the operation of deterrence. Proposals for a nuclear weapons-free zone in ECE have surfaced in Russian debates but do not appear to have had much practical consideration at the policy level.

Military reform in Russia

Russian military reform and the development of military doctrine are both crucial to the demilitarization process. While the new military-political situation in Europe has undoubtedly reduced the need for large-scale forces evidence points to the fact that, unlike the 'foreign policy-led' Strategic Defence Review in the UK, military reform in Russia has been determined as much by internal political, economic and social developments. A shift in emphasis in the defence debate from internationally oriented issues of military strategy and arms control to internal issues such as reducing the defence burden and reforming the armed forces had, in fact, already taken place under Gorbachev, and military reform remains a dominant theme in Russian defence debates. Russia's position on adapting the CFE Treaty and building upon other demilitarization initiatives will necessarily be influenced both by how defence planners in Moscow perceive future military-political developments in Europe and by the demands of military reform at home.

This domestic dimension, however, has been far from straightforward. Russian defence planners were for some time reluctant to accept reductions to 1.5 million personnel set by a September 1992 Law on Defence, despite a growing realization that high personnel levels place a massive strain on the economy. A strength in excess of 1.5 million would, in theory, allow the retention of the 1.45 million troops permitted by the CFE-1A agreement (the agreement only pertains to that part of Russia within the ATTU region). However, as one source points out, 'in practice such a large force could not easily be fitted into combat-capable military

Table 7.1   Military expenditure in the Soviet Union and Russia, 1987–98

	Total military expenditure (bn. current Rubles)	Total military exp. as % of	
		Total budget	GNP/GDP
USSR			
1987	137.3	31.9	16.6
1988	138.3	30.1	15.8
1989	133.7	27.7	14.2
1990	123.4	24.0	12.3
Russia			
1992	1 049	17.6	5.5
1993	9 037	15.7	5.3
1994	35 409	15.1	5.8
1995	60 542	11.3	3.7
1996	82 310	10.7	3.7
1997	93 647	–	3.6
1998 (budget)	79 100		

Sources: 1987–96 – J. M. Cooper, 'The Military Expenditure of the USSR and the Russian Federation, 1987–97', *SIPRI Yearbook 1998. Armaments, Disarmament and International Security* (Oxford: Oxford University Press/Frösunda, Sweden: Stockholm International Peace Research Institute, 1998), p. 258; 1997–98 – data communicated to the OSCE. Total military expenditure figure includes spending on paramilitary forces.

structures and [...] implie[s] a longer-term presence and a slower reduction plan – or a freezing of such reductions – in regions such as the Kaliningrad enclave'.[37] Attempts to maintain a large number of troops while retaining a measure of parity with former adversaries in conventional and nuclear weaponry also meant spending over 15 per cent of the federal budget, equating to well over 5 per cent of gross domestic product (GDP), on military expenditure in 1992–94 (see Table 7.1). These figures come from an authoritative western source calculated from available data. In fact, some Russian analysts have estimated real defence spending at 20 per cent of the federal budget or 6–7 per cent of GDP as the Defence Ministry accumulated substantial debts and effectively ignored the ceilings on spending stipulated in the budget. There were, in fact, clear reasons for continuing high levels of expenditure, not least the redeployment of troops from abroad after 1991 and the execution of the military campaign in Chechnya. However, in GDP terms, spending of this order was far higher than in developed western countries and was clearly unsustainable as the economy came under pressure.

Recent studies by leading policy analysts have attempted a more realistic appraisal of Russia's military prospects based on a sober analysis of realistic security requirements and economic capabilities.[38] Such studies have, generally speaking, concluded that since 1991 the widening gap between the shrinking economic base and federal budget and the inflated structure of the armed forces – reduced in size but retaining the basic features of the armed forces supported by the larger Soviet economy and budget – must be closed and sustainable force levels established. In fact figures from 1995 onwards (see Table 7.1) suggest that the struggle waged by the military for higher levels of defence spending has already been lost and that more realistic levels have been imposed. As of mid-1999 there was no indication that NATO action in Kosovo had prompted any reversal of this trend.

Despite the absence at the time of writing of a formally adopted new military doctrine to replace that drawn up in 1993, the programme of reform of the Russian armed forces launched in the summer of 1997 and a document on military development (*voennoe stroitel'stvo*) drawn up by the Russian government in August 1998 reflect much of the current official thinking on Russia's strategic position and tackle some of the main problems outlined above.[39] Russia's geostrategic position – in particular, its long land borders, growing threats posed by terrorism, extremism and national separatism, instability in regions adjacent to Russian territory, and the enlargement of NATO and the development of its military capabilities – are key factors which defence planners have in view. They have concluded that large-scale military aggression against Russia is unlikely in the foreseeable future but that the likelihood of regional wars and conflicts is quite high. The latter poses a potential threat to Russia, especially if the military-political and economic situation inside the country deteriorates further. Existing and potential threats are to be repulsed through measures designed, on the one hand, to deepen integration within the CIS and to develop partnership relations with leading regional powers (the political response) and, on the other, to maintain the readiness of the armed forces, including its nuclear arm (the military response). The aim of the military reform is to rationalize and create well-equipped, combat-ready and mobile armed forces, eventually leading to a three-branch (land, air-space and naval forces) structure capable of effective deterrence against aggression. It also aims to strengthen the officer corps, to establish a sound legal framework for military development, and to boost morale in, and political support for, the military. Ultimately the creation of a fully professional army is envisaged, although this is not likely to happen for at least 25 years.

In pursuit of these goals the main reform measures to be carried out are seen as follows: in the period 1997–2000 – a merging of the Strategic

Missile Forces, the Military Space Forces and the Missile Space Defence troops into a single force; a reform of the Land Forces and the creation of ten full-strength, combat-ready divisions including one specially designed for peacekeeping operations; the establishment of operational strategic commands on a territorial basis in six (reduced from eight) military districts; a reduction of the numerical levels of the armed forces to 1.2 million personnel; a merging and rationalization of the air defence troops and the air force; and the retention of the structure of the navy albeit making it more compact and narrowing the range of its tasks. An additional measure is to disband or rationalize a number of the armed paramilitary organizations not subordinate to the Defence Ministry and to reduce their personnel levels.[40] Detailed data on the hardware in the possession of these paramilitary forces (which, incidentally, are not covered by the CFE Treaty) are lacking, but it may be that in view of their extensive nature it is difficult to talk of a real demilitarization in Russia. As such, this reflects the nature of Russia's security environment (as outlined in the 1997 Russian National Security Concept) whereby internal security threats are perceived as the most pressing.[41]

In the period 2001–2005, it is envisaged that the transition to a three-branch structure will be completed and far-reaching qualitative improvements in the armed forces effected, including the delivery of new, modern weapons systems. Thoroughgoing re-equipping of the armed forces is planned from 2010–15 with completion by the year 2025. This last objective is particularly controversial. Major changes in methods of warfare expected in the first quarter of the next century, perhaps constituting a 'revolution in military affairs', will require leading powers both to make organizational changes and to develop and exploit new technologies to maintain their position, involving a restructuring of defence industries.[42] The problems faced by all governments in determining the scale of effort for, and allocating resources to, military security are even more acute in contemporary Russia. If recent prognoses concerning the development of the Russian economy over the next 20 years or so are accurate, large-scale rearmament of the Russian armed forces with the most modern conventional weapons and command and control equipment will be unrealistic in the short to medium term unless there is a drastic shift in the country's priorities or the introduction of large-scale burden-sharing collaboration with western defence industries. Priority seems likely to be accorded to strategic nuclear forces and selected other items, such as fighter aircraft. More extensive re-equipping is possible in the long term only if the Russian economy makes a qualitative and quantitative leap forward, something that at present is far from assured.

Ultimately, a clear vision of Russia's role in the world and its political relations with key states is crucial in determining the scale of defence requirements and thus the success of military reform. Since the appearance in November 1993 of the 'Main Provisions of the Russian Military Doctrine', defence planners have struggled to develop a coherent concept of Russia's defence requirements based on an assessment of international political relations, economic indicators, military-technical capabilities and, indeed, social factors. The last of these – rarely considered in traditional 'strategic' studies – has received a huge amount of attention in Russian domestic politics. Concerns of Soviet military leaders in the late 1980s that cuts in forces might leave officers 'literally in the street'[43] anticipated what has become a massive social and psychological upheaval for the country's armed forces. The rapid deterioration in traditional discipline and morale is the result both of a lack of reform and of the changing weight of military factors in Russian society. Allied to poor provisioning and recruitment, it has resulted in a situation whereby the combat readiness of the Russian armed forces has been under serious threat.

It is in this sphere that debate in Russia has raged most fiercely and where a weak Russian government has largely failed to formulate priorities which satisfy substantial sections of élite opinion.[44] There has been much criticism of a reform which, apart from maintaining the strategic nuclear deterrent to counter large-scale aggression, appears to reduce the tasks of the armed forces to dealing with local conflicts and carrying out peacekeeping operations. There are influential voices who think that this constitutes too narrow a view of Russia's role and that its geostrategic position, the diversity of potential threats in the longer term and the safeguarding of national state interests, demand a far greater military presence – in effect, the capability of force projection.

Russia and the current military-political situation in Europe

Much has been achieved in the military-political sphere since the process of demilitarization in Europe started to gather pace a decade or so ago. Capabilities for initiating large-scale surprise offensive actions with conventional forces have, broadly speaking, been eliminated and do not enter into likely military-political scenarios. Furthermore, although the establishment of a stable balance of forces was rendered difficult to achieve by the twin break-up of the Warsaw Pact and the Soviet Union and consequent changes in the European security map, lower force levels have contributed to a sense of greater security between Russia and the major European states.

This altered situation is reflected in the establishment of a 'Framework for Arms Control' under the auspices of the OSCE and described in its 1996 'Lisbon Document'. As the latter makes clear, however, many vital challenges and risks in the field of military security remain to be addressed. Several of these reflect Russia's most immediate security concerns: military imbalances that may contribute to instability, inter-state tensions and conflicts (particularly in border areas), internal disputes which may escalate into military tension between states, enhancing transparency regarding the military intentions of states, ensuring democratic political control of military and security forces, and ensuring that the evolution of multinational military and political organizations is compatible with the OSCE's comprehensive and cooperative concept of security and with arms control objectives.[45]

The widening of military disparities is also a cause of concern for Moscow. NATO has far greater resources available to carry out force modernization and qualitative improvements in military capabilities, something not yet covered by the CFE Treaty. The Alliance's ability to carry out sustained offensive operations out-of-area using a range of the most modern capabilities (conventional, nuclear and new information processing and communications technologies) has – particularly given unease over NATO's new missions – also unnerved Russian defence planners.[46] A Russian defence official recently expressed the military establishment's concern over the rapid development of US combat technology suggesting that 'we are trying to talk about European security in terms of the fourth or even third generation weapons systems with which we are armed. [However t]here has been a shift in the basic concepts of predictable security which existed before. In the new situation we can not calculate within a framework of units of armaments or of standard schemes of reckoning the strategic balance.'[47] Numerous articles in the Russian press dealing with military issues have also focused on NATO military activities in areas close to Russian territory, including Ukraine, with the implication that these pose a threat to Russia's national security. The application of NATO military power in areas further removed from Russia has also generated suspicion and resentment in Moscow, as comments on air-strikes against Serbia/Yugoslavia have attested (see Chapter 8).

There may well be a considerable element of bias and misperception in Russian attitudes, but these attitudes nevertheless exist and remain to be addressed. Verification measures, which provide information about intentions as well as capabilities, allied to mechanisms designed to promote cooperation and coordination of activities in the military sphere, including those outside of arms control processes, are, therefore, crucial. Valid security considerations in both Russia and among NATO states mean that there are inevitable limitations on transparency, particularly where operational measures to tackle crisis situations are concerned, but military-political relations can only proceed if both sides aim at transparency in the defence planning process and cooperation in crisis management. The breakthroughs in arms control, which effectively sealed the end of the Cold War, were dramatic but building confidence remains an inherently incremental process and requires constant attention. The development of CSBMs among parties to conflicts (as in their sub-regional application in Bosnia) can be seen, in this light, as an important element of further demilitarization.

The role of arms control has not ended, but it has to be seen within the wider context of military-political, and to an extent social and economic, developments on the European stage. This is reflected in the Founding Act, which, for all the current difficulties in Russian–NATO relations, recognizes the military-political tasks faced by the signatories. Primakov's insistence in July 1998 that the CFE Treaty be discussed within the NATO–Russia PJC parallel to negotiations in Vienna[48] emphasizes that CFE is not just part of the 'technical' arms control agenda but is central to political relations between the major powers.

Whether the relatively stable situation created by the CFE Treaty persists will, to a considerable degree, depend on developments in regions bordering Russia and the security problems these pose for Moscow. Former Russian Prime Minister Viktor Chernomyrdin made an explicit link between security in the Baltic region and NATO enlargement in proposing Russian security guarantees for the Baltic states while leaving them outside of the Alliance.[49] In announcing cuts in forces in Russia's northwest region in December 1997 Yeltsin echoed these proposals and talked of 'going beyond the boundaries defined by the Vienna document [CFE Treaty]'.[50] The reductions outlined by Yeltsin have reportedly since been completed.[51] Clearly there are prospects for some kind of regional security initiative in the Baltics.

The greater immediate threat to Russia's security lies to the south. Continuing instability in Nagorno-Karabakh (Azerbaijan) and the conflicts in Georgia require urgent political solutions as well as additional measures for transparency in armaments and military equipment. Whether Russia will play a longer-term active military role in the successor states, particularly in Armenia and Georgia, and what form this role will take is uncertain. The difficulties involved have been well documented in reports from the area.[52] The fact that Russian forces are not properly equipped, either in the technical or the psychological sense, to deal with peacekeeping tasks, where a mix of low-intensity combat and policing functions are needed, is generally accepted.[53] The creation of greater concentrations of combat units in the North Caucasus creates an ambiguous situation in which a rapid reaction peacekeeping force has to deter threats pending the deployment of larger forces, which themselves might also be used for 'peacekeeping' purposes.[54]

Conclusions

The process of demilitarization that followed the end of the Cold War has had, above and beyond a reduction in military forces and the disengagement of two hostile alliances, a positive effect on the European strategic environment. There are certainly grounds for optimism in that this process has happened in spite of the strategic disadvantages which Russia has faced as a result of the imbalance in conventional forces and the cardinal political shifts in Europe after 1989. While it would be premature to claim that 'a Eurasian–Atlantic security community has been formed that would institutionalize joint management of the military aspects of the transition from the Cold War to a new world order',[55] its prerequisites – in the form of an arms control framework and multiple fora for dialogue – have been established. Furthermore, compromises reached over revisions to the CFE Treaty, allied to reductions in NATO's tactical nuclear forces have at least partially assuaged Russian concerns over vulnerability in the European theatre. Even in the case of the Open Skies Treaty, not yet ratified by Moscow due to the unequal burden it imposes, Russia has participated on an informal basis.[56] Furthermore, as the demilitarization process develops, routine and closer contacts between Russian defence experts and their counterparts in the West could potentially make an important contribution to overcoming differences in perception.

Nevertheless, disagreements which still remain on specific points of the CFE Treaty, the gaps in control over TNWs, the growing disparity between Russian and NATO operational capabilities, and the new security risks which Russia faces have all meant that demilitarization and the security-building process in Europe are far from secure. This is particularly so at a time when the problems posed by tumultuous social and economic change in Russia are absorbing much of the attention of the political leadership, engendering a bitter domestic political debate, something that is having an uneven effect upon foreign policy. It remains to be seen whether even an amended CFE Treaty is flexible enough to accommodate these new challenges. Much work also remains to be done to reconcile divergent views on nuclear issues and establish a formal framework for a warhead-transparency regime.[57]

Perfecting mechanisms to address military-political issues is a necessary starting-point. Particularly with the first wave of NATO enlargement and CFE Treaty revision negotiations taking place, there has been a need for a period of consolidation in which CSBMs can flourish and engender greater transparency so that Russian security relations with Europe can develop into a genuine partnership. The danger exists that further NATO enlargement will encourage a zero-sum mentality. Even though Russia is at present scarcely capable of rebuilding a conventional force which might threaten Europe, the limited trust and confidence built up over the last decade could still be undermined. Russia's political interests in cooperating with its Euro-Atlantic partners have to be seen against the strategic uncertainties posed by its degraded armed forces in a potentially unstable environment. As J. Steinbrunner has suggested, '[a] coherently planned reduction [in Russian force levels] will not be undertaken if those who are doing it believe the consequence is indefinite exposure to [an] unmanageable external threat. Systematic reassurance of the sort that Russia requires is not an adversarial process and in that sense it is fundamentally different from the traditional practice of arms control which was designed to constrain a continuing confrontation.'[58]

At present there is still sufficient flexible and progressive thinking on both sides to avoid stalling progress on military-political cooperation, but constant attention must be paid not only to the technical aspects of arms control but also to broader political relations among the European powers. It may be the case that arms control agreements can only be properly reviewed once greater clarity emerges with regard to Russian military doctrine and force structure planning, and the full implications of NATO's new missions and strategic concept become clear.

A final word returns us to the starting-point of this chapter. For the Gorbachev leadership conventional arms reductions had two main functions: first, to free resources for economic development, and second, to undercut western threat perceptions through a reorientation of Soviet military doctrine.[59] The strategic threat from Russia is perceived in Europe to have diminished and the security dilemma has become less acute. However, the perception among many Russians is that a loss of military-political weight over the last decade and a growing economic dependence on the West represents a danger to national security. The array of different threats which has emerged and which a weak Russian state is poorly equipped to manage has made further progress on arms control problematic. Certainly, Russian policy in the demilitarization sphere is still vulnerable to domestic pressures. Identifying and understanding the ambitions and concerns of new Russian political and security élites remains a major task for western scholars and policy-makers.

Notes

1. S. Koulik and R. Kokoski, *Conventional Arms Control: Perspectives on Verification* (Oxford: Oxford University Press, 1994) p. 211. This source reproduces the CFE Treaty in full.
2. B. Buzan, *People, States and Fear*, 2nd edn. (Hemel Hempstead: Harvester Wheatsheaf, 1991) p. 166.
3. Koulik and Kokoski, *op. cit.*, p. 90.
4. R. A. Falkenrath, *Shaping Europe's Military Order: the Origins and Consequences of the CFE Treaty* (Cambridge, Mass.: MIT Press, CSIA Studies in International Security, No. 6, 1995), p. 29.
5. A. R. Collins, 'GRIT, Gorbachev and the End of the Cold War', *Review of International Studies*, Vol. 24, No. 2, 1998, pp. 209–12.
6. See M. MccGwire, *Perestroika and Soviet National Security* (Washington D.C.: Brookings Institution, 1991) pp. 164–5, 312, 325–6; Falkenrath, *op. cit.*, pp. 41–2; G. Snel, '"A (More) Defensive Strategy": the Reconceptualisation of Soviet Conventional Strategy in the 1980s', *Europe-Asia Studies*, Vol. 50, No. 2, 1998, pp. 205–39.
7. In fact, the Soviet Union eventually accepted ceilings on artillery pieces and tanks in spite of objections by its military. See Falkenrath, *op. cit.*, p. 100.
8. Koulik and Kokoski, *op. cit.*, p. 150.
9. For details see R. Fieldhouse, R. S. Norris and W. M. Arkin, 'Nuclear Weapon Developments and Unilateral Reduction Initiatives', *SIPRI Yearbook 1992: Armaments, Disarmament and International Security* (Oxford: Oxford University Press/Frösunda, Sweden, Stockholm International Peace Research Institute, 1992), pp. 71–3. Yeltsin announced that Russia would destroy nuclear warheads for tactical ground-launched systems (and not produce new warheads to replace them) and eliminate up to a third of its tactical sea-launched and half of its air-launched and anti-aircraft missiles warheads.
10. The Warsaw Pact was formally dissolved in July 1991 but had been in terminal decline since 1989 following demands in Hungary and the then Czechoslavakia for the removal of Soviet troops, the assertion across ECE of full command of national armies and the relinquishing of a unified military doctrine.
11. Falkenrath, *op. cit.*, p. 117.
12. *The Military Balance, 1992–1993* (London: The International Institute of Strategic Studies/Brassey's, 1992), pp. 237–41.
13. Koulik and Kokoski, *op. cit.*, pp. 120–1; Falkenrath, *op. cit.*, pp. 92–5.

14. See R. Allison, 'The Russian Armed Forces: Structures, Roles and Policies', in V. Baranovsky (ed.), *Russia and Europe: the Emerging Security Agenda* (Oxford: Oxford University Press/Frösunda, Sweden: Stockholm International Peace Research Institute, 1997), pp. 188–9.

15. BBC, Summary of World Broadcasts (henceforth SWB), 4 August 1997, p. F/2; Z. Lachowski, 'Conventional Arms Control', *SIPRI Yearbook 1998: Armaments, Disarmaments and International Security* (Oxford: Oxford University Press/Frösunda, Sweden: Stockholm International Peace Research Institute, 1998), pp. 503–4.

16. Due primarily to the lack of necessary funding and cannibalization of equipment, Russian holdings of major conventional weapons in Europe were, in fact, by 1996 lower than the ceilings permitted by the CFE Treaty (5 per cent lower for artillery pieces, 14 per cent for ACVs and attack helicopters and 15 per cent for tanks) and shortages of manpower meant that Russian forces were 44 per cent below levels stipulated by the CFE-1A agreement. See S. Rogov, *Military Reform and the Defense Budget of the Russian Federation* (Alexandria, Virginia: Centre for Naval Analyses, August 1997), p. 44. Numerous other sources have described the 'involuntary demilitarization' of Russia due to underfinancing and the poor quality of the draft. See V. Serebryannikov, 'Armies in a Changing World', *Svobodnaya mysl'*, No. 2, 1998, pp. 20–8; C. J. Dick, 'Past Cruelties Hinder the Taming of the Bear', *Jane's Intelligence Review*, December 1998, p. 5.

17. Z. Lachowski, 'Conventional Arms Control', *SIPRI Yearbook 1997: Armaments, Disarmament and International Security* (Oxford: Oxford University Press/Frösunda, Sweden: Stockholm International Peace Research Institute, 1997), pp. 476–9; S. Walkling, 'CFE "Flank" Accord Enters into Force – Senate Warns Russia on Deployments', *Arms Control Today*, May 1997, pp. 26–7; C. Bluth, 'Arms Control and Proliferation', in R. Allison and C. Bluth (eds.), *Security Dilemmas in Russia and Eurasia* (London: Royal Institute of International Affairs, 1998), p. 310.

18. *Study on NATO Enlargement*, September 1995, <http:www.nato.int/docu/basictxt/enl-9503.htm>, paragraph 21.

19. *Nezavisimaya gazeta*, 18 December 1997; SWB, 7 January 1999, p. B/10. For a detailed account of the issues involved see Yu. Fedorov, 'NATO Expansion and the "Modernisation" of the CFE Treaty', *Yadernyi kontrol'*, Nos. 28–9, 1998.

20. 'Founding Act on Mutual Relations, Cooperation and Security between NATO and the Russian Federation', *NATO Review*, Vol. 45, No. 4, 1997.

21. S. Walkling, 'NATO Presents Initial Proposal for Adaptation of CFE Treaty', *Arms Control Today*, March 1997, pp. 24–5.

22. Lachowski, 'Conventional Arms Control', *SIPRI Yearbook 1998, op. cit.*, p. 510.

23. V. Kuznetsov, 'Treaty on Conventional Forces in Europe. Reasons for its Revision and Problems Involved', *Military Parade*, November–December 1997, pp. 81–2; V. Kuznetsov, 'Difficult Decisions', *Nezavisimoe voennoe obozrenie*, No. 24, 1997, p. 1 (Kuznetsov was writing in his capacity as head of the Russian Defence Ministry International Treaty Directorate of the Main Directorate for International Military Cooperation).

24. *Kommersant-Daily*, 25 July 1997, p. 4; C. Hain-Cole, 'Taking up the Challenge of CFE Treaty Adaptation', *NATO Review*, Vol. 45, No. 6, 1997, pp. 16–19. The document is reprinted in full in *SIPRI Yearbook 1998, op. cit.*, pp. 541–3.

25. The Arms Control Association, Fact Sheet – April 1999, <http://www.arms-control.org/FACTS/cfe499.htm>; R. Eggleston, 'New Arms Agreement Aims to Ease Russian Fears', Radio Free Liberty/Radio Free Europe, *Newsline*, Endnote (newsline@list.rferl.org), 25 May 1999.
26. The conclusion of this agreement was, for a time, jeopardized by the Kosovo crisis. In early May, for instance, Defence Minister Igor Sergeyev suggested that Russia might reconsider the terms of the preliminary adaptation agreement. See *International Herald Tribune*, 5 May 1999.
27. START I was signed between the Soviet Union and the US in June 1991; START II was signed by Russia and the US in January 1993. Although START II has not been ratified by the Russian Duma, Presidents Yeltsin and Clinton have agreed (in March 1997 and June 1999) to authorize negotiations on a follow-on START III treaty. START I sets limits of 6000 strategic nuclear warheads, a limit which must be reached by December 2001. START II sets a subsequent and lower limit of 3500 strategic warheads. Under an agreement reached in September 1997, this limit has to be reached by 2007. In that START has been a largely bilateral Russian–American issue it is not treated in detail in this chapter.
28. The US had 7450 strategic and 970 non-strategic warheads operational and 3650 in reserve or awaiting dismantling at the same point in time. At the Helsinki summit in March 1997 Clinton and Yeltsin called for a forum to discuss measures related to TNW and sea-launched cruise missiles. S. Kile, 'Nuclear Arms Control', *SIPRI Yearbook 1998, op. cit.*, pp. 416, note 41 and 433, note 114.
29. See A. D'yakov, E. Myasnikov, 'A Way out of the Deadlock', *Nezavisimoe voennoe obozrenie*, No. 34, 1998, pp. 1, 4; *SWB*, 17 December 1998, pp. S/1–2.
30. For a summary of these arguments see chapters by S. Miller and J. W. R. Lepingwell in G. Quester (ed.), *The Nuclear Challenge in Russia and the New States of Eurasia* (New York: M. E. Sharpe, 1995).
31. 'Osnovnye polozheniye voennoy doktriny Russiskoy Federatsii', *Krasnaya zvezda*, 19 November 1993.
32. V. Belous, 'Key Aspects of the Russian Nuclear Strategy', *Security Dialogue*, Vol. 28, No. 2, 1997, p. 170.
33. N. Sokov, 'Tactical Nuclear Weapons Elimination: Next Step for Arms Control', *The Nonproliferation Review*, Winter 1997, p. 18.
34. *The Guardian*, 30 April 1999.
35. *SWB*, 24 November 1998, p. S1/1; Sokov, *op. cit.*, p. 18.
36. 'Ministerial Meeting of the Defence Planning Committee and the Nuclear Planning Group, Final Communiqué, Brussels, 11 June 1998', *NATO Review*, Vol. 46, No. 3, 1998, p. D13.
37. Allison, *op. cit.*, p. 172.
38. Rogov, *op. cit.*
39. *SWB*, 5 August 1997, pp. S1/1–2. For discussions of key points see I. Sergeev, 'Over the Next Eight Years Russia's Armed Forces will be Completely Reformed', *Nezavisimoe voennoe obozrenie*, No. 35, 1997, p. 1, 3; V. Solov'ev, 'Russia has Received a Detailed Conception of Military Reform' (Review of the 'Bases [Conception] of State Policy on Russia's Military Development in the Period to 2005'), *Nezavisimoe voennoe obozrenie*, No. 29, 1998, pp. 1, 3; V. L. Manilov, 'Military Reform: Parameters and Priorities', *Vooruzhenie, politika, konversiya*, Nos. 3–4, 1998, pp. 4–8.

40. Then Internal Affairs Minister, Sergei Stepashin was reported as stating that his personnel would be cut from 250 000 to 120 000. See *SWB*, 17 August 1998, p. S1/1.
41. *Diplomaticheskii vestnik*, No. 2, 1998, pp. 7–9.
42. See, for example, *The Strategic Defence Review* (London: The Stationery Office, 1998), pp. 54–6; W. Q. Bowen, 'New Technologies and Their Impact on Nuclear Policies' (Chilworth Manor Validation Meeting, No. 2, 5 June 1998), pp. 10–12.
43. C. Kennedy, 'The Soviet Union and CFE', in S. Croft (ed.), *The Conventional Armed Forces in Europe Treaty: the Cold War Endgame* (Aldershot, Vermont: Dartmouth Publishing Company, 1994), p. 48.
44. One source from early 1998 argued that 'the project for a conception of military development is falling apart before the public's very eyes [. . .] reform is being carried out by a small group of officials relying not on carefully checked calculations but on their personal feelings in this sphere [. . .] the aim of military reform should be determined by military doctrine – a conceptual state document. Everyone, including the Defence Minister, has forgotten about it.' V. Solov'ev, 'Secrecy of Military Reform Leads to Crisis', *Nezavisimoe voennoe obozrenie*, No. 4, 1998, p. 1.
45. *Lisbon Document 1996* (Lisbon: OSCE, 1996), pp. 16–17.
46. The contrast between combined NATO capabilities and those of Russia is clear when one compares the desultory Russian effort in Chechnya in 1994–96 with the force mobilized by the Alliance in its air campaign against Serbia/Yugoslavia in the spring of 1999.
47. 'European Security: Theory and Practice', *Mirovaya ekonomika i mezhdunarodnye otnosheniya*, No. 1, 1998, p. 63.
48. *SWB*, 10 July 1998, p. B/11.
49. Chernomyrdin suggested confidence- and stability-enhancing measures to a conference in Vilnius in September 1997. These included a 'hot line' between military commands in Kaliningrad and the Baltic states, reciprocal notification about military exercises taking place in the region, additional limits on exercises being carried out both on land and sea, arms control based on an adapted CFE Treaty, and common control of air space in the Baltics and wider adjacent territory. *Diplomaticheskii vestnik*, No. 10, 1997, pp. 10–11.
50. *SWB*, 4 December 1997 p. B/3.
51. *SWB*, 7 December 1998, p. B/15.
52. See for example A. Shaburkin, 'Between Two Lines of Fire', *Nezavisimoe voennoe obozrenie*, No. 32, 1998, p. 2.
53. M. J. Orr, 'The Russian Armed Forces as a Factor in Regional Stability' (Conflict Studies Research Centre, Sandhurst, Paper C99, June 1998) p. 7.
54. Allison, *op. cit.*, p. 188.
55. J. L. Twigg, 'Defence Planning: the Potential for Transparency and Cooperation', in J. E. Goodby and B. Morel, *The Limited Partnership: Building a Russian–US Security Community* (Oxford: Oxford University Press, 1993), p. 272.
56. Lachowski, 'Conventional Arms Control', *SIPRI Yearbook 1998, op. cit.*, p. 525.
57. One source notes that there are no ongoing negotiations over a warhead transparency regime which might address concerns over Russian TNW stockpiles and Russian worries over the US strategic redeployment potential,

as well as secrecy requirements and asymmetries in nuclear weapons pro-
duction. See 'Conclusions from the Russia–US Workshop on Warhead
Transparency' (Centre for Arms Control, Energy and Environmental Studies,
Moscow Institute of Physics and Technology, 9–10 November 1998),
<http://www.armscontrol.ru/start/publications/tr1198.htm>.

58. J. Steinbrunner, 'Can the United States Lead the World?', in K. Booth (ed.),
Statecraft and Security: the Cold War and Beyond (Cambridge: Cambridge University Press, 1998), p. 141.

59. Kennedy, *op. cit.*, pp. 42–3.

8
Russia and the Former Yugoslavia

Michael Andersen

Introduction

In line with the overall theme of this volume, the central question for this chapter is: has Russia cooperated with or confronted Europe and the West over the 'former Yugoslavia'?[1] This, in turn, has a wider contextual importance because, in a number of ways, the wars in that region represent a 'mini-cosmos' of European security both at present and in years to come. First of all, they constitute an important case of post-Cold War European security management – perhaps the most serious test of the so-called 'European security architecture' since the demise of the Soviet Union, and the emergence of Russia. These wars amount to a regrettable but nonetheless probably persistent threat to European stability; a threat premised not on nuclear exchanges or large-scale conventional warfare between states, but on 'low level', house-to-house ethnic cleansing, raping and pillaging. Secondly, issues surrounding the former Yugoslavia have generated a very heated political debate in Russia. The development of Russia's role in the region is thus a particularly good prism through which to examine Russia's new foreign policy and the formulation process behind it. Thirdly, a similar thing can be said about the West. In our part of the world, the debate about what to do in the former Yugoslavia has become a very important part of the wider debate about the future of the western Alliance – about means and modes of cooperating, about partners, dangers and dividing lines.[2]

As for the overall theme of this book – 'conflict or cooperation?' – the analysis in this chapter, focusing on Russian policy, suggests three conclusions. The good news is that there is no inherent reason why the issue of 'Yugoslavia' should lead to confrontation between Russia and Europe (and the West more generally). Despite the sometimes rather confrontational rhetoric from Moscow, cooperation with, or at least acceptance of, western policies, has been the dominant Russian behaviour. This will become apparent in the analysis below. Furthermore despite the much-hyped suggestion in Moscow as well as in the West, about a pan-Slavic 'special relationship' between Russia and Serbia, in the real world Russia has only very limited interests and even fewer resources to invest in the Balkans. The dominant pattern in the cases of both Bosnia and Kosovo was that of Russia condemning but ultimately following the western lead. Moscow's primary motive in both cases was to avoid exclusion from the decision-makers' table rather than any specific goals in Bosnia and Kosovo *per se*. As such, Russia wanted the United Nations (UN) and not the North Atlantic Treaty Organization (NATO) to be the primary organization of intervention, but was forced to compromise and tacitly cooperate with the Alliance when its greater influence upon events became manifest. This was complemented by a parallel policy of sympathy for Serbia and the Bosnian Serbs, but this should be understood as a means to an end: it was the only way in which a weakened Russia could create some distance from the West and thus claim to be playing an independent role on the international stage.

The potentially worrying news, however, is that issues surrounding the former Yugoslavia do have the potential to impact in a most serious way on wider relations between Moscow and the West. This has been particularly so when events there have aggravated an already vexed security agenda (hence the linkage in Moscow's eyes between NATO intervention in Bosnia and Kosovo and the Alliance's unilateral determination to manage wider European security affairs). However, there is also a positive side to this as shown by the day-to-day cooperation between Russian and NATO peacekeepers in, first, Bosnia following the 1995 Dayton Accord and, second (and to a lesser degree, admittedly), in Kosovo from June 1999.

The definitive bad news is that the complicated political dynamic affecting Russian involvement in the former Yugoslavia has been under-appreciated in Europe and the West. If stable, long-term Russian cooperation is indeed the aim of western policies, it must be said that too often policies, among the NATO states especially, have been counter-productive. In the former Yugoslavia, NATO has either excluded Russia or marginalized it, something which has led Moscow as a consequence to protest at or to oppose many European and American initiatives. In this connection it is interesting – and very worrying – to compare Russian–NATO relations during the wars in Bosnia and Kosovo, respectively. Two things spring to mind. Firstly, the chain of events in the two episodes is very similar. In both cases, Russian opposition to military intervention was followed by unilateral NATO actions, which, in turn, triggered highly strung Russian protests followed by a desperate search for a Russian role in the peace settlement. Secondly, it is also important to recognize that the compounded effect of disagreements over the former Yugoslavia has eroded the very basis of a truly pan-European security order and understanding which would include Russia.

In what follows, these themes will be elaborated. The chapter will first situate the issues provoked by Russian policy toward the former Yugoslavia in its wider context. It will then look at the central argument concerning the alleged special relationship between Russia and Serbia, before turning to analyse in some detail some of the main turning points of the wars in the region.

Much more than meets the eye: placing the debate about Russia and the former Yugoslavia in context

The debate about Russia's role in the former Yugoslavia is about much more than just whether Russia has taken a cooperative or confrontational approach *vis-à-vis* the West. In Moscow, Washington and European capitals, the question of Russia's role has, to a certain extent, been a surrogate debate: the immediate focus has been the former Yugoslavia, but in reality only as a component of a much wider-ranging set of issues.

In Russia, the issue of the former Yugoslavia has formed an important part of the broader debate on Russia's foreign policy and national interests. In the first half of the 1990s, two main schools of thought emerged in this connection. The first, dubbed the 'Slavophiles' (a group which overlapped to some degree with the 'Eurasianists') stressed the importance of Russia's long-standing links (ethnic, linguistic and cultural) with the Serbs. The second – the 'Atlanticists' – stressed, by contrast, the importance of good relations with the West, and cooperation with and integration into western institutions (see also Chapter 2). During this period, the question of Russia's role in the former Yugoslavia was quickly turned into a political football with personal overtones. Nationalists sympathetic to the Slavophile cause used the issue to criticize President Yeltsin and his reformist team in the domestic power struggle. Many of the attacks on Foreign Minister Andrei Kozyrev in particular, were highly personal in character as not a few of his most vocal critics were eyeing his job.[3] During Yeltsin's second term after 1996, the shape of the debate in Russia altered somewhat. The Atlanticists had, in effect, left the political stage and Yeltsin more firmly adopted a nationalist agenda. This shift did not, however, completely satisfy his more vocal critics. Influential groups such as the Communist Party of the Russian Federation, and contenders for presidential office such as the communist leader Gennadi Zyuganov, the mayor of Moscow Yuri Luzhkov and the governor of Krasnoyarsk (and erstwhile Secretary of the Security Council) Aleksandr Lebed, continued to attack Yeltsin's foreign policy in general, and policy toward the former Yugoslavia in particular. These criticisms were usually couched in terms of a failure on the part of the Yeltsin administration to promote Russian interests and a parallel lack of conviction in opposing western (i.e. NATO) interventionism.

In the West, considerations regarding Russia and the former Yugoslavia have formed part of a broader, longer-standing debate that has focused on what motivates Russian foreign policy. This wider debate thus situates the Russian role in the former Yugoslavia alongside issues pertaining to the Russian attitude toward issues such as the expansion of NATO, the role of the US in European security affairs and the use of force in international affairs. All of these issues share three foci: Russian (Soviet) ideology, interests and capabilities. While the terms 'interests' and 'capabilities' speak for themselves, a couple of words on the term 'ideology' is required. The main point in this connection is the fact that ideological assumptions have often been seen as determining or at least influencing policy choices. With regard to the Soviet case, analyses of foreign policy along these lines were commonplace given the ideological claims of the Soviet state itself. A classic of this type of approach was George Kennan's article dating from 1947 on the 'Sources of Soviet Conduct'. In this piece Kennan described how the Soviet leadership, while having interests and capabilities which restrained its policy options, nonetheless still read the world in a particular way owing to the influence of Marxist-Leninist ideology. This compelled Moscow to act in a specific fashion, namely to prepare for what was seen as an inevitable attack by the West.[4] Post-Soviet Russia lacks such a firm ideological foundation; however, in connection with its role in the former Yugoslavia, some have suggested that the concept of pan-Slavism does perform quasi-ideological functions. In this regard, a good deal of commentary focuses on the historic (and current) bonds between Russia and Serbia, bonds which, it is argued, compel Moscow to act in a particular manner and to pursue certain objectives.[5] This theme will be taken up in the following section.

The myth about the Slavic brethren

Much has been made of the pan-Slavic 'special relationship', the instinctive, 'traditional link' between the 'Slavic brethren' of Russia and

Serbia. It is important to keep an eye on the ball here: the question is not whether Russia's relationship with Serbia is different from its relationship with, say, Britain or Italy (it is), but whether it affects Russia's policy in the former Yugoslavia. To this question, the answer would be a qualified 'no'. True, Russia has shown a certain favouritism towards Serbia and has been one of the few defenders of the Serb cause outside of the former Yugoslavia. Yet whether such a bias in policy stems from a long-cultivated special relationship is much more questionable.[6] In short, the pan-Slavic argument, which identifies a particular bond between Russia and Serbia based on religious (Christian-Orthodox), cultural, linguistic and ethnic ties is spurious. To understand why requires a brief historical overview.

Taking a broad sweep, pan-Slavic ideas have never had a common focus in Russia and Serbia. While Russian pan-Slavism was directed against Germany, especially after Prussia's defeat of Austria in 1866, Serbian pan-Slavism was always more occupied with anti-Turkish sentiment. As a matter of fact, during the last 200 years, Russia and Serbia have been allies for fewer than two decades. Russia's primary reason for involving itself in the Balkans has been primarily strategic in nature. From the time of its emergence as a great European power after 1815 this meant a preoccupying desire to gain open access to the Turkish Straits and the Dardanelles (the only warm water outlet from the Black Sea). In parallel, Russia sought to block German and Austria-Hungarian expansion into this region, and to achieve gains in an ongoing confrontation with Turkey. Russia repeatedly used Serbia as a pawn in this game. The war with Turkey and the resulting San Stefano peace treaty of 1878 facilitated Serbian independence but at the same time led to the creation of a large independent state of Bulgaria (a rival of Serbia in the Balkans) and the establishment of Bosnia-Herzegovina as an Austro-Hungarian protectorate (again, something not fondly regarded by Serbia). During the Second Balkan War between Bulgaria and Serbia (in 1913), Russia took the side of the former.

In 1914 Russia did side with Serbia against the ultimatum from Austria-Hungary, which triggered World War I. But the 1917 Revolution ended such cordial relations; between 1918 and 1941 there was not even mutual diplomatic recognition between the Serbian/Yugoslavia Kingdom and the Soviet Union. In World War II, the Soviet Union did not support the Serbian nationalists under Draza Mihailovic but the forces led by the communist Josep Tito, a Croat. In 1948 this alliance, in turn, broke down, and Yugoslavia was expelled from the Cominform. From then on, Tito tried to maintain a balanced or 'non-aligned' position between the Warsaw Pact and NATO, while the Soviet Union's only close ally in the Balkans was Bulgaria. It is also worth noting that Tito repeatedly invoked the threat of a Soviet invasion to calm down separatist movements, as in Croatia in 1970–71, and that the system of territorial defence developed by the Yugoslavian armed forces was directed first and foremost against the possibility of Soviet, not Western, intervention. During the Brezhnev period, relations did not improve. The Soviet invasion of Czechoslovakia in 1968 did not exactly send a positive signal to countries like Yugoslavia.

Given his own attempts to maintain the territorial integrity of the Soviet Union, Mikhail Gorbachev's response to the separatist developments in Yugoslavia in the late 1980s and beginning of the 1990s was to stress the need to preserve the Yugoslav federation. In this, Gorbachev was on the same wavelength as the United States (US) and the European Community (EC). He strongly endorsed the mediation efforts by the latter in 1991 aimed at a cessation of hostilities between the Yugoslavian military and the secessionist republics of Slovenia and Croatia. Gorbachev also consistently supported the reformist programme of the federal-oriented Yugoslav Prime Minister Ante Markovic.[7]

In the late 1980s and beginning of the 1990s, closer ties were being established between the churches and various nationalist groupings of Serbia and Russia. And during a trip to Moscow in March 1991, high-ranking Yugoslav military officials (traditionally the Yugoslav army was heavily dominated by Serbians and Montenegrins) made secret arrangements with their sympathizers in Moscow to have armaments delivered to the Yugoslav army, without Gorbachev's knowledge.[8] Gorbachev, still nominally in charge of the Soviet Union, continued his policy of advocating a federal Yugoslavia, to the extent of playing host to a fruitless meeting between the Croatian President Franjo Tudjman and his Serbian counterpart Slobodan Milosevic in the autumn of 1991 when his own country was falling to pieces.

Initially, Boris Yeltsin was on par with the line of Gorbachev, supporting a federal Yugoslavia. Following the aborted coup in August 1991, Yeltsin increased his voice for Russian self-determination, and his stand on Yugoslavia began to change as well. In fact, there is little love lost between Yeltsin and Milosevic, the primary proponent of a federal state. The Serb leader had initially supported the anti-reformist coup attempt in Moscow in August 1991, and subsequently flirted with Yeltsin's nationalist opponents in the Russian Parliament and armed forces.[9] Throughout the Yeltsin presidency, the administration has rarely articulated Russian policy in the language of Slavic solidarity. This is not to deny (as we shall see below) that Moscow has pandered to pro-Serb sentiment within Russian political circles (and within the Russian Parliament specifically) nor that it has totally eschewed Serbian interests in the former Yugoslavia. However, as the remainder of the chapter will show, beneath the pan-Slavic rhetorical veneer more concrete Russian objectives have been in evidence.

Historically, Russia has used Serbia as a pawn to protect and increase its interest and influence in the Balkans. This is a case of great power *realpolitik*, something which, in many ways, is the direct opposite of the quasi-ideological functions of pan-Slavism. Moreover, by the 1990s, Serbia (and the Balkans in general) was far down the list of Russian priorities, and Russia was, in essence, left without the resources to influence developments there. At the political level, however, events in the former Yugoslavia have connected with the wider matter of Russia's declining international stature and it is in this way that developments there have had their greatest impact on Russian policy.

Russian policy toward the former Yugoslavia: the record of the 1990s

Repeatedly during the period since 1992, the world has witnessed President Yeltsin and his foreign policy team struggling to perform a difficult balancing act between maintaining a working relationship with the West, crucial for the Russian reform process, while at the same time avoiding policies which would allow nationalist and conservative forces in Moscow to build the case that he was bowing down to outside pressures. To avoid marginalization and to prevent NATO dominance have consistently been Russian priorities.

1992–93: cooperation and strategic partnership

Following the collapse of the Soviet Union, Russia continued Gorbachev's policy of close cooperation with the West and adherence to the norms of the international community. During this period, Kozyrev, the main proponent of the 'Atlanticist' approach, repeatedly rejected the argument that Russia should be the protector of Serbia because of ethnic or religious ties. Reflecting a more cosmopolitan outlook than many of his political opponents, Kozyrev argued that an unashamedly pro-Serb line not only threatened to isolate Russia internationally but was replete with unwelcome domestic consequences. Russia, he insisted, was, after all, a multinational and multi-confessional state. To pursue a foreign policy based on alleged Slavic and Orthodox affinities with Serbia threatened to alienate Russia's own minority and particularly Muslim populations. It would thus be 'tantamount to shifting the civil war from Yugoslavia to our own motherland'.[10]

Seeking to stay in line with international opinion, Moscow committed troops to a UN Protection Force (UNPROFOR) mandated in February,[11] followed the EC's policy of recognizing the independence of Slovenia and Croatia in May and, later that same month, lent its support to a UN Security Council Resolution (UNSCR) mandating sanctions against the 'rump' Federal Republic of Yugoslavia (FRY) of Serbia and Montenegro. This latter step in particular led to strong domestic attacks on Yeltsin and more vociferously on Kozyrev, for betraying Serbia and slavishly following an American and European line. The influential chair of the Russian Parliament's Committee for International Relations and Foreign Economic Relations, Yevgeni Ambartsumov, for example, argued that '[i]t would hardly seem obligatory that Russia, which naturally has its own interests, duplicate the US position in all respects'.[12] Yeltsin and Kozyrev, however, had only decided to back sanctions against Serbia/ Montenegro after having worked hard to avoid the FRY's suspension from the Conference on Security and Cooperation in Europe (CSCE)[13] and following the collapse of a ceasefire in Bosnia negotiated by Kozyrev during a visit there earlier in May. The reason Yeltsin and Kozyrev eventually backed sanctions was two-fold. By May they had concluded that militant Serb forces in Bosnia and in Belgrade were, in Kozyrev's words, responsible for 'waging a war of extermination against their [...] neighbours'[14] and that consequently, uncritically supporting a Serb cause was both unpalatable in its own right and a danger to Moscow's cordial relations with the West. Kozyrev still argued, however, that isolating the FRY internationally would only harm any efforts to achieve a settlement in Bosnia and in the former Yugoslavia in general. Second, as intimated above, a prolonged power struggle was underway at this point between the Yeltsin administration and the Russian Parliament. Support for sanctions can, in this light, be read as a deliberate attempt on Yeltsin's part to assert presidential prerogative.

Decisiveness of this order was not, however, always apparent. The strength of feeling in the Russian Parliament in favour of a more independent Russian foreign policy meant that the Yeltsin administration often felt the need to pander to domestic pressures.[15] This resulted in a policy which alternated, on the one hand, between a willingness to cooperate with the West (on sanctions, for example) and, on the other, a distance from the western agenda. Hence, Moscow's argument that the Serbs should not be singled out as the main aggressor in Bosnia and (support for the establishment of a 'no-fly zone' over Bosnia in October notwithstanding) its opposition to any use of force outside of UN auspices to impose a settlement either in Bosnia or in neighbouring Croatia.[16]

The Russian leadership also tried repeatedly to communicate to the West that it was under domestic pressure over the Yugoslav issue. Kozyrev, in what was to become a diplomatic *cause célèbre*, issued a warning to a meeting of CSCE Foreign Ministers in December 1992 of what Russian foreign policy toward the former Yugoslavia might look like in the event of a conservative take-over in Moscow.[17] This was followed by Yeltsin suggesting, in meetings with American presidents George Bush and Bill Clinton, respectively in January and April 1993, that real differences existed between the US and Russia over the former Yugoslavia. At the same time, however, Russia was also lending its support to international efforts on Bosnia, most notably the Vance–Owen Plan.[18] In similar Janus-like fashion, in April 1993 Russia abstained on a UN Security Council vote tightening sanctions against the FRY, in part, at least, because Yeltsin wished to court nationalist opinion in the run-up to a national referendum on his domestic policies. Once the referendum had been won, the Yeltsin administration reiterated its support for sanctions and, for good measure, signed up in May to the Washington Declaration (along with the US, France, the UK and Spain) on the creation of UN 'safe areas' in Bosnia.[19]

Yeltsin's exasperation with his domestic opponents brought about the violent dissolution of the Russian Parliament in early October 1993. This left Yeltsin and Kozyrev with a temporary free hand before parliamentary elections in December of that year. On the very same day that troops loyal to Yeltsin were storming the Russian Parliament building, Russia voted for a UNSCR extending the mandate of the UNPROFOR in Croatia, a resolution which only days before Russian diplomats had questioned because of its implicit references to further sanctions against Serbia.[20] Of course, this was only to be a short-lived reprieve. Following gains by the ultra-nationalist Liberal Democratic Party of Russia (LDPR) in the elections to the new Russian Parliament (the Duma) in December, the Yeltsin administration was once again placed under pressure to assert itself in the former Yugoslavia. Actual policy, however, remained relatively unchanged as Kozyrev continued to work behind the scenes in order to avoid a break with the West over Bosnia.

During the period 1991–93, a high priority for the NATO states was to support the Russian President, and to demonstrate this publicly. This consideration left Russia with not insignificant room for maneouvre. Yeltsin and Kozyrev were given the benefit of the doubt when their rhetoric seemingly indicated an imminent break with the Europeans and the US over the former Yugoslavia.[21] Russia was also helped in its policy of rejecting any form of military intervention by a lack of will-ingness on the part of the West itself to become militarily involved in Bosnia. The Americans and French were at this stage lukewarm, while Britain was decidedly against any such operation.[22] This, however, would change. Up until the end of 1993 the contours of what would be a dividing line between Russia and the West over military, as opposed to simply diplomatic intervention, was not readily apparent. After 1993, as the West, led by the US, would warm to, or rather feel forced to, intervene militarily, a gap would open up between NATO and Russia.

February 1994: Sarajevo – Russia's finest hour

The complex web of factors constituting Russia's role in the former Yugoslavia was well illustrated by developments during the short space of two months, from February to April 1994. On 5 February 1994 a shell exploded in a marketplace in the centre of Sarajevo, killing 68 people and injuring 200 others. An outraged Bill Clinton forced his NATO allies into issuing an ultimatum to the Bosnian Serbs to remove their forces from a 20 kilometre radius around Sarajevo within ten days or face air attacks. NATO issued this ultimatum without having determined the responsibility for the shell[23] or consulting Russia. The Bosnian Serbs did not make any signs of complying, Russia voted against air-strikes in the UN Security Council and Yeltsin criticized NATO for 'trying to solve the problems in Bosnia without Russia'.[24]

The Yeltsin administration appeared to be in a 'no win' situation, trying to balance its preferred policy of cooperating with the West against a background of humiliation at not having been consulted by NATO and domestic pressure to throw in its lot with the Serb cause. Vladimir Zhirinovsky, the leader of the LDPR, chose this moment to warn that air-strikes would amount to a declaration of war against Russia.[25] While such statements can be written off as nothing more that alarmist hyperbole, it remained the case that the NATO ultimatum did put signi-ficant pressure upon Moscow to come up with a policy response. Anything other than a clear opposition to NATO's *démarche* could only be seen in Russia as 'anti-Serb'.

In this difficult situation, Yeltsin and his foreign policy team initiated what was to amount to 'their finest hour' during the war in Bosnia. After talks with Milosevic, Yeltsin's Balkan envoy, Vitaliy Churkin, suggested to the Bosnian Serbs that Russia was prepared to deploy troops around Sarajevo under the auspices of the UN in order to separate the Serb and the Muslim-led Bosnian forces, if the Serbs would comply with the NATO ultimatum. The Serbs agreed to this. The result was that while NATO's ultimatum was fulfilled, the Russian intervention allowed the Serbs to look as if they had ignored NATO and instead had accepted a Russian plan within a UN framework. This allowed the Serbs to save face and the Russians to celebrate one of their most successful diplomatic initiatives since the demise of the Soviet Union. In addition, Russia was given the rare pleasure of having stolen a march on European and American efforts to resolve the conflict. As the Belgrade weekly, *Nedeljne Informativne Novine*, boasted, 'NATO was left swimming in an empty pool'.[26]

As Lenard Cohen has pointed out, Churkin's description of the Russian initiative provides an interesting insight into the line of thinking and priorities of the Yeltsin foreign policy team in the early spring of 1994. Churkin stressed that Russia's intervention showed it to be an equal of the other major powers. He drew a parallel with World War II and argued that Sarajevo represented 'the Elbe of the 1990s' where the Russians stood together with the Americans and their European allies. In this light, he was very open about the motives for the Russian intervention, stating that:

> when I was working on this problem the main thing I was trying to prevent was a national humiliation for Russia. Not a further escalation in Bosnia – although I didn't want that, of course – but a humiliation for Russia. After all given our current low self-esteem, if everything had been done without us this time, too, if we [had] allowed others to ignore us yet again, the consequences would have been greater for us than the Bosnians.[27]

There is no reason why Churkin should not be believed. After all, he and Yeltsin received praise both internationally (by arguing that Moscow had acted out of considerations for human life or international norms) and at home for demonstrating Russia's great-power credentials.[28]

Thus, the Russian initiative was driven primarily by considerations of its status in international affairs, and not by pro-Serb or pan-Slavic impulses.[29] More specifically, Russia's objective was to avoid exclusion, to establish that Russia, as a major power, should be fully consulted by the western powers and, to this end, that the UN should not be usurped by NATO as the main international actor in the Bosnian conflict. At the same time, during the spring of 1994, constraining NATO's role in Bosnia become important in another connection, because Russia feared that deeper NATO involvement would strengthen the Alliance's claim to be the dominant security organization in post-Cold War Europe, a role Russia wanted the CSCE to fulfil (see Chapter 5).

April 1994–November 1995: the waning of Russian influence

In the wake of the Sarajevo episode, Russian involvement in the former Yugoslavia appeared to be on a high. Having demonstrated its ability to influence events on this occasion, Moscow repeated the success (albeit on a more limited scale) persuading Serb forces in March 1994 to lift a blockade of Tuzla airport and to accept a ceasefire agreement in the Serb-held Krajina region in Croatia.[30] Moscow, moreover, managed to balance its new-found influence while remaining within the parameters of international cooperation. Thus, at the end of February it expressed qualified backing for NATO's first military activity in the former Yugoslavia (the interception of Bosnian Serb aircraft over the 'no-fly zone')[31] and in February–March lent its support to agreements brokered by the US and Germany establishing a ceasefire between Bosnian Muslims and Croats, and outlining the creation of a Muslim–Croat Federation within Bosnia.[32] In April, Russia was included as one of only five members in the Contact Group (alongside the US, the UK, France and Germany) set up to expedite international diplomacy in Bosnia.

Russian satisfaction was, however, short-lived. Only two months after the Russian triumph at Sarajevo, the limits of Russian influence were illustrated and a pattern of events was introduced, which would be repeated again and again over the following eighteen months. From the spring of 1994, developments in Bosnia would continuously force the NATO states, led principally by the US, to take steps which would undermine Russian influence. From this point, the US (and to a lesser extent the rest of NATO) became increasingly disillusioned with what was regarded as UN impotence in dealing with the conflict – leading to episodes of American unilateralism and to the focus being moved to NATO intervention. Furthermore, the Bosnian Serbs showed no signs of complying with peace proposals (a plan put forward by the Contact Group was rejected by the Bosnian Serb leadership in August) and strong media coverage forced Clinton to take an increasingly pro-Muslim and thus, implicitly, anti-Serbian stance. This placed added pressure on the Yeltsin administration to stand up for Russia and the Serbs.

In these circumstances, Russian influence was squeezed in two ways. First, an increased emphasis on NATO meant a marginalization of the UN, the one organization in which Moscow had a real influence. Second, military-strategic changes undermined the position of the Bosnian

Serbs forcing them (and the Milosevic regime in Serbia) to deal directly with NATO without the necessity of Russian mediation.

The situation around the so-called 'safe haven' of Gorazde (a Muslim-populated region in Bosnia) in April illustrates well this change in the balance of forces. In a situation similar to that in Sarejevo in February, Bosnian Serb forces had advanced on the area, and the Clinton administration chose not to consult Moscow before NATO launched air-strikes in retaliation. Yeltsin warned that this could mean 'eternal war' in the Balkans.[33] NATO intervention was, however, only half of the humiliation for Russian policy. A few days after the air-strikes the Bosnian Serbs broke their promises to Moscow, the latter having designed a plan to halt NATO action in exchange for Serbian withdrawal of heavy artillery from an agreed exclusion zone. Churkin, who had assured NATO that the Serbs would fulfil their part of the agreement, did not hold back his frustration, charging that 'the Bosnian Serbs had used Russian policy as a shield', and demanding that they 'realize that Russia is a great power, not a banana republic'.[34]

This course of events – NATO led by an increasingly belligerent US executing air-strikes against the Bosnian Serbs without informing Russia, or achieving Moscow's support for such action – would be repeated in November 1994, and again in May, July and August 1995. These actions, moreover, came at a point when the NATO enlargement issue had begun to seriously test Russia's relations with the West. Cooperation on Yugoslavia fell victim as a consequence. A communiqué of NATO's North Atlantic Council of 1 December 1994 unequivocally welcomed the expansion of the Alliance 'to our east'.[35] That same day Russia vetoed a UNSCR prolonging sanctions against the Bosnian Serbs. At the CSCE summit later in December Russia vetoed a number of statements on Bosnia because, it was argued, they were too critical of Serbia. Yet for all this, Russia's outrage did not mean a complete departure from western policy. It is well worth noting that in reacting to NATO air-strikes the rhetoric of the Yeltsin administration was aggressive while its actions were much less so. In response to the strikes against Bosnian Serbs in August 1995, for instance, Yeltsin denounced NATO action as a 'cruel bombardment' and called for an immediate convocation of the UN Security Council.[36] Almost simultaneously, however, he vetoed a Duma resolution that would have unilaterally removed Russia from the campaign of international sanctions against Serbia.

It became increasing clear during 1994 that NATO, and the US in particular, had chosen sides in the former Yugoslavia. Serbia and the Bosnian Serbs were labelled as the aggressors, and Washington set out to shift the military balance in Bosnia and Croatia. This policy of taking sides came in a number of guises all of which illustrated Moscow's marginal role. The first move, the creation of the Croat–Muslim Federation in Bosnia, was noted above. Secondly, from 1994 the Americans had allegedly begun to secretly supply weapons to the Muslims in Bosnia (in blatant disregard of the UN arms embargo) and did nothing to hinder Iran from doing the same.[37] Thirdly, the NATO states stood idly by while the Croatian military inflicted defeats upon Serb forces in the Serbian-populated Croatian territories of western Slavonia (in May 1995), and Krajina (in August). This completely altered the military-strategic situation to the detriment of the Serb cause. Serb control of Croatian territory abutting Bosnia was lost and the position of Bosnian Serb forces severely weakened as a consequence. The offensive in western Slavonia, meanwhile, ethnically cleansed the area of 90 per cent of the Serbs who lived there. This provoked condemnation but no forceful reaction by the West against Croatia. Michael Ignatieff probably got it just about right when he argued that 'the Americans have concluded that Tudjman may be a bastard, but he is their bastard'.[38]

President Yeltsin, to all intents and purposes sidelined, tried to save the last grain of Russian influence, and to cover his back from domestic ridicule, by inviting the presidents of Croatia and Serbia to peace talks in Moscow in August 1995. Milosevic showed up, Tudjman, now with the upper hand, did not. Moscow, having frozen relations with the Bosnian Serb leadership following its rejection of the Contact Group plan, had, by this point, focused its efforts on Serbia proper in the hope that Milosevic would prove central to a settlement in Bosnia, thus allowing Moscow to claim the role of broker of any agreement. As part of this strategy (and, indeed, mindful also of the need to counter the prospect of NATO enlargement), Moscow was careful to retain its links with the Milosevic regime. In March the Russian Defence Minister Pavel Grachev signed an agreement with his Yugoslav counterpart providing for large-sale military cooperation once the arms boycott against the FRY had been lifted. Two months later, Kozyrev's successor Yevgenni Primakov suggested during a visit to Belgrade that Russia and Serbia should develop a 'strategic partnership'.[39]

These face-saving measures and rhetorical noises notwithstanding, any further progress towards a settlement was only made as a result of a more assertive and independent American diplomacy led by President Clinton's special envoy to the Balkans, Richard Holbrooke. This was a policy which, in effect, sidelined both the Contact Group and Russia. US diplomacy, moreover, was backed by force. In late August NATO launched 'Operation Deliberate Force' – air raids and artillery attacks on Bosnian Serb positions (see above). At the same time, forces of the Bosnian Muslim–Croat Federation, taking advantage of the NATO bombings and their own improved firepower, launched renewed attacks to win back large parts of territory from the Bosnian Serbs. Claims from the Russian Foreign Ministry that the latter were threatened with 'genocide' were completely ignored.[40]

The military-strategic shifts of the summer of 1995 tilted the balance toward a settlement in Bosnia. A formal ceasefire was agreed in early October and in late November the Dayton Accord was signed.

The Dayton Accord: Russia a junior partner, at most

The events of 1994–95 illustrated that Russia was, at best, a junior partner in efforts to bring some sort of resolution to the conflict in Bosnia.[41] Holbrooke's entry into the fray was accompanied by an American insistence that Milosevic negotiate on behalf of the Bosnian Serbs and that these negotiations be brokered by him personally. Russian representatives were thus not even present when a ceasefire was signed on 5 October 1995.

Paradoxically, however, Russia and NATO shared an interest in making the Russian contribution seem important: Yeltsin, for the various reasons discussed in detail above; the NATO states because of a realization that a loss of Russian face in Bosnia would hurt Yeltsin's reforms at home. Washington, furthermore, wanted the settlement in Bosnia to look as if it enjoyed widespread international support. Russia, consequently, was given a nominally important role.[42] At Yeltsin's insistence, the presidents of Serbia, Croatia and Bosnia were invited to attend a politically inconsequential, but symbolically important, pre-Dayton summit in Moscow (although this was subsequently cancelled owing to Yeltsin's ill-health). Russia was also nominated as a co-chair of the conference location in Dayton and was one of the signatories of the resulting accord. The accord itself recognized Bosnia as a sovereign state containing two parts – the Muslim–Croat Federation and the Bosnian Serb Republic (Republika Srpska), both having their own presidents, parliaments and armed forces. Sarajevo would be a part of the Muslim–Croat Federation. A whole raft of political and humanitarian measures was also outlined, the implementation and oversight of which was delegated to the UN and the Organization for Security and Cooperation in Europe (OSCE). This was designed, in part at least, to relieve Moscow of any anxieties it may have felt at NATO's seeming usurpation of the UN in 1994–95.[43] As for Dayton's military provisions, NATO, supported by other states, would deploy 55 000 peacekeepers as I-For (Implementation Force) in Bosnia, later to be reduced to 35 000 when I-For would be replaced by S-For (Stabilization Force) in December 1996. Russia was to contribute 1400 personnel and this would be the first time since 1945 that Russian troops would serve alongside forces from the US and western Europe.[44]

When it came to the actual Russian military deployment, however, Yeltsin deemed it imperative that Russian troops formally did not serve under NATO command. Lengthy negotiations ended with a compromise between NATO and the Russian Defence Minister in November 1995. The Russian troops in Bosnia would not be subordinated to NATO, but to an American general as commander of I-For, who, in turn, would issue orders through his deputy, Russian Colonel-General Leonti Shevtsov. However, as the American general in charge of I-For was at the same time also the commander-in-chief of NATO forces in Europe, it was not very difficult to see through this face-saving maneouvre.[45]

Despite these initial wranglings, on the ground, so to speak, there have been surprisingly few problems in the everyday dealings between NATO and the Russian contingent. NATO's Secretary-General, Javier Solana, has referred to Moscow's participation in I-For and later S-For as models of cooperation between NATO and Russia.[46] There have been minor episodes, most notably when Moscow protested at British troops shooting an indicted war criminal in July 1997,[47] but overall NATO officials agree that the Russian contingent has shown itself capable and willing.[48] The Russian political and military leaderships have also commended the operation, Shevtsov, for instance referring to it as 'the first real, tangible achievement' in relations between Russia and NATO 'since the Second World War'.[49]

Kosovo

In many ways Russia's relationship with the West over Kosovo is similar to the situation over Bosnia, although with the very important difference that this time Moscow's tone when trying to make itself heard seems to have been some pitches higher and more desperate.

There are at least three interrelated, reasons for this. First of all, the situation in Kosovo has forced political leaders, principally in Europe and the US, to act more swiftly and decisively than in Bosnia – not least because of the ugly Bosnian precedent itself. In ethical terms, the events in Kosovo leading up to the launch of air-strikes in March 1999 appeared as clear-cut as any in the former Yugoslavia: an indisputable case of violent ethnic cleansing perpetrated on the orders of an internationally vilified leader. The NATO states, although not as one over Kosovo and still tugged along by Washington, were nonetheless prepared to act with considerable force to resolve (as they saw it) the crisis which was brewing during 1998. Secondly, the crisis over Kosovo came to a head at a point when Russia's relations with the NATO states generally were much more strained than at the time of the Bosnian *dénouement* at Dayton in 1995 (see Chapter 3). Thirdly, the situation in Russia, politically and economically, had by 1998–99 deteriorated still further, thereby giving added cause for the articulation of anti-western sentiment and forcing the Yeltsin administration to appear tough in its conduct of conflict diplomacy. These factors left little room for positive maneouvre between Russia and the West. They did not, however, totally rule out cooperation. Yet in Kosovo, more so than in Bosnia, cooperation has tended to be fragile, accompanied by painful compromises (on Russia's part) and tarnished by near irresolvable disagreements concerning the use of force and the precise role of outside actors (most controversially NATO).

The status of Kosovo had, prior to 1999, often been referred to as the 'unfinished business' of the Balkans. A province of Serbia (rather than a republic of the former Yugoslavia in its own right) its case for independence was, legally speaking, more tenuous than the likes of Slovenia, Croatia, Bosnia and Macedonia, and its ability to resist the Milosevic regime in Belgrade much more constrained. Attempts to address the issue of Kosovo's status had been made in the early 1990s but were placed in abeyance following the termination of an OSCE mission by the FRY authorities in 1993. Kosovo was not placed on the agenda of the Dayton negotiations in 1995 in part, at least, to win over Milosevic to what at the time were more pressing issues concerning Bosnia. Only with the launch of attacks by the Kosovo Liberation Army (KLA) in the autumn of 1997 and subsequent reprisals by the Serb/FRY military and special forces did international attention focus upon the province.[50]

Throughout 1998 and during the first three months of 1999, various diplomatic efforts were undertaken to resolve the crisis. During this period, Russian policy was framed by similar objectives to those that it had pursued earlier in Bosnia and Croatia. Russia was, throughout, in favour of a diplomatic solution, but one which preferably did not depend on NATO enforcement and preserved a determining role for international bodies in which Moscow retained an influence (the UN Security Council, the OSCE and the Contact Group). Moscow's priorities, in other words, were to frustrate NATO from asserting its role as Europe's principal institute of European security and to retain for itself a say in the diplomatic decision-making process of any settlement. Beyond this,

Moscow was adamant in its opposition to the cause of Kosovan seces-sion and lukewarm in its attitude toward the further imposition of sanc-tions against Belgrade. While coincident with the interests of Serbia itself, such a stance need not be seen as indicative of a natural Moscow–Belgrade axis. The Yeltsin administration was sensitive to the secession issue owing to its own recent troubles in Chechnya and saw sanctions as detrimental to its own drive to promote civil and military exports fol-lowing the relaxation, post-Dayton, of the boycott of the FRY.

While Russia had clear objectives, these were distinctly reactive in nature. As in Bosnia and Croatia, Russia's influence over events was cir-cumscribed by the lead role played by the US, followed by the Europeans. Total opposition to American and European initiatives might have curried favour in Serbia but would render Moscow isolated in the establishment and implementation of any settlement. If Russia was to have any influ-ence over events it had to recognize, however unpalatable, this secondary status. In sum, then, Russian policy was once again finely balanced between a need for independence and assertiveness and the unavoid-able necessity of involvement with western efforts.

This balance of interests became increasingly clear during 1998. During a visit to Belgrade in mid-March, Primakov stated that while Russia supported greater Kosovan autonomy, the FRY's continuing territorial integrity was paramount.[51] Moscow, did, however, sign up to a Contact Group statement earlier that month demanding the withdrawal of special Serb forces from Kosovo and shortly after voted in favour of UNSCR 1160 re-imposing the arms boycott on Serbia that had been lifted fol-lowing the Dayton Accord. In June, Russia sought to retain some credib-ility as an independent interlocutor by inviting Milosevic to talks in Moscow. This was not an entirely unhelpful exercise in that it yielded an undertaking by Milosevic to resume negotiations with Kosovan rep-resentatives (these having been initiated and immediately terminated the previous month) that would include consideration of forms of auto-nomy for Kosovo.[52] These pledges, however, did not stop the violence and Moscow was consequently prepared to endorse other more robust efforts. These included a further UNSCR (1199) of September demanding a withdrawal of FRY forces and autonomy for Kosovo; an agreement reached between the US envoy Holbrooke and Milosevic in mid-October which provided *inter alia* for the deployment of OSCE monitors to oversee the withdrawal of Serb/FRY forces; and the convening of peace talks in February 1999 at Rambouillet (Paris) between Serb/FRY and Kosovan representatives. This latter move was accompanied by a Contact Group document signed by all its members (including Russia) of 'non-negotiable principles/basic elements' for a settlement that foresaw Yugoslavia's continued integrity but with a high degree of Kosovan self-rule. The Contact Group also appointed three negotiators, representing the US, the European Union (EU) and Russia, to facilitate the talks.[53]

The use of force, was, however, an issue upon which Moscow and NATO could find no common ground. Throughout 1998 and 1999 leading figures within the Yeltsin administration had warned against NATO's preparations for the deployment of air-strikes. Yeltsin, in October 1998, for instance, suggested that such measures would be 'disastrous for global peace', while his Foreign Minister Igor Ivanov indicated that they would totally undermine the post-Cold War basis of improved relations between Russia and the West.[54] Such statements were accompanied by admonitions that any intervention related to Kosovo required a proper mandate from the UN Security Council (a process, of course, subject to a Russian veto).[55]

Moscow's position on this matter placed a practical limit on how far it was prepared to sanction international (i.e. western) efforts at dealing with the Kosovo issue. Any move that intimated (directly or by implication) a use of force by NATO failed to attract its sympathy. Thus, on two occasions during 1998 it issued declarative statements after voting for UNSCRs 1160 and 1199 that references to 'further action' in the event of FRY non-compliance should not be interpreted as authorizing a use of force.[56] On the occasion of voting on UNSCR 1203, sanctioning the terms of the Holbrooke–Milosevic agreement, Russia abstained on the grounds that the document left open the possibility of coercive measures for its enforcement. Russia, similarly, was unprepared to fully endorse the Rambouillet accords of February 1999. While firm in their insistence on Kosovan autonomy within a federated Yugoslavia (the Contact Group formula Moscow had supported) certain of the agreement's military provisions proved totally unacceptable. The principal bone of contention in this regard concerned the organization of peacekeepers in Kosovo. A role for Russia was envisaged in this force, but Moscow baulked at the demand that this be NATO-led and commanded (even though its mandate would come from the UN Security Council).[57] Belgrade's own rejection of this stipulation (and indeed, the accords in general), along with further attacks by Serb forces in Kosovo prompted the launch of NATO's 'Operation Allied Force' against Serb targets in the FRY in late March.

Reaction in Russia to this action was of a pitch unheard in the entire post-Cold War period. A statement issued by Yeltsin on the same day as the operation was launched, accused NATO of violating the UN Charter and the 1997 NATO–Russia Founding Act, of subverting international law, of destabilizing the Balkans, and of setting NATO up as a 'world policeman'. In the event of the situation worsening, Russia, he warned, retained 'the right to take adequate measures, including military ones, to defend itself and the overall security of Europe'. Simultaneously, Yeltsin ordered the suspension of virtually all cooperative links between Russia and NATO (see Chapter 3).[58] As NATO strikes escalated, Yeltsin became even more forthright. In mid-April he was reported as stating that NATO was preparing a ground offensive in order to seize Yugoslavia as a western protectorate. Russia, he declared, 'cannot permit that' and would be prepared to take military counter-measures to prevent it.[59]

Outside of the Yeltsin administration, Russian comment was even more threatening. Zhirinovsky referred to events as the beginning of World War III, Zyuganov compared NATO to Nazi Germany, and Lebed suggested that NATO was bent on global control.[60] The Alliance's actions, it was demanded, also required a robust response. Zhirinovsky's LDPR began a recruitment campaign for Russian volunteers to fight alongside Serb forces; mayor Luzhkov and Deputy Speaker of the Duma, Sergei Baburin, meanwhile, both suggested that Russia unilaterally break the UN arms embargo and supply military assistance to the FRY.[61] Along these lines, Viktor Chechevatov, commander of Russia's Far East Military District wrote to the Russian President outlining his readiness to lead a detachment of Russian volunteers to serve alongside Serb units.[62]

Yeltsin's own pronouncements were, in part, a reaction to such outrage. Their ferocity was influenced by the fact that he was, at this juncture, facing an impeachment vote in the Duma (scheduled for mid-May) and needed to boost his nationalist credentials. That said, there did remain real substance to Moscow's opposition to NATO action. A number of points are relevant here. Perhaps most importantly, Operation Allied Force seemingly justified Moscow's worst fears concerning NATO's dominance in European and, indeed, international security affairs.[63] Not only was the scale of the operation seen as a disproportionate, but NATO was also condemned for its circumvention of the UN (no explicit Security Council mandate had been sought by the Alliance) and for the extension of its military tasks beyond the traditional mission of collective defence of its members. NATO action had, after all, entailed intervention in the internal affairs of a sovereign state.[64] A readiness to use force in this manner came, moreover, at a crucial point in NATO's evolution – shortly after having admitted three new member states (the Czech Republic, Hungary and Poland) and just prior to the adoption of a new 'Strategic Concept' in April, which outlined an intention to undertake tasks essential to the stability of the entire 'Euro-Atlantic area' (see Chapter 3).

The corollary of NATO dominance was, of course, the sidelining of Russia and the consequent injury to Moscow's assumed status as a European power. The 1997 NATO–Russia Founding Act had attempted to assuage Russian concerns on this score by offering institutionalized dialogue. As pointed out in Chapter 3, the absence of any consultation with Moscow prior to Operation Allied Force was seen as an undermining the principles of cooperation upon which these channels had been established. This meant, as Celeste Wallander has argued, that Russia had been excluded 'from the single most important decision about European security that has been made since the end of the Cold War'.[65] Consultation would not have removed Russia's opposition to air-strikes, but it would at least have allowed it the opportunity to voice that opposition in a timely fashion. As Ivanov was to declare shortly after their launch, 'we just don't want to be left in a situation where we are not informed'.[66]

Russia had also consistently argued that diplomacy rather than force was the best method for dealing with the situation in the former Yugoslavia. In light of the humanitarian consequences of the NATO campaign this stricture may appear well meant. It was, however, partly self-serving. The Yeltsin administration by its own actions had already demonstrated that it was not opposed to a use of force in principle. Moscow had resorted to large-scale military action in Chechnya in 1996; and while it could claim that here it was acting within its own borders, the Russian armed forces have also played an interventionist role against the wishes of the host governments in Georgia and Moldova. This suggests that Russia's real concerns lay elsewhere. Anxiety in relation to Kosovo was felt, first, because the use of force was employed by NATO specifically, and second, because it meant a downgrading of diplomatic efforts and thus concrete Russian participation. In this light, a return to diplomacy was the best option for Russia. It would allow it a certain role in events and would detract from NATO's clear supremacy. Diplomacy also offered Russia the best opportunity to demonstrate its credentials as an important actor in European affairs, and, the rhetoric of the Yeltsin administration notwithstanding, the best chance for the preservation of a modicum of broad cooperation with the West (not least, because at this juncture Russia was negotiating a package of assistance with the International Monetary Fund, entry into the World Trade Organization, a free trade agreement with the EU and a revision of the Conventional Forces in Europe Treaty).

From the very beginning of the crisis, Russian policy was thus informed by the central objective of promoting diplomacy and thus Moscow's involvement in conflict resolution efforts. During its early stages, this was a largely fruitless exercise. Yeltsin's first statement, which included a call for a halt to military action and the convening of the UN Security Council and the Contact Group in emergency session had absolutely no effect.[67] Four days later Primakov (now Prime Minister) embarked upon a mission to Belgrade. He returned with a six-point peace plan from Milosevic which NATO promptly rejected.[68]

A crucial turning point occurred, however, in mid-April. The campaign of air-strikes by this point had had no obvious effect on the resolve of the Milosevic regime and certain European NATO member states (France, Germany, Greece, Italy, Portugal and Spain) were becoming increasingly predisposed to a return to political solutions. This culmin-ated in a German peace plan envisaging a withdrawal of Serb forces from Kosovo and the installation of an interim administration under UN auspices.[69] The German Foreign Minister Joschka Fischer, suggested also that a future Kosovo peacekeeping force could include Russian units.[70] While the plan gained little enthusiasm in Washington, by this point the Clinton administration was, nonetheless, keen to involve Russia in the search for a diplomatic breakthrough, hence a meeting in Oslo between Ivanov and US Secretary of State Madeleine Albright. This did little to resolve differences on either the composition and command of a future peacekeeping force or the issue of how long NATO's bombing campaign should be pursued. It did, however, provide the occasion for a restatement of points on which no disagreement existed (a withdrawal of Serb forces from Kosovo, the safe return of refugees and the entry of international humanitarian organizations).[71] Shortly after this meeting Yeltsin appointed former Prime Minister Viktor Chernomyrdin as his special representative on the Kosovo issue, a move interpreted as signal-ling a Russian determination to seek a joint diplomatic solution with NATO.[72]

By the end of April, Russia's role in a settlement was being openly acknowledged by NATO states. Gerhard Schröder, the German Chancellor, suggested that there could be 'no lasting peace without Russia'. In a similar vein, British Foreign Secretary Robin Cook referred to Russia as part of any solution to the Kosovo crisis.[73] By this point Chernomyrdin was working intensely with US Deputy Secretary of State Strobe Talbott in seeking a formula for a diplomatic solution. These efforts bore fruit in early May when Russia joined the other Group of Eight (G8) Foreign Ministers in agreeing to seven principles on a Kosovo settlement. These referred to an 'international security presence' but left its exact composition to be resolved (it would, however, be endorsed by the UN) and was silent on the cessation of NATO air-strikes. In other respects it was more acceptable to Moscow, reiterating certain provisions of the German peace plan and the Rambouillet formula for Kosovon autonomy within the FRY.[74]

Following the G8 statement, the subsequent two months witnessed a series of shuttle missions by Chernomyrdin to Belgrade and a number of Russian proposals concerning, first, peacekeeping, and second, the sequencing of a Serb withdrawal with any cessation of NATO action (the two central points disputed between Russia and NATO).[75] Throughout, the Alliance remained adamant that any peacekeeping force (the 'international security presence' of the G8 statement) be under a single NATO command and that air-strikes would stop only after the terms of a settlement had been accepted by Belgrade. Moscow was clearly unhappy with these conditions and continued to criticize the bombing campaign as detrimental to peace diplomacy.[76] It did, nonetheless, come to recognize that NATO's position was immovable. NATO, for its part, faced with the possibility of a ground offensive was ever keener for Moscow to influence Milosevic in favour of suing for peace. The climax was finally reached in early June when a peace plan formulated jointly by Talbott, Chernomyrdin and the Finnish President and EU representative Marti Ahtisaari was delivered to Belgrade and accepted by Milosevic. This capitulation was influenced by the accumulated impact of the NATO campaign and KLA gains within Kosovo, but Russia also played a role. Chernomyrdin intimated to Milosevic that NATO was prepared to mount a ground invasion (even though NATO itself was reluctant to do so) and that Russia was in agreement with the peace plan, something that seemingly allowed the Serb leader no further scope for exploiting Russian quibbling over issues of peacekeeping and sequencing.[77] One week later and following the personal intervention of Yeltsin, Russia agreed to a UNSCR 1244 that endorsed a fuller settlement while also incorporating the Ahtisaari–Chernomyrdin–Talbott document and the May G8 principles.[78]

From Moscow's point of view the *dénouement* in Kosovo was, in some respects a beneficial outcome. Russia won plaudits from the US and the European powers for its vital diplomatic contribution,[79] demonstrated its utility as an international actor in crisis situations, and promoted its image as an upholder of international law in contrast to an image of NATO as more concerned with force than persuasion. The final settlement, moreover, represented much that Russia had stood for in the period leading up to the Rambouillet accords and prior to NATO's bombing campaign. Thus, even though in reality Kosovo would succumb to the status of an international protectorate, in formal terms it was to remain part of the FRY. The settlement also resurrected a role for the UN (in mandating the peacekeeping force and in running an interim administration) and provided for the demilitarization of the KLA. Coincidentally, Russia had taken upon itself no obligations for the post-war reconstruction of Kosovo. It could sit back and watch NATO states take on the burdensome tasks of returning refugees, disarming the KLA and reviving the Kosovan economy.[80]

Its cooperation in framing the settlement did, however, carry a certain price in that Russia also conceded vital points, most notably on the composition of the security presence or peacekeeping force. Having rejected at Rambouillet NATO command of a Kosovan deployment, it conceded in the deal offered to Milosevic that the security presence in Kosovo would entail 'substantial NATO participation' and would be deployed under 'unified command and control'. In the final UNSCR 1244, Russia also conceded on three other issues. First, a reference to Chapter VII of the UN Charter (thus implicitly permitting further coercive enforcement in Kosovo regardless of the objections of its still legally sovereign government in the FRY). Second, language which suggested that the UN civilian presence foreseen in Kosovo would have no jurisdiction over NATO peacekeepers. And third, a clause that allowed the 'security presence' (i.e. NATO) to arrest Serbs suspected of war crimes.[81] As Vladimir Lukin, Chair of the Duma Committee for International Affairs, pointed out at the time, concessions of this type reflected the still obvious fact that the balance of influence remained in NATO's favour owing to Russia's economic and military weakness.[82] In fact, since the launch of air-strikes, figures in the Yeltsin administration had been open and frank on this score. Although the Russian President had, as noted above, threatened military counter-measures, these never materialized. The arms embargo was not breached and prior to the settlement of early June Russia's only significant military activity was to send a single reconnaissance ship to the Adriatic. It should also be noted that, a few outbursts aside, Yeltsin was equally forthright in stating that Russia would not be dragged into a conflict in the Balkans.[83] Such sentiment reflected, in part, Russia's own limited capabilities. As Vladimir Putin, then Secretary of the Russian Security Council suggested in late March, Russia may have had sympathy with the interests of the FRY but its own interests in avoiding a conflict had to come first. Russia, he continued, could not 'engage in any military action [...] in its present state'.[84] Equally, it reflected an appreciation for Russia of the dangers of a widening Balkan war. Chernomyrdin, when explaining his motives for involvement in the diplomatic effort, argued that Russia had stood by Serbia in 1914, but had lost seven million dead in World War I as a result. It was in Russia's interests to avoid any such repetition.[85]

Russia's involvement in the Kosovo settlement of June 1999 was thus an uneasy one. A modicum of cooperation was preserved with the West despite the heightened atmosphere of a crisis in relations, and certain benefits accrued to Moscow as a result. Yet as with the events surrounding Bosnia and the Dayton Accord, Russia clearly participated as junior partner; it had followed rather than shaped events.

This state of affairs – fragile cooperation and limited scope for Russian action – was also apparent after the diplomatic settlement, in a series of wranglings concerning Russian participation in Kosovan peacekeeping. The agreements of June had been clear in suggesting that NATO would play the principal role in this force (dubbed 'K-For'). Moscow had let it be known that it wished to play some part, and this had been accepted by NATO leaders. The terms of Russian participation, however, soon emerged as an object of contention. Two issues stood out: Moscow's demand for its own sector in Kosovo (preferably in the north abutting Serbia) and its insistence that Russian peacekeepers would not serve under a NATO command.[86] Of the two demands, the former was the most difficult to resolve. The NATO side expressly rejected the Russian claim on the grounds that it would lead to a *de facto* partition of Kosovo and an undermining of unified command. Negotiations on the issue were rendered particularly difficult, moreover, by an assertion of influence on the part of the Russian military. Chernomyrdin played no part and the main interlocutors with NATO were Defence Minister Igor Sergeyev, Colonel-General Leonid Ivashov (responsible for international cooperation within the Russian Ministry of Defence) and Foreign Minister Ivanov. Ivashov, in particular, had made known his displeasure with the terms of the June peace settlement. To make matters worse, while final preparations were being made for NATO to enter Kosovo, a 200-strong Russian detachment based in Bosnia made a dash through Serbia and subsequently entered the main airport outside the Kosovan capital Pristina. This caused consternation among a British detachment which arrived at the same location just hours later. The move was seemingly designed to strengthen the Russian position in negotiations and, according to US military sources, as the beginning of a unilateral attempt to set up a Russian sector.[87] Both Russian and other sources reported that while having the formal approval of Yeltsin, it was a step taken on the initiative of the Russian General Staff, without consultation with the Russian Foreign Ministry.[88]

Whatever its motives, however, the dash to Pristina had no positive impact on the Russian position in Kosovo. The advance unit soon became cut off (and thus dependent on NATO/K-For troops for basic provisions) after Romania, Hungary and Bulgaria refused Russia permission to cross their airspace with supplies and reinforcements. The complications raised by the maneouvre also delayed an agreement on a larger Russian presence in Kosovo. Russian troops were, therefore, absent as NATO/K-For took up positions throughout the province. Furthermore, while in July a final agreement was eventually worked out with NATO for Russian participation in K-For, this entailed no advance toward Russia's demands. A convoluted chain of command was established similar to that relating to the Russian contingent in I-For/S-For in Bosnia. This preserved a semblance of Russian independence but was a thinly disguised arrangement that preserved NATO's operational control.[89] There was also to be no Russian sector. Instead Russian peacekeepers were to be spread across the German, French and US sectors with a unit also based at Pristina airport in the British sector. Russians were to be absent from the strategically significant northern sector allocated to Italy. The final Russian deployment was projected at 3600 personnel; clearly of a far lesser order than NATO's planned force of 55000.[90]

Conclusion

The former Yugoslavia has presented ample opportunity for disagreement between Russia and the West. Indeed, next to the issue of NATO enlargement, events there have caused the greatest rift in Russia's relations with Europe and the US since the birth of the Russian Federation in late 1991. The strength of feeling in Russia, at least within the presidential administration, has not been the result of some deep-seated sympathy toward the Serb cause. Neither has it sprung from any appreciation of the inherent strategic significance of the Balkan region. It has been shaped, rather, by an antipathy toward the methods of western intervention (principally, the use of NATO military force) and an assessment that preserving Russia's credentials as a European power required involvement and the articulation of an independent voice. The wars in the region have, after all, represented the greatest crisis in Europe's international affairs since the end of the Cold War, and perhaps in the entire post-World War II period. For Russia not to have had a say in their resolution would clearly have given the lie to its claims to status and would also have established the unwelcome precedent that American/NATO intervention was the ultimate arbiter of events. In this respect, Russia's achievements were modest. Moscow's actions aimed to minimize the worst effects of NATO predominance and in consequence, to back, up to a point, the position of Serbia/FRY. Yet, ultimately, Moscow was also prepared to support the vast majority of sanctions, to partake in the diplomatic isolation of Belgrade and to give way in favour of diplomatic solutions (principally the Dayton Accord and the measures ending the war in Kosovo) that, while containing concessions to Russian feeling, encapsulated, unaltered, core western positions. This represented a begrudging, but nonetheless very material form of cooperation on Moscow's part. In the final analysis, Russia was too weak, its interests in the Balkans too uncertain and its overriding concern with preserving a broadly cooperative relationship with the US and European powers too clear-cut for it to use the wars in the former Yugoslavia as a cause for mobilizing against the West.

Notes

1. The phrase 'the former Yugoslavia' is used throughout this chapter in order to refer to conflicts in the territory once occupied by the Socialist Federative Republic of Yugoslavia prior to the beginnings of its dismemberment in 1991. The main conflicts in this connection are those that waged in the former Yugoslav republics of Bosnia and, to a lesser degree, Croatia in the period 1992–95, and that in Kosovo in 1998–99. Strictly speaking the war in Kosovo occurred in latter-day Yugoslavia in that it was at the time a province of Serbia, one of two republics (the other being Montenegro) which made up the surviving Federal Republic of Yugoslavia (FRY). However, for the sake of analytical convenience, it is seen as falling under the moniker 'former Yugoslavia' in order that it bear comparison with the Bosnian and Croatian cases.
2. A somewhat polemic point, perhaps, but it should be pointed out that although western analysts are apt to view a Russian inclination toward cooperation rather than confrontation as a positive outcome, not all of the western actions and inactions during the wars in the former Yugoslavia were 'good' policies. In this sense, Russian opposition to such policies should not *ipso facto* be seen as wrong.
3. Author's interviews with close advisers to a number of Kozyrev's critics, Moscow, October–December 1995.
4. 'X' (G. Kennan), 'The Sources of Soviet Conduct', *Foreign Affairs*, Vol. 25, No. 4, 1947, pp. 566–82.
5. See, for instance, the editorial in the *Christian Science Monitor*, 30 March 1999 as carried by *Johnson's Russia List* (davidjohnson@erols.com), 30 March 1999 and B. Anderson, 'Milosevic Has Kosovo, NATO Has No Idea', *The Spectator*, 3 April 1999, p. 11.

6. There is a string of good articles and books, which together constitute a sub-stantial and convincing refutation of the pan-Slavic argument behind Russia's policy in the former Yugoslavia. See for example C. Jelavich, *Tsarist Russia and Balkan Nationalism* (Berkeley: University of California Press, 1958); D. Geyer, *Russian Imperialism: the Interaction of Domestic and Foreign Policy, 1860–1914* (Yale University Press, 1987); V. Sobell, 'NATO, Russia and the Yugoslav War', *The World Today*, Vol. 51, No. 11, 1995, pp. 210–15; I. Traynor, 'Expedient Band of Brothers', *The Guardian*, 15 April 1999.

7. L. Cohen, 'Russia and the Balkans: Pan-Slavism, Partnership and Power', *International Journal*, Vol. 49, No. 4, 1994, pp. 817, 820.

8. *Ibid.*, p. 819.

9. M. Glenny, 'The Return of the Great Powers', *New Left Review*, No. 205, 1994, p. 130.

10. *Nezavisimaya gazeta*, 20 August 1992.

11. UNPROFOR was initially deployed in Croatia. It was extended to Bosnia in September 1992. A 900-strong Russian contingent was deployed in the Serb-populated enclave of Krajina in Croatia.

12. Cited in S. Crow, 'Russia's Response to the Yugoslav Crisis', *Radio Free Europe/Radio Liberty (RFE/RL) Research Report*, Vol. 1, No. 30, 1992, p. 33.

13. Russia had, under the consensus provisions of the CSCE, vetoed suspension in May and early July. At the CSCE summit in mid-July, however, Russia, sensitive to its isolation on the issue, acceded to Yugoslavia's suspension.

14. Cited in Crow, *op. cit.*, p. 33.

15. In December 1992, the Supreme Soviet (the working Parliament of the Russian Congress of People's Deputies) called on the Yeltsin administration to resist any outside military intervention in the former Yugoslavia, to prevent a lifting of the arms embargo on Bosnia and to ensure that sanctions were imposed equally on all sides in the conflict. For an overview of criticisms mounted by voices in the Parliament see A. Lynch and R. Lukic, 'Russian Foreign Policy and the Wars in the Former Yugoslavia', *RFE/RL Research Report*, Vol. 2, No. 41, 1993, pp. 29–31.

16. J. Gow, *Triumph of the Lack of Will. International Diplomacy and the Yugoslav War* (London: Hurst and Co., 1997), pp. 192–200.

17. *The Independent*, 15 December 1992. Kozyrev's speech is reprinted in full in *RFE/RL Research Report*, Vol. 3, No. 18, 1994, p. 2.

18. The plan had been unveiled in January 1993 on the initiative of the joint UN and EC mediators Cyrus Vance and David Owen. For Russian support see D. Owen, *Balkan Odyssey* (London: Viktor Gollancz, 1995), p. 112.

19. Gow, *op. cit.*, p. 248.

20. RFE/RL, *News Briefs*, 4–8 October 1993, p. 11.

21. Thus, in response to Kozyrev's tilt toward nationalist opinion in late 1993, one British diplomat commented: '[h]e remains an important interlocutor for us. He sees a domestic mood and as Foreign Minister he has to take account of it. Some of what he says is trimming to the political wind. But his essential mood is the same.' See *The Guardian*, 20 January 1994.

22. Gow, *op. cit.*, pp. 156–222, passim.

23. In fact, later investigations showed that it was Bosnian Moslem forces which had launched the offending weapon. See *The Sunday Times*, 1 October 1995.

24. RFE/RL, *News Briefs*, 14–18 February 1994, pp. 2–3.

25. RFE/RL, *News Briefs*, 7–11 February 1994, p. 4.
26. Cited in Cohen, *op. cit.*, p. 838.
27. Cited in *ibid.*, p. 839.
28. *Krasnaya zvezda*, the newspaper of the Russian Ministry of Defence wrote in its 19 February edition that Russia's initiative on Sarajevo had demonstrated that 'if the West really wants peace in the Balkans, it must understand and accept the position of Russia; it must be seen as a great power and an equal partner'. Cited in RFE/RL, *News Briefs*, 21–25 February 1994, p. 1.
29. Cohen, *op. cit.*, p. 839.
30. *Keesing's Record of World Events*, March 1994, pp. 39926–7; RFE/RL, *News Briefs*, 28 February–4 March 1994, p. 4.
31. Kozyrev, Churkin and Defence Minister Pavel Grachev cited in RFE/RL, *News Briefs*, 28 February–4 March 1994, p. 2.
32. Churkin cited in RFE/RL, *News Briefs*, 28 February–4 March 1994, p. 5.
33. *Pravda*, 13 April 1994.
34. Cited in Cohen, *op. cit.*, p. 842.
35. Cited in S. Croft, J. Redmond, G. Wyn Rees and M. Webber, *The Enlargement of Europe* (Manchester and New York: Manchester University Press, 1999), p. 34.
36. *Keesing's Record of World Events*, August 1995, p. 40691.
37. C. Jacobsen, 'Yugoslavia's Wars: a Reappraisal', *European Security*, Vol. 4, No. 4, 1995, p. 674, note 25; *The Independent*, 6 April 1996.
38. *The Independent*, 22 November 1995.
39. H.-J. Hoppe, 'Russia's Balkan Policy', *Aussenpolitik*, Vol. 49, No. 1, 1998, p. 41.
40. *Financial Times*, 13 September 1995.
41. See also H.-J. Hoppe, 'Moscow and the Conflicts in Former Yugoslavia', *Aussenpolitik*, Vol. 48, No. 3, 1997, p. 271 and S. Parrish, 'Russia's Marginal Role', *Transitions*, Vol. 2, No. 14, 1996, pp. 21–2.
42. R. Holbrooke, *To End A War* (New York: Random House, 1998), pp. 213–14.
43. A. Konovalov, 'Creating the European Security System in the Post-Cold War Period' (NATO Research Fellowship Report, June 1996), <http://www.nato.int/acad/fellow94-96/konovalo/home.htm>.
44. M. Bowker, 'The Wars in Yugoslavia: Russia and the International Community', *Europe-Asia Studies*, Vol. 50, No. 7, 1998, pp. 1254–5. The full text of the Dayton Accord can be found in *SIPRI Yearbook 1996: Armaments, Disarmament and International Security* (Oxford: Oxford University Press/Frösunda, Sweden: Stockholm International Peace Research Institute, 1996), pp. 232–50.
45. Bowker, *op. cit.*, p. 1255; Parrish, *op. cit.*, p. 22.
46. J. Solana, 'NATO's Role in Bosnia: Charting a New Role for the Alliance', *NATO Review*, Vol. 44, No. 2, 1996, pp. 3–6.
47. Bowker, *op. cit.*, p. 1255.
48. Author's interviews with Pentagon officials, Washington D.C., July 1998. See also U. Brandenburg (Head of Partnership and Cooperation in NATO's Political Affairs Division), 'NATO and Russia: a Natural Partnership', *NATO Review*, Vol. 45, No. 4, 1997, p. 18 and M. Meckel (general rapportuer), 'NATO on the Threshold of the 21st Century: a New Strategy for Peace, Security and Stability' (North Atlantic Assembly, Political Committee, 6 May 1999), paragraph 32.
49. Col.-Gen. L. P. Shevtsov, 'Russian–NATO Military Cooperation in Bosnia: a Basis for the Future?', *NATO Review*, Vol. 45, No. 2, 1997, p. 21.

50. M. Weller, 'The Rambouillet Conference on Kosovo', *International Affairs*, Vol. 75, No. 2, 1998, pp. 218–19.
51. The Jamestown Foundation, *Monitor* (webmaster@jamestown.org), 18 March 1998.
52. This amounted to the first, albeit implicit, public commitment by Milosevic to enhanced Kosovan self-government. For a positive assessment of the Yeltsin–Milosevic meeting see G.-M. Chauveau, 'Conflict Management in Europe: the Case of Kosovo' (North Atlantic Assembly, Civilian Affairs Committee, 14 April 1999), paragraph 8.
53. Weller, *op. cit.*, pp. 225–7.
54. *The Independent*, 8 October 1998; RFE/RL, *Newsline* (newsline@list.rferl.org), 12 October 1998.
55. And Moscow had made it clear that it would veto any draft resolution legitimizing NATO air-strikes. See Ivanov cited in *The Guardian*, 7 October 1998.
56. C. Guicherd, 'International Law and the War in Kosovo', *Survival*, Vol. 41, No. 2, 1999, p. 26.
57. Weller, *op. cit.*, pp. 246–7.
58. *Russia Today*, 25 March 1999, <http://www.russiatoday.com/rtodayspecial/yeltsnato.html>.
59. *The Guardian*, 10 April 1999.
60. *Boston Globe*, 28 March 1999; Reuters, 28 March 1999; *Hindustan Times*, 31 March 1999 as carried by *Johnson's Russia List* (davidjohnson@erols.com), 28 March, 29 March and 1 April 1999.
61. Interfax, 6 April 1999; Associated Press, 6 April 1999 both in *Johnson's Russia List* (davidjohnson@erols.com), 6 April; *The Independent*, 15 April 1999.
62. *Rossiyskaya gazeta*, 27 March 1999.
63. E. A. Stepanova, 'Explaining Russia's Dissension on Kosovo' (Programme on New Approaches to Russian Security, Harvard University), Memo No. 57, March 1999, <http://www.fas.harvard.edu/~ponars/POLICY%20MEMOS/stepanova57.html>.
64. 'Memorandum of the Permanent Mission of the Russian Federation to the Organization for Security and Cooperation in Europe' (Vienna: 23 April 1999).
65. C. A. Wallander, 'Russia, Kosovo, and Security Cooperation' (Programme on New Approaches to Russian Security, Harvard University), Memo No. 58, April 1999, <http://www.fas.harvard.edu/~ponars/POLICY%20MEMOS/Wallander58.html>.
66. As reported in *Johnson's Russia List* (davidjohnson@erols.com), 2 April 1999.
67. See footnote 58 above.
68. *The Guardian*, 31 March 1999.
69. *The Guardian*, 15 April 1999.
70. *The Guardian*, 16 April 1999.
71. *The Independent*, 14 April 1999.
72. *The Guardian*, 15 April 1999.
73. *The Guardian* , 26 and 28 April 1999.
74. *The Guardian*, 7 May 1999.
75. See, for instance, the proposals reported in the *Financial Times*, 20 May 1999, *The Independent*, 29 May 1999 and *The Guardian*, 1 and 2 June 1999.
76. V. Chernomyrdin, 'Impossible to Talk Peace with Bombs Falling', *The Washington Post*, 27 May 1999.

77. *The Observer*, 6 June 1999; J. McGeary, 'Why He Blinked', *Time*, 14 June 1999; *The Guardian*, 30 June 1999.
78. <http://www.un.org/Docs/scres/1999/99sc1244.htm>. The adoption of the Security Council resolution and the simultaneous signing of a military-technical agreement between NATO and the Serb military finally resulted in the suspension of NATO's campaign of air-strikes.
79. *The New York Times*, 4 June 1999.
80. For this positive assessment see the comments of M. McFaul as reported in *Johnson's Russia List* (davidjohnson@erols.com), 5 June 1999.
81. *The Guardian*, 9 June 1999.
82. *Moscow News*, 9–15 June 1999, p. 5. Others in the Duma were even more forthright. Zyuganov accused Chernomyrdin of treachery and a Duma resolution urged that Yeltsin sack his special representative. The resolution went on to say that Russia had permitted the 'defeat of a strategic ally [. . .] in the Balkans [something that has] sharply worsened Russia's geopolitical position and created a serious threat to its national security'. *The Guardian*, 11 June 1999.
83. See his annual 'state of the federation' address as reported by Reuters, 30 March 1999 and carried on *Johnson's Russia List* (davidjohnson@erols.com), 30 March 1999.
84. Itar-Tass, 30 March 1999 as carried by *Johnson's Russia List* (davidjohnson @erols.com), 30 March 1999.
85. As reported in *Johnson's Russia List* (davidjohnson@erols.com), 7 June 1999.
86. *The Guardian*, 11 June 1999.
87. *The Washington Post*, 25 June 1999.
88. *Komsomolskaya pravda*, 15 June 1999; *The Washington Post*, 25 June 1999.
89. For details see RFE/RL, *Newsline* (newsline@list.rferl.org), 7 July 1999.
90. *The Guardian*, 6 July 1999; RFE/RL, *Newsline* (newsline@list.rferl.org), 7 July 1999.

9
Conclusion: Russia and Europe – Trajectories of Development

Mark Webber

The celebratory, even euphoric language that was once used to describe Russia's relations with Europe (and indeed the West more generally) has been out of currency for several years. The vocabulary of analysis, since at least 1994, has tended toward either neutral terms that hint at a balanced, but nonetheless competitive relationship ('pragmatism' and 'realism'), or labels suggestive of some fundamental schism (Russian foreign policy as 'rigidly anti-western').[1] The use of such vocabulary is not without merit. Russia and the states of Europe (most obviously those centred on the North Atlantic Treaty Organization (NATO) and the European Union (EU)) have experienced differences over a large number of issues. Several of these disputes have been covered in this volume and there are others beside (the west European states, for instance, have objected to Russian sales of nuclear technology to Iran and anti-aircraft missiles to Cyprus).

The existence of divisions, then, is undeniable. Whether or not these develop into a prolonged, even indefinite crisis in Russian–European relations remains, however, an open question. On the basis of the record to date, there are at least two major reasons for thinking that such a state of affairs can be avoided. The first concerns the changed context of the relationship in the post-Cold War period. This new environment was outlined in some detail in Chapter 1 and several of its features have been touched upon in the case-study chapters. It does not, therefore, require elaborate recapitulation here. Suffice it to say, that for all the evidence of friction, an equally compelling set of examples can be found of how Russia's incorporation in multilateral settings has given rise to abundant (and ongoing) instances of joint action and cooperation. These include adaptation of the Conventional Forces in Europe (CFE) Treaty, the development of a partnership with the EU, Russian involvement in initiatives relating to the former Yugoslavia (the Contact Group, I-For/ S-For and K-For), and NATO-related activities linked to the Founding Act and the Permanent Joint Council (PJC). They also include Russian involvement with bodies not covered in this volume, but in which European states are dominant or important. The Western European Union (WEU) has increased its outreach activities toward Russia,[2] and the Group of Seven (G7), has, since 1997, been effectively converted into the G8 owing to the incorporation of Russia.[3] The latter is particularly notable because it confers upon Russia a standing undeserved in terms of economic prowess and international influence. These instances may not always be indicative of a genuine meeting of minds between Russia and Europe but neither do they suggest unalleviated animosity. Furthermore, the existence of various channels of communication and interaction have a long-term significance, offering as they do an institutionalized means of dealing with – and in some cases, resolving – ongoing and future instances of friction in the Russian–European relationship.

Second, and related, it could be argued that the occurrence of divisions may, in fact, reflect an increasing but manageable normality in relations between Russia and the states of Europe. Just as France, or for that matter Turkey, Greece and the United Kingdom (UK) are often at odds with their European counterparts, so too is Russia. None of this is to minimize the qualitative differences that attach to Russia, differences which make the management of disagreements that much more vexing. However, what it does suggest is that disagreement is not *ipso facto* wrong, unnatural or incompatible with the survival of otherwise constructive relations. What is more, the statecraft of the continent has become increasingly adept at dealing with these differences without relapsing into general crisis. This was clearly apparent over the two issues which have so far threatened such a crisis – NATO enlargement and NATO's 1999 air-campaign in relation to Kosovo. In both instances, Russia was opposed in principle to NATO action and threatened dire consequences in retaliation. Yet in both, it found itself isolated, bereft of realizable policy alternatives and ready, ultimately, to accept compromises and agreements which, while preserving a role for itself, recognized NATO predominance. Neither instance, moreover, spelled the end of broader-based cooperation. To take just the latter, the Kosovo crisis of March–June 1999 did, it is true, provoke a suspension of Russian participation in certain NATO-related activities. Yet, as was pointed out in Chapter 8, in persuading the Serbian leadership to accept NATO's demand for a Serb withdrawal from Kosovo, Russia did eventually prove itself to be a useful diplomatic partner of the Alliance. Moreover, despite the strains the crisis placed upon Russia's relations with Europe (and the West more generally), during this same period substantial progress was registered in other fields. In late March a preliminary agreement was reached on the adaptation of the CFE Treaty and in May the EU launched its 'Common Strategy' on Russia (see Chapters 4 and 7).

If one accepts, then, that discord is not automatic in the Russia–Europe relationship it would, nonetheless, be wrong to jump to the opposite conclusion that the two sides engage with one another in a totally harmonious fashion. While there has been much progress during the 1990s in the development of a context favourable to cooperation, it is clear that as time has passed such cooperation has become increasingly conditional and subject to difficulty. The likelihood of these difficulties assuming a critical mass sufficient to push the relationship in a totally confrontational direction is, however, slim. Likely future trends (both inside and outside of Russia) suggest that although frictions will persist and perhaps even intensify, a relapse of such magnitude will probably be avoided. The remainder of this chapter will consider three areas likely to have a bearing in this respect.

The Russian economy

Russia has experienced an economic collapse of staggering proportions. Despite the location of huge natural reserves and a relatively well-educated and skilled workforce (a legacy of the Soviet period), Russia at present barely functions as modern economy. It lacks a reliable base of taxation, a properly regulated commercial financial sector and a vibrant, wealth-generating industrial and manufacturing base. During the period 1989–98, it registered only a single year of positive growth (a minuscule 0.8 per cent in 1997) and, overall, by the end of 1997 its real gross domestic product (GDP) stood at only 58.6 per cent of its 1989 level. In comparative terms, this is not out of line with the experience of other Soviet successor states (the average real GDP of the states of the Commonwealth of Independent States (CIS) in 1997 was 56.3 per cent of the 1989 level).[4] However, it is far worse than the performance of states in east-central Europe (ECE) (only war-hit Bosnia and the Federal Republic of Yugoslavia have performed as badly) and, in broader terms, represents a precipitate drop in Russia's economic standing in the world. Measured by gross national product (GNP) per capita, Russia ranked a lowly 51st in the world in 1997, on a par with Thailand, Costa Rica and Peru. Its position is somewhat better in absolute terms (measured by total GNP, the Russian economy was ranked 12th in 1997, comparable in size to that of the Republic of Korea, Australia and the Netherlands) but this too looks less impressive when one considers those ranked above it. The United States (US) has an economy nineteen times larger than that of Russia's, Japan's is twelve times bigger, Germany's nearly six times, those of France and the UK some three to four times, and that of China two and a half times.[5] Even if one assumes Russia is capable of resuming growth, it will take decades for it to close these gaps. At a growth rate of 4–5 per cent per annum, it has been estimated that it will take until the year 2025 before the Russian economy is comparable to that of the UK, currently the world's fifth largest economy.[6] More realistically, a stagnant or low rate of growth will see Russia slip further behind. By 2025 it may well have slipped to a world ranking of 20th in total GNP terms, equivalent to middle-ranking European states such as Sweden, Austria and Belgium.[7]

Certain foreign policy consequences follow from this sorry picture. In the first place, Russia simply lacks an economy commensurate with playing the role of a great power, something that constrains its ability and desire to break with the West. Moscow has been able to hold onto the vestiges of influence by virtue of its nuclear capability and its diplomatic standing as the Soviet Union's 'continuing state' (hence its permanent seat in the UN Security Council), but the influence and reach which follow from relative economic advantage is simply absent beyond a handful of Soviet successor states. Furthermore, Russia has become increasingly reliant upon western sources of finance. The International Monetary Fund (IMF) and the US have played the lead roles in providing and scheduling this assistance but there has also been an important European dimension, both through bilateral channels (France, Germany and the UK are large official lenders, while German banks, in particular, are among the largest providers of commercial credits) and through technical and other forms of assistance provided by the EU. Dependency of this sort has not been welcomed in Moscow, yet it has, at least during the Yeltsin years, been viewed as almost inescapable. Furthermore, one of the few remaining strengths of the Russian economy, that of foreign trade, will keep Russia fixed upon western and particularly European markets. Russia's trade profile, involving a heavy reliance on commodity exports, has increasingly come to resemble that of a developing nation, but it has managed to deliver healthy surpluses every year since 1992. Overall, these developments have meant that Russian foreign policy has become 'economized'. Russia has a clear and vested interest in maintaining access to sources of finance, furthering its integration into the global economy and maintaining good relations with its major trading partners.[8] Europe, of course, is and will remain central to this priority.

A second foreign policy consequence of economic collapse is that the 'guns versus butter' dilemma has been presented ever more acutely to the Russian leadership. It would be perverse to suggest that the latter part of this equation has been preferred given the desperate collapse in Russian living standards since 1991. Yet neither is it the case that the armed forces have enjoyed any favouritism. As the figures in Chapter 7 amply illustrate, the Russian military budget has fallen as a proportion of (an already declining) GDP and even allowing for optimistic projections of future growth it is unlikely that Russia will be able to convincingly alter this trend any time soon. The consequence has been (and will continue to be) an emasculated conventional military force and an increasing reliance on ageing nuclear weapons for national defence. The latter does hold the potential to introduce a degree of tension into relations with Europe, however, it has thus far remained a largely bilateral issue with the US and even here has been partly accommodated within the START process (see Chapter 7). Far more significant for Europe is Russia's denuded conventional profile, something that has denied to Moscow the wherewithal to threaten the continent and which has limited its military presence to all but a handful of states along its immediate periphery. As in the cases of Tajikistan, Georgia and Armenia, these are states largely removed from European concerns. The Russian presence in Belarus and Ukraine is far more sensitive, but to date only the former has shown a preference for alliance with Russia, and even if political developments in Ukraine were to give rise to a regime more congenial to Russian interests, the military component of a Slavic union would still remain problematic. Ukrainian and Belorus's economic situation is as bad as that of Russia and the projections of future developments are no better. The ability to construct anything comparable to the Soviet armed forces or NATO can, therefore, be ruled out in the short-to-medium term.

The Russian political system

An early casualty of political upheaval in Russia was the notion of a successful and swift transition to democracy. The *demokritizatsii* of the late Gorbachev years followed by the seemingly decisive moves toward decommunization under Boris Yeltsin initially gave rise to hopes that a clear shift had occurred away from authoritarianism.[9] The subsequent history of the Yeltsin presidency, however, resulted in a considerable sobering of such judgements. Not only were certain practices of his tenure anti-democratic in tone (the storming of the Russian Parliament in October 1993 and the 1994–96 war in Chechnya) but the very nature of the transition in Russia can now be seen as problematic to democratic consolidation. In common with other post-communist states, Russia has undergone not just one transition (that at the political level), but at least two others: of social relations and of the economy. In combination, these amount in Claus Offe's phrase to a 'triple transition', the negotiation of which has given rise to stable, proto-democratic states in only a handful of cases (Poland, Hungary and the Czech Republic).[10] In Russia, moreover, these upheavals have been compounded by some specific conditions – an authoritarian political culture, a polarized political élite, a non-consensual and highly competitive form of political intercourse – none of which is propitious for democratic consolidation.[11] Indeed, these conditions have proven averse not just to democracy but to governance and political order itself, a state of affairs increasingly evident from a destatization of political life (the breakdown of the rule of law, unregulated federal decentralization, and the inability, noted above, to extract resources from the economy through taxation).[12]

Amidst such turbulence it may seem perverse to speak of Russia as possessing a consolidated polity. Yet there is a sense in which the contours of an established political system can be seen. This may well be an inherently unstable and ineffectual system but it has, nonetheless, a durable and recognizable form. Although its bases were laid amidst the peculiarities of Yeltsin's rule, it also has a more deep-rooted structure that is an outgrowth of the particular social, political and economic conditions of post-Soviet life. In institutional terms this has involved a tendency toward 'super-presidentialism', a waxing and waning of the position of the Prime Minister, a cleavage between President and Parliament, the haphazard development of Russian federalism, and a constant battle for influence between well-connected political and economic élites within the governmental arena. Such a system has some obvious authoritarian characteristics, but it is also one whose logic of development (the vested interest of élites in a circulation of power) has allowed the continuation of at least some democratic features, most importantly the holding of relatively free and regular elections.[13]

What then is the significance of this political picture for Russia's external orientation? Specifically, it suggests a certain unpredictability. The fact that the Russian political system has been characterized by a bureaucratic and personal competition for influence has clearly affected the institutional context of foreign policy decision-making and implementation. The lines of authority connecting President, Foreign Ministry, the Ministry of Defence, Parliament and other actors have often been blurred and the institutions themselves often at loggerheads. Thus, the

Foreign and Defence Ministries have often been in disagreement or working at cross purposes (tellingly illustrated by the military intervention in Pristina, Kosovo, noted in Chapter 8); the President has, at times, actively undermined his Foreign Minister (such was the fate of Andrei Kozyrev during 1994–95); and the Russian Parliament has periodically sought to frustrate presidential prerogative.

Amidst this battle for influence, the central source of power in foreign policy has remained that of the office of President. This potentially has a stabilizing effect, both in fixing the broad content of policy, and in cohering the decision-making process that contributes to it. Yet by the same token it can also have more disruptive or radical consequences. Policy can become exposed to the idiosyncrasies and weaknesses of the presidential incumbent (something clearly apparent under Yeltsin) and can be subject to sudden change should the incumbent be replaced. Furthermore, sudden changes of policy are possible because, unlike settled democracies, the polarized nature of political discourse in Russia means that foreign policy is an object of fierce political debate. Vague commitments such as the need to preserve Russia's great power status are apparent, but practical issues of orientation are far more divisive. A single electoral outcome, therefore, can conceivably have a far-reaching effect. Presidential hopefuls such as the communist Gennadi Zyuganov, the nationalist mayor of Moscow Yuri Luzhkov or the patriotic governor of Krasnoyarsk Aleksandr Lebed adhere to a view of Russia's national interests and a vision of foreign policy somewhat different from those of Yeltsin. All three, and Zyuganov in particular, view cooperation with Europe, and the West more broadly, with a sceptical eye.[14]

How far this scepticism might be translated into actual policy, however, is at present unclear, for whoever holds power after the elections in 2000 will have to labour under similar economic constraints to those noted above, something that will limit the possibilities for developing a foreign policy based on assertiveness and hostility. However, if not outright confrontation, what is conceivable is a much greater circumsription of cooperation (on say commitments undertaken with regard to CFE and the Council of Europe, involvement in NATO and EU structures, and on matters relating to Bosnia and Kosovo) than that in evidence under Yeltsin's tenure. This may also be accompanied by far more qualified attitudes toward marketization and Russia's exposure to the international economy. All would clearly spell a far more troubled relationship with Europe. It need not, however, mean the end of cooperation. In domestic terms, it is unlikely that a post-Yeltsin regime will effect a meaningful turnaround of the economy or of Russia's political fortunes in the four-year period of a single presidential term. As a consequence, the course favoured by a Zyuganov, Lebed or Luzhkov may come to be regarded as just as unpopular and ineffective as that associated with Yeltsin in his second term. This in itself could lead to a tempering of policy (both domestic and foreign) or even to a new presidential incumbent in 2004. The political complexion of this figure is, of course, a complete uncertainty but after four years of post-Yeltsin hardship, the assumption of an identifiably liberal figure cannot be ruled out. It is also worth bearing in mind that whoever is President (be this in the year 2000 or 2004) that individual operates within certain political limits. All of the three figures noted may have to work with a Parliament, a Prime Minister/government and federal governors less than enamoured with their political programme. The maximalist language of opposition should not blind one to the pragmatism, trade-offs and compromises that may follow from actually holding presidential office.

External incentives toward cooperation

Clearly, domestic factors inside of Russia can influence the course of the Russia–Europe relationship. However, it should also be remembered that the route of influence also works in the other direction: that Russia resides in a cooperative external setting can influence its own foreign policy responses. Of some importance, therefore, is the manner in which the European states relate to Russia; the incentives they offer, in other words, for the survival of a cooperative framework. And on this score, it can reasonably be argued that the states of western Europe in particular have shown a fair degree of sensitivity toward Russia. Indeed, as the case studies in this volume have suggested, accommodation and compromise have so far been the order of the day. This is not to say that the European states have blithely ignored their own interests for the sake of comforting Russia, a fact clearly borne out by the stance of the EU in relation to certain trade disputes with Russia (noted in Chapter 4) and the difficulties that attended the follow-on CFE negotiations (noted in Chapter 7). What matters, however, is that such disputes have not derailed cooperation in broad terms and have been addressed in a manner that leaves open the possibility of mutually acceptable solutions. Hence, in relation to the examples cited: the holding of trade talks within the institutional framework of the Partnership and Cooperation Agreement, and the preliminary agreement of March 1999 on adapting the CFE Treaty.

Of a somewhat different order have been controversies relating to NATO enlargement and military action in the former Yugoslavia, where the states of the continent (east as well as west) have supported courses of action that have provoked sustained protest in Moscow. Yet as noted above (and see also Chapters 3 and 8), even here compromises have been reached which partly address Russian concerns. Looking ahead, however, the Russian–NATO relationship still has great potential for friction. The institutional framework established under the 1997 NATO–Russia Founding Act was severely tested by the Kosovo crisis of 1999 and, at least on the Russian side, found severely wanting. A major litmus test for the relationship will, therefore, be how far the credentials of the NATO–Russia PJC are re-established following the marginalization of that body over the Kosovo issue. As for the equally vexing matter of enlargement, while Moscow seemingly reconciled itself to the entry of Poland, Hungary and the Czech Republic into the Alliance in 1999, it has remained opposed to any subsequent wave of enlargement. What will be crucial here is the geographic location of any new members. A second wave that incorporates only, say, Romania and Slovenia could be swallowed in Moscow, but any incorporation of the former Soviet republics (the Baltic states or Ukraine) would, as Kennedy-Pipe suggests, be met with unprecedented hostility and thus consequent injury to the Russia–Europe relationship. Baltic membership is very much desired in the states concerned and NATO itself has not ruled it out. However, it may, in fact, be precisely because of its grave consequences that the Alliance is unlikely to take such a precipitate step in the foreseeable future.[15]

Developments beyond Europe are also likely to be important. Of particular note here is relations with the US. Of course, this has a very obvious European dimension – the US is heavily involved in European-based issues, not least those relating to the Balkans and NATO, that touch upon Russian concerns. However, Russia does view America through a particular lens. An intercourse with the US is important for all manner of reasons: because it buttresses Russia's claim to great power status, because of American influence in global affairs and institutions (and specifically those such as the IMF heavily involved in Russia), and because of important bilateral issues such as nuclear arms control which remain the preserve of Moscow and Washington. Yet for all this, there has, since the mid-1990s, been a growing disillusionment in Moscow with American actions. Some of this feeling is aimed at matters of a strictly bilateral nature (US retaliation at Russian arms sales to India and nuclear technology transfers to Iran, American demands for a revision of the 1972 Anti-Ballistic Missile Treaty, and what are seen as encroachments by the US in Russia's own sphere of influence in Ukraine, Central

Asia and the Transcaucasus). Some, however, bear directly upon European issues. The US, for instance, has been viewed as having taken the lead role in pressing for NATO enlargement, in supporting punitive military action in the Balkans, and in hindering the development of the OSCE.[16]

The significance of these strains with the US is that they have increased the incentives on Russia's part for a closer relationship with the European states. This may be read, in part, as a rather crude wedge-driving strategy. During the NATO enlargement debates of 1996–97, for instance, Russia made a concerted attempt to court Greece and struck up what was seen as a special relationship with France.[17] Yeltsin's suggestion in October 1997 that the Europeans were able to manage their own affairs without the assistance of 'an uncle from elsewhere', followed six months later by the Moscow 'troika' summit of Russia, France and Germany can also be read in a similar fashion. However, the Soviet Union before 1991 had long tried such strategies to little obvious effect and they have proven no more successful subsequently.

In this light, at least two other reasons suggest themselves as to why, in relation to the US, Europe may, in the long term, assume a greater profile in Russian foreign policy. First, and rather straightforwardly, Moscow may have calculated that in light of US assertiveness, the European states are simply more open to Russian concerns. NATO's European members have been less forthright, for instance, in their support of an enlargement of the Alliance and less 'hawkish' in advocating military action in Bosnia and (the British excepted) in Kosovo. Analysis in Russia often portrays the US as dragging its NATO allies toward actions which the latter view with something less than enthusiasm.[18] Second, Russia may well come to appreciate the increasing diplomatic and military significance of the EU and NATO's European members. Although still in the shadow of the US, the UK, France and Germany acquitted themselves relatively well in the Kosovo military operations and have subsequently played a significant role in the post-conflict stabilization of the province. Furthermore, should the much-vaunted European Security and Defence Identity of NATO assume real flesh and, in parallel, the EU develop a more robust Common Foreign and Security Policy (two possibilities given a significant boost in 1998–99[19]) then Russia will clearly have an interest in an enhanced dialogue with European states on a range of security related issues.

Further afield still from Europe, China too has some relevance. Since Russia's turn away from the unashamed courting of the West in 1992, it has sought to develop ties with regional centres of power around its Asian periphery. This strategy has focused upon China and to some extent India and Iran. It has some very concrete bases in Russian national interests (securing the long Russian–Chinese border and developing trade links and military contacts) and also serves to justify Russian claims to regional, even global weight. There is also a seeming strategic logic. What a 1996 joint Sino-Russian communiqué referred to as a 'strategic partnership' between Moscow and Beijing and what Prime Minister Yevgenni Primakov in December 1998 hailed as a 'strategic triangle' comprising Russia, China and India has, in part, evolved over common anxieties regarding American global influence.[20] Furthermore, while this bloc has little chance of developing into a formal military alliance, it does offer opportunities for enhanced military cooperation in the sale and joint manufacture of arms and related technologies. Such ties have been boosted by NATO enlargement and NATO's Kosovo engagement.[21]

Such a bloc does, however, have limitations of its own and is unlikely to provide the basis of a concerted turn away from Europe on Russia's part. China does, after all, pose a very real threat to Russia. It is, in military, geostrategic and economic terms, in a position of relative buoyancy and is a competitor with Russia for influence in Central Asia and (border agreements and confidence-building measures notwithstanding) Russia's own far eastern regions. Significantly, for these very reasons many in Russia's senior military consider that China rather than NATO poses the greater threat to Russia.[22] In the simple logic of military balancing, therefore, Russia has a greater incentive for cooperative relations with the US and the European states of NATO than it does with China. The long-term economic benefits of a turn to the East are also far smaller than those offered by cooperation with Europe and the West. China cannot offer to Russia the finances sufficient for economic stabilization and, while it is of some significance as a trading partner, it hardly stands as a surrogate for the Europeans. Not only is trade with China a mere fraction of that with Europe but the goods involved are hardly those likely to contribute to Russia's modernization. (Russia's trade with Europe comprises high technology goods and services that with China tend to be in commodities, semi-finished goods and arms). Furthermore, China itself (and for that matter, India) is less than enthusiastic about a special relationship with Russia based on anti-westernism, simply because such an alignment would jeopardize its own relations with west European states, the US and to some extent Japan.[23]

Closer to home for Russia, the successor states are of significance in the context of Russia's relations with Europe on at least two grounds. In the first place, the Yeltsin leadership (and even more so Yeltsin's possible successors) has posited the successor states (and the regional organization to which most of them belong – the CIS) as yet one more alternative orientation in Russian foreign policy. However, the scope for Russian action in this regard is rather limited. Russia has good relations with only a minority of its neighbours and as for the CIS itself, the organization has displayed little viability as a military alliance or potential as a substitute market for continental Europe.[24] A post-Yeltsin leadership may seek to alter this situation by a more vigorous policy toward Russia's neighbours, but, as noted above, Russia's depleted resource base is likely to remain a significant impediment to such a strategy.[25] One should also bear in mind that Russia does not enjoy a free hand in the region. Several of the successor states have unilaterally resisted or limited Russian encroachment (Azerbaijan, Uzbekistan and Ukraine are of particular note here) while collectively, sub-groups have emerged premised, in part at least, on promoting autonomous efforts at cooperation without Russia.[26]

Second, the region does have the potential to complicate relations with Europe. As already noted, the Baltic states have loomed large in debates on NATO. In addition, energy issues in the Caspian Sea region have been a source of competition between Russian and European concerns. Russia has also been highly suspicious of European efforts geared toward closer relations with Ukraine. Yet while tensions have not been absent, Russia and the European states have, thus far at least, been able to maintain a degree of cooperation and mutual restraint in regard to the Soviet successor states. This can be seen in the relaxed attitude of the West toward Russian peacekeeping and military intervention in Georgia, Moldova and Tajikistan, and the effective rejection of requests on the part of Georgia and Azerbaijan for the emplacement of NATO peacekeepers in their respective internal conflicts. There is, arguably, an unspoken assumption in Europe (and to some extent the US) that Russia has legitimate interests in the successor states and, linked to this, that the western capitals have no compelling strategic or political reasons to compete with Russia in a damaging tustle for spheres of influence around the latter's borders. Of course, the perception in Moscow may well be different. Commercial competition and low-level political-military contacts such as those channelled through NATO's Partnership for Peace and the Euro-Atlantic Partnership Council have been viewed as indicative of some wider intent (and it is fair to assume that a post-Yeltsin leadership is likely to be even more suspicious). However, in that the most obvious material expression of such intent – that of a NATO enlargement into the successor states – is unlikely to occur for several years, if at all, then the single most likely cause of a wholesale deterioration in Russian–European relations will remain moot.

Conclusion

This volume began by positing two alternative images of Russia's relations with Europe: one based on confrontation, division and difference; the other centred on cooperation, accommodation and inclusion. As a full and accurate characterization, the latter of these alternatives only held true for a short time after the birth of the new Russia in 1991. Since then the relationship has been troubled by a number of controversies. These are unlikely to disappear.

Yet while a degree of competition has clearly emerged and may now be considered a permanent feature of the relationship, it is important to remember that this has done so in a European setting that has remained favourably disposed to cooperative behaviour and the peaceful management of those differences that do exist between Moscow and its western neighbours. Russia, it is true, has been and will be excluded from two of the most important developments on the continent (the enlargement of NATO and the future enlargement of the EU) but this does not constitute for Moscow sufficient cause to subvert the post-Cold War European order itself. Russia may well have reasons for challenging the precise institutional form that this order has taken and the terms of its own participation in it, but importantly, its grievance has not been born of ideology, territorial ambition or nationalist mobilization. For all the talk of a 'Weimar scenario' in Russia on account of economic hardship, political paralysis and a loss of international influence,[27] the country has not developed any sense of national solidarity based on an aggressive, *revanchist* nationalism.[28] Certain developments could change this: a further, long-term deterioration of the economy and a wilful disregard for Russian sensitivities on the part of an enlarging NATO and EU. However, even then a paucity of resources, the limitations of regional alternatives and calculations of simple pragmatism will conspire to deter almost any Russian leadership from embarking upon a course of policy that is unrelievedly antagonistic toward Europe.

Furthermore, even allowing for the fact that in the post-Cold War period Russia has found itself constantly trying to catch up with (rather than shape) the emerging European order, its engagement thus far with the continent has nonetheless been productive. The multilateral setting of the relationship has after all produced certain benefits in particular policy areas, and, overall, has acted to inflate Russia's international importance. The Russian political élite may well be as one in arguing for the pursuit of status, but in Europe at least such status has and continues to be recognized. Russian diplomacy, moreover, can take some credit for this. It has successfully 'punched above its weight' in order to win concessions where arguably these were unwarranted and to impress upon European states, east and west, that it has a legitimate interest in the continent's orientation. Finding itself in 1991 excluded from some institutions and marginal to others Russia has, in the intervening years, achieved a fairly full and active participation in their subsequent development.

Of course, a post-Yeltsin leadership may well have a different appreciation of these achievements and the European states whose concessions made them possible may well adopt a more conditional attitude that narrows the range of possibilities for further Russian gains. Two general considerations, however, point to a logic of continuity for cooperation even in these less propitious circumstances. In the first place, it can be argued that cooperation within multilateral settings is much harder to create than it is to maintain.[29] If this is the case, then it is best that the conditions favourable for cooperation are loaded toward the beginning of the process; such conditions are less critical once that process is underway. In this light, the so-called 'Atlanticist' phase in Russian foreign policy (and to some degree Gorbachev's 'new political thinking' upon which it built) now appears particularly fortuitous. The decision of the Yeltsin administration in late 1991 to opt for rapid market reform and (what appeared at the time at least) a consolidation of democracy was based on the assumption that Russia's domestic transformation could only be furthered by integrating Russia with the West externally. This then presented a window of opportunity both for an intensification of Gorbachev-era cooperation and the inauguration of new initiatives, the fundamentals of which have continued to this day.[30]

Second, and related, once institutionalized cooperation is underway it is costly to terminate. This stems from the fact that all sides recognize it affords them certain benefits (many of which could not be obtained in other settings, cooperative or otherwise) and because it acquires a certain bureaucratic life of its own, all sides having invested in it a modicum of political capital and human (and sometimes economic) resources. Granted, cooperation on this basis is hardly exciting. But in a European context it is crucially important nonetheless, pointing as it does to the long-term routinization of Russia's engagement with the continent.

Notes

1. C. Walker, 'Russia's Internal Crisis Imperils Cooperation with the West', Radio Free Europe/Radio Liberty, *Newsline*, Endnote (newsline@list.rferl.org), 21 September 1998.
2. D. Danilov and S. de Spiegeleire, 'From Decoupling to Recoupling. Russia and Western Europe: a New Security Relationship?' *Chaillot Paper*, No. 31 (Paris: Institute for Security Studies of the Western European Union, April 1998).
3. Russia remains excluded from discussion of certain financial matters, but on most other business it is a full participant. This has meant its involvement in the G8's broadening security and political agenda.
4. United Nations Economic Commission for Europe, *Economic Survey of Europe, 1998*, No. 2 (New York and Geneva, 1998), p. 146.
5. World Bank, *World Development Report, 1998/99* (New York: World Bank, 1998), pp. 190–1.
6. J. Cooper, 'The Russian Federation as a Lower Middle Income Economy' (paper presented to the annual conference of the Centre for Russian and East European Studies, University of Birmingham, June 1998), p. 2.
7. *The Economist*, 12 June 1999, p. 122; *The Washington Post*, 6 June 1999.
8. C. A. Wallander, 'The Economization, Rationalization, and Normalization of Russian Foreign Policy' (Programme on New Approaches to Russian Security, Harvard University), Memo No. 1, July 1997, <http://www.fas.harvard.edu/~ponars/POLICYMEMOS/wallander.html>.
9. J. Lloyd, 'Democracy in Russia', *The Political Quarterly*, Vol. 64, No. 3, 1993, pp. 147–9.
10. C. Offe, 'Capitalism by Democratic Design? Democratic Theory Facing the Triple Transition in East Central Europe', *Social Research*, Vol. 58, No. 4, 1991, pp. 865–92.
11. H. Eckstein, 'Russia and the Conditions of Democracy', in H. Eckstein, F. J. Fleron Jr., E. P. Hoffmann and W. M. Reisinger, *Can Democracy Take Root in Post-Soviet Russia? Explorations in State–Society Relations* (Lanham: Rowman and Littlefield Publishers, 1998), pp. 376–7.
12. J. Snyder, 'Introduction: Reconstructing Politics Amidst the Wreckage of Empire', in B. R. Rubin and J. Snyder (eds.), *Post-Soviet Political Order. Conflict and State Building* (London: Routledge, 1998), pp. 1–13.
13. For an overview of the Russian system of rule see D. N. Jensen, *How Russia Is Ruled* (Radio Free Europe/Radio Liberty, 1998), <http://euro.rferl.org/nca/special/ruwhorules/index.html>. For the argument that the system in Russia has increasingly established features see A. Karatnycky, 'Nations in Transit: From Change to Permanence', in *Nations in Transit. 1998* (New York: Freedom House, 1999), pp. 10–13, 17.
14. It is also a possibility that a candidate associated with Yeltsin's pragmatic, cooperative approach toward Europe and the West might win the 2000 presidential elections. Two such possibilities are Yevgenni Primakov, former Foreign and Prime Minister, and Vladimir Putin who was appointed Prime Minister in August 1999. If this were the case, then a clear continuity would exist between Yeltsin's second presidential term from 1996–2000 and the first term of the new President.
15. J. Hoekema (general rapportuer), 'NATO Policy and NATO Strategy in Light of the Kosovo Conflict' (North Atlantic Assembly, Defence and Security

Committee, Draft General Report, 7 May 1999), paragraph 54. As well as its effects upon Russia, at least two other factors are likely to forestall a future enlargement of NATO into the successor states. First, the incorporation of the Czech Republic, Hungary and Poland, following their entry in March 1999, will tie up NATO resources and political energies and thereby strengthen the case for caution. On this score, in March 1999 both the German Chancellor Gerhard Schröder and the US Secretary of Defence William Cohen alluded to the need for a consolidation of membership. Second, even if one supposes that NATO was to continue to enlarge, it may well do so at a rate and with a geographic focus that precludes the accession of any of the successor states. Thus, while the three Baltic states have been emboldened by Czech, Hungarian and Polish entry, it may be the case that a second and even a third wave will be limited to the Balkans and south ECE, Slovenia, Romania, Bulgaria, Macedonia, Slovakia and even Albania being admitted in an ad hoc sequence and over a period of several years. This so-called 'southern strategy' has gained added credibility in the wake of the Kosovo campaign, the thinking among certain NATO officials being that Alliance membership is one route toward stability in the Balkans and surrounding region. See NATO Secretary General Javier Solana as cited in *The Washington Post*, 7 July 1999.

16. P. J. Stavrakis, 'After the Fall: US-Russian Relations in the Next Stage of Post-Soviet History' (Washington D.C.: The Atlantic Council of the United States, Occasional Paper, December 1998), passim.

17. See, for instance, the press coverage of the visits of President Jacques Chirac and Prime Minister Lionel Jospin to Moscow in 1997 in *Izvestiya*, 27 September 1997, pp. 1, 3, and *The Straits Times*, 1 November 1997 as carried by *Johnson's Russia List* (davidjohnson@erols.com), 2 November 1997.

18. B. Kazentsev (Deputy Director of the Department of European Cooperation of the Russian Ministry of Foreign Affairs), 'Serious Concern over New NATO Strategy', *International Affairs* (Moscow), Vol. 45, No. 2, 1999, electronic edition <http://home.mosinfo.ru/news/intaff/1999/data/002azan.htm>.

19. See Chapter 3.

20. The Jamestown Foundation, *Monitor* (webmaster@jamestown.org), 26 April 1996; *Financial Times*, 22 December 1998.

21. *Moscow News*, 16–22 June 1999, p. 2.

22. V. Baranovsky, 'Russia', in A. Khron (ed.), *The Baltic Sea Region* (Baden-Baden: Nomos Verlagsgesellschaft, 1996), pp. 166–7.

23. R. J. Art, 'Creating a Disaster: NATO's Open Door Policy', *Political Science Quarterly*, Vol. 113, No. 3, 1998, pp. 392–3.

24. R. Sakwa and M. Webber, 'The Commonwealth of Independent States 1991–1998: Stagnation and Survival', *Europe-Asia Studies*, Vol. 52, No. 3, 1999, pp. 379–415.

25. See also H. E. Hale, 'The Rise of Russian Anti-Imperialism', *Orbis*, Vol. 43, No. 1, 1999, pp. 111–25.

26. The two most important groups in this regard are 'GUUAM' comprising Georgia, Ukraine, Uzbekistan, Azerbaijan and Moldova, and the Central Asian Economic Community of Kazakhstan, Kyrgyzstan, Tajikistan and Uzbekistan.

27. S. E. Hanson and J. S. Kopstein, 'The Weimar/Russia Comparison', *Post-Soviet Affairs*, Vol. 13, No. 3, 1997, pp. 252–83.

28. A. Lieven, 'The Weakness of Russian Nationalism', *Survival*, Vol. 41, No. 2, 1999, pp. 53–70.
29. This is so because the former requires greater practical application, risk-taking and, importantly, convergence of interests. See R. O. Keohane, *After Hegemony: Cooperation and Discord in the World Political Economy* (Princeton: Princeton University Press,1984), p. 100.
30. For a similar argument see C. D. Blacker, 'Russia and the West', in M. Mandelbaum (ed.), *The New Russian Foreign Policy* (New York: Council on Foreign Relations, 1998), pp. 167–93.

Index